WORK OF A GUARDIAN ANGEL

By Annie Stillwater Gray

For permission, serialization, condensation, adaptions, or for our catalog of other publications, write to Ozark Mountain Publishing, Inc., P.O. box 754, Huntsville, AR 72740, ATTN: Permissions Department.

Library of Congress Cataloging-in-Publication Data

Gray, Annie Stillwater – 1946 -

Work of a Guardian Angel by Annie Stillwater Gray

This the sequel to "Education of a Guardian Angel" is the continuing story of the relationship with Angel and the true story of a remarkable elfin being and her mission.

1. Spirit Guides 2. Metaphysics 3. Elementals 4. Guardian Angels

I. Gray, Annie Stillwater 1946- II. Spirit Guides III. Metaphysics IV. Title

Library of Congress Catalog Card Number: 2016960049

ISBN: 9781940265414

Cover Art and Layout: www.vril8.com

Book set in: Times New Roman, Ringbearer

Book Design: Tab Pillar

PO Box 754, Huntsville, AR 72740

800-935-0045 or 479-738-2348; fax 479-738-2448

WWW.OZARKMT.COM

Printed in the United States of America

CONTENTS

INTRODUCTION

Many do not realize that there is much unseen activity on Earth. What I speak of goes far beyond the wind or the force of gravity, for there are many subtle layers of existence and many invisible beings who call Earth their home. Humans spend time and energy exploring outer space when the most fascinating unknown worlds exist right here.

The subtle plane that has the most influence and is most important to understand is the realm of the elementals, such as elves and faeries, because it is the one most closely tied to Earth. Indeed, this planet would not be what she is and would not have such resiliency without the activity of the elementals. I am privileged to have ties to this magical world.

My name is Darcimon Stillwater, Darci for short. I am a Spirit Guide, also known as a guardian angel. I have agreed to help my human charge, named Angel, in any way I am able. Also, we Spirit Guides often assist elemental beings, especially when one is entering or leaving the earth plane. This is part of the work of a guardian angel. The following is the continuing story of my relationship with Angel, and the true story of a remarkable elfin being and her mission.

CHAPTER ONE
NYNA SERAHN

My first day as the guardian of a human was much different from what I expected. The birth of my charge was traumatic, which left me wondering why I had chosen the path of a Spirit Guide. During my long and arduous training, I had been shown many ways to guide a human being, but as I sat by the crib of this newborn, I felt utterly helpless. Only hours before, dear Angel, the soul I had agreed to watch over and protect, had been perfect as all souls are. Now this beautiful spirit was trapped in the body of a human baby, a body that had been drugged, twisted in the birth canal, and scarred with a tong-like tool called forceps. She had been held upside down and spanked until she cried. Although other Guides present at the birth assured me that these events were all part of Angel's life lessons and the taking on of her karma as it were, the birth left me downhearted.

That evening was also the time of my first interaction on Earth with an elemental being. The night of July 4, 1946, was quiet after the Independence Day fireworks celebrations. The atmosphere in the hospital nursery was warm and humid, so one of the attendants opened the window. I was so focused on the newborn, staying close to her crib, that I did not see the grandmother elf appear.

"You think you know her destiny. You do not know all."

Startled, I turned to see a glowing being at my left elbow. The size of a small human, perhaps five feet tall, she had eyes that sparkled like emeralds in the midday sun. Her white hair was wound neatly into a bun, and she wore a rich purple cape with gold trim. I was so taken aback I could not speak.

1

She glared at me. "I can see you have not met an elfin being before."

"Not on Earth," I managed to answer.

"I am Nyna Serahn. I know about you, Darci Stillwater, and your charge. Communication is especially good among elves."

"I am honored to meet you, Nyna. Who told you about us?"

"My dear friend and comrade, Chilliwon Mac."

"Ah, yes! I came to know the fellow on the Spirit Guide Plane at meetings of the Elevated Council."

As she nodded, sparkles effervesced from her hair. "While you were training to become a Guide."

"Nyna, what do you mean I do not know Angel's destiny? I helped her prepare for the earth lifetime she has just begun."

"Her potential is great." The grandmother elf stepped closer and looked at the babe. "Do you remember the line in her Soul Contract: 'I will dedicate myself to serving the Earth Mother'?"

"Of course I do."

"That makes this precious babe a friend to all elves."

"You also serve the earth?"

Her eyes twinkled. "That is the reason for our existence."

We both stared silently at the sleeping baby. Finally, I asked, "How can Angel help?"

Nyna smiled. "In many, many ways—as can you." She turned and glanced toward the window. "I must take my leave, Mr. Stillwater. I will visit again soon."

And she vanished leaving a trail of purple and gold luminescence that wound from the crib to the tree outside and beyond.

Several weeks later as the air hung heavy on a humid August evening, I was at my usual post by Angel's bassinette. It was late, the house quiet, when effulgence on the windowsill caught my eye. The radiance spilled into the room and spiraled vertically until before me stood Nyna Serahn.

"Good evening, Mr. Stillwater," she said as she smiled and curtsied. She looked very elegant in a deep green dress that rippled and flowed around her like water.

"Please call me Darci." I bowed.

"How is our Angel?"

"She sleeps quietly. I'm glad you have returned. I have many questions for you."

She smiled wisely. "And I have much to relate to you. The more you know, the better you will be able to help us."

"You are speaking of the elves?"

"I include all of the elemental beings and the Earth Mother herself."

"Tell me about Angel's destiny." I settled myself to hear the details.

"That is not where to begin, Darci. I must first tell you about the gifts."

"Gifts for Angel?"

"For Angel and for all upon the earth. The Master Guides have informed you that Earth is moving toward a great transition."

"Yes. It will occur in Angel's lifetime."

"You also know of the ray of energy that will be given to help with this time of change."

"I do. It will increase the vibration of the planet. I believe Angel and I are to write about it."

"Good. Good." The grandmother elf stepped nearer and sat by me. "This ray will bring many gifts, not just increased energy and vibration."

"Tell me of these gifts."

Her eyes gleamed with joy. "Any time of transition needs leaders, and since the changes on Earth will affect all life forms, there will be highly evolved leaders for every level. These are known as the Seven Avatars."

"Seven Avatars. It has been centuries since such leaders came to Earth."

"The Buddha, the Christ, and Mohammed were all human avatars, and there will be another who comes to lead humankind." Her eyes crinkled at the corners as she grinned. "I'm here to tell you that these avatars will arrive on every level of existence here on Earth."

"So not all will be human."

"No. Only one will manifest for humans. We elves are joyfully preparing for the arrival of ours. And one more thing, Darci." She paused, came closer, and looked me in the eyes. "All seven will be female."

I inadvertently raised my eyebrows. "Is there a reason for this?"

"Of course. The Creator does not act randomly, though sometimes it may seem so. These seven female leaders will help to bring the earth back into balance."

"So that leadership roles in the future will go to women?"

"Leadership will include women on an equal basis with men. No, we will not return to the matriarchal days when the Great Yin Energy was the dominant force on the planet, though the Great Yang Force that exists now must be controlled and balanced."

"Yes," I mused. "War is yang and there has just been a second terrible world war."

"I caution that the avatars will not arrive until the new ray makes some fundamental changes in the energy on the planet. These beings are highly evolved and will wait for the climate to be more agreeable to them."

"When will this be?"

"As you know there is no precise timetable for Earth, as there is free will here on every level, but I will venture to say fifty years."

"Fifty years! Why, that will be very close to the new millennium!"

"Yes, Darci. A new decade, a new century, a new millennium, a new age. All the cogs in the great cycles are meshing to make this one of the most important times on this planet. That is why Earth is being gifted with these new leaders. It is a joyous time for you and your charge to be working together."

"You know of our mission?"

"Oh yes. Do you not remember? My friend, Chilliwon Mac, is overseer of all communications between realms. He informed me of the work you and Angel have been asked to do. You will help usher in a new golden age on this planet."

"I hope this will be so." I sighed. "I've learned that nothing is certain on Earth."

"There are a few constants, Darci. The most important one is love from the Creator."

The babe began to stir. I nodded toward the bassinette. "She will wake soon. Her belly is empty and she will cry."

"Such potential in that little one." Nyna spoke with a serious tone. "Much lies ahead of her."

"Yes, I know. She has personal karma to resolve as well as the mission to address."

"You both will have the opportunity to help us as well. Would you be willing to assist us with the arrival of the elfin avatar?"

I sat speechless. Before I could ask what such assistance would entail, Nyna winked, twirled, and once again became a helix of luminescent sparkles that spiraled out the window.

∞

Each night as I sat close by the sleeping baby, I awaited Nyna's return. She had stirred so many questions in my heart and mind that I eagerly anticipated speaking with her again. In fact, I sent several telepathic messages asking her to visit. It was not until Angel's first birthday that I again saw the grandmother elf.

Angel and her parents were living on the second floor of a large Victorian farmhouse that had been in the family for generations. Her great-grandmother and a nurse occupied the first floor; a friend and caretaker was in residence on the third. The grand old house was perched atop a hill surrounded by lovely rolling landscape. Majestic oaks graced the front lawn and several giant barns stood at the back. When I saw the farm for the first time, I thought it was a wonderful home for Angel as well as a friendly place for elves. At the time I did not know much about the world of the elementals, though I was soon to learn.

It had been a big day for my little charge. At a family party she had received gifts and enjoyed cake, and had taken her first steps without assistance. The little one lay exhausted in her crib clutching a brand-new teddy bear. As I was giving her my gift, a love bath of vibrant rose light, Nyna appeared by my side.

I was startled. "Nyna! You found us!"

"Greetings, Darci. Have you enjoyed your first year on Earth as a Spirit Guide?"

"There have been ups and downs."

Nyna chuckled. "Yes, this little one is learning to walk. Soon you will have to pay attention every moment as she will be walking, talking, and getting into everything."

"Why were you gone so long? Why didn't I hear from you? I thought perhaps you didn't know where we were."

"We elves have an excellent communication network. I was informed of your move to the country, but I have been very busy. After all, I am an honored elfin elder and one of the leaders on this continent."

"I did not know that, Nyna. I'm very glad to see you again."

"You may not be once I've told you what I came here to say."

I felt a strange compression of my energy. "What is it, Nyna?"

She gazed into the crib. "This little darling, your dear charge, has many rough years ahead."

"I know her karma."

"But you do not know the circumstances. There will be days when you encounter frustration beyond anything you have ever known."

"Due to circumstances?"

"Or because of the influence of the people who surround her, or because of her choices."

"This is true of all Spirit Guides, is it not? When I was an apprentice guide here on Earth, I had several disconcerting experiences." Sighing, I felt heaviness descend upon me. "If only humans knew that we are here trying to help them. If only they could see or hear us!"

"It does seem odd," she said as she motioned toward the sleeping toddler, "that when they are babies they can see us, yet when they are older and out in the world, they forget we are here. We are invisible to them."

"You say we, Nyna—but elves are different from Spirit Guides."

"We are the same in that we are energetic beings with spirit bodies. What is different is our purpose."

"Mine is to watch over, guide, and protect Angel. I promised when I signed the records."

"And mine is to watch over, protect, and aid the Earth Mother. We elves specialize in flora, the very life breath of the planet."

"Because plants and trees produce oxygen."

"Very good, Darci. Of course, everything on this plane is interconnected, the seen and the unseen."

"So when the changes you spoke of arrive on Earth, everyone and everything will be affected."

Raising one eyebrow, she smiled. "You remember our previous conversations."

"I've thought much about them—and have questions, many questions."

"I will answer one, for I cannot dally. My duties call me."

"One! How can I choose?"

She glided gracefully around the crib as I tried to decide what, at that moment, I most wanted to know, finally blurting, "Please tell me something I do not know about Angel's destiny."

She moved toward me. "Have you heard of the Sabian Symbols?"

I shook my head.

"There is a symbol for each degree of the zodiac."

I wanted to make sure I understood. "For each of the 360 degrees of the sky surrounding Earth?"

"Yes. Examine the one that pertains to the degree where the sun was located from the vantage point of Earth on the day Angel was born."

I was about to ask how I might find information on these symbols when she vaporized into a stream of luminous energy, which quickly flowed out the window and disappeared into the night.

Because all Spirit Guides have connections with their teachers and advisors, on occasion I would call on my mentor and dear friend, Sottrol. After Nyna's departure, I sent him a telepathic message asking to see the Sabian Symbols.

His voice came into my mind. "Darci, know that these symbols were divinely inspired."

Instantly there was a glow in the room, which brightened until it took the shape and appearance of my mentor. There he stood, clad in a phosphorescent purple robe and cap, the crystals in his white beard glittering.

"Sottrol! Thank you so much for responding! I'm glad to see you."

"And I, you, Darci. Birthday greetings to Angel. I see she sleeps soundly."

"Yes. She has had a busy day."

"You ask about the Sabian Symbols. They were given by spirit in 1925 and are currently being interpreted by some of the finest minds working today in psychology, philosophy, theology, and astrology."

"Can you show me these symbols?"

"Of course, though I can see that you are specifically interested in the symbol that relates to Angel's day of birth."

"Yes. May I see it?"

"It is the symbol for degree one hundred two of the Great Wheel."

His aura became brighter until I could no longer see him. Slowly a picture manifested in the radiance. I was astonished. Three Tibetan monks sat at the feet of a mother who was nursing a baby. The newborn in her arms glowed with incandescent brilliance. I fixed my eyes on the image until it faded from view. Sottrol was also gone.

I sat dumbfounded. How did this symbol relate to Angel's destiny? Alas, I was left with more questions than answers.

Chapter Two

Celebration of the Rose Moon

Nyna had spoken the truth; my charge kept me very busy. Even at night when Angel slept, I found I had my hands full healing and revitalizing her. The grandmother elf was right about the frustration, too. Angel was a shy but independent child who acted and reacted from a place of insecurity and low self-esteem. These were weaknesses she was destined to face and, at this point, she allowed them to run her life. How I longed to talk with her, to explain her karma, to show her how to face the challenges and resolve them.

At age seven, Angel became very ill with pneumonia and was in bed for weeks. Her fever was so high a doctor visited the house, a cottage just up the road from the old family farm, which had been sold. Of course I stayed by her bedside and continuously sent healing energy to her; I didn't have much else to do—or that I wanted to do.

On one of these quiet evenings as Angel lay in fevered sleep, the ceiling began to glow. I thought perhaps Sottrol or one of my other teachers had come to help heal my charge. The radiance brightened until light rained down precipitating two golden forms. A moment later Nyna stood before me with a male elf by her side. Both wore forest-green cloaks. He was slightly taller with hair so blond it was almost as white as hers. He appeared young and quite fit.

"Greetings, Mr. Stillwater. May I introduce Orillo Benaye?"

I nodded from my seated position by Angel's bed. "Welcome, Orillo. Good to see you again, Nyna."

Nyna stepped closer, her eyes glistening, her cloak shimmering with thousands of tiny stars. "Orillo is elfin royalty," she announced. "He is interested in helping protect your charge."

I was surprised. "I know that this is my first time as a Spirit Guide and I am inexperienced, but I do not think I need help," I replied, perhaps a bit too defensively.

Orillo grinned. "You are doing a fine job, Mr. Stillwater. My assistance will allow you time to study."

Now I was confused. "Study what?"

Nyna winked at me. "You must educate yourself on Earth matters."

"I cannot leave her, not for any reason. I have sworn to be her Guide. I have signed the records!"

"Yes, yes." Nyna looked at the sick child with much compassion. "There is a higher purpose here, Darci. We elves wish you and Angel to work with us, to be a part of something very great. We do not want you to be distracted from your duties, so we have come to offer assistance. Prince Orillo volunteered."

"Thank you." I nodded toward him.

His stance was regal, legs apart, hands on his hips so that his cape was parted revealing a golden belt, which seemed animated with swirling light. He did indeed look like a prince.

Their visit was brief, though I thought about them often as Angel recovered.

∞

The following summer they came again to the cottage. It was the evening of a full moon, and the sweet floral essence that floated on the breeze lured me to the open window of Angel's bedroom. Just as I was trying to determine the source of the intoxicating fragrance, two luminescent spheres of energy appeared in the yard below. In a moment the light crystallized into the elder elf and her royal companion.

"Come join us, Darci," called Nyna as she waved.

I glanced at the sleeping child. "You know I cannot—will not—leave my post."

Suddenly Orillo manifested beside me. "She sleeps soundly. I will stay with her." He nodded toward the window. "You go."

My heart urged me to remain by Angel's side, but curiosity drew me to the grandmother elf, who, I knew, had much wisdom to impart. Taking a deep breath, I floated down to her.

"You will be back soon," Nyna assured, beckoning me to follow.

We moved quickly through the field by the house. The smell of freshly cut hay, newly raked, filled the air. The dewy atmosphere created a magical mist that snaked about us as we descended into a glen and approached a stand of glowing trees. The elder elf escorted me into this incandescent forest. I heard singing and laughter and, upon reaching a well-protected clearing, saw a gathering of several dozen, colorfully dressed elves in all shapes and sizes. All eyes were upon us as Nyna led me into the circle.

She raised her hand and the group quieted. "May I introduce Darci Stillwater? He is here to learn more about us, for I believe he will choose to assist us in the days to come."

As a murmur rose from the clan, an elder gentleman stepped forward using a tree branch as a cane. His white beard, plaited into several braids, hung to his waist. He wore a green jacket that appeared to be made of fresh leaves, and his trousers were the color of fieldstone. He looked me up and down, then poked with his twisted stick.

"What do you wish to know, Stillwater?"

I hesitated.

The old elf fixed his earth-colored eyes upon me. "There are many stories, Spirit Guide. I ask again, what do you wish to know?"

"W-wh-whatever you wish to tell," I managed to sputter.

The elves, including Nyna, quietly seated themselves in a circle. Patting the ground beside her, the elfin grandmother indicated I should join them.

The old elf surveyed his audience. "Most of you know me. I am Grandfather Jekaht, and this is the Celebration of the Rose Moon. I have now observed seven hundred and forty such celebrations." He turned in my direction. "That is the first thing you must know about us, Stillwater. We elves are spirits with souls—as are you—as are humans. However, we come but once to the earth in this form, and because this is our one elfin lifetime, we stay for hundreds of years."

At that moment a child who looked to be about two or three, toddled to Jekaht's side. "Gee-pah!" she chirped gleefully.

He stroked her fuzzy auburn hair and smiled. "Here is a little one who will witness many changes on this planet."

"Tell the guide about our avatar!" The voice came from the back of the group.

The old elf guided the toddler back to her family, then settled himself on a log. "That is not where to begin," he replied, stroking his snowy beard. "Let us first talk about how a soul is chosen to become an enlightened being, an avatar."

Although I was fascinated by the way the glowing trees and bushes lit the clearing and by the radiant faces of the elfin beings that surrounded me, my attention was focused on this grandfather elf. Realizing that he had inhabited the earth since the thirteenth century, I followed his gaze around the circle.

"We earn our gifts and we earn our challenges." His voice seemed to deepen as he continued. "Our avatar has earned her place as our enlightened leader."

"You know the soul who is to come?" I blurted.

"Yes, Stillwater. We elders do. Tonight I will tell you a story about this soul, the one who will arrive to lead us into the new time. This being has walked the earth many times as a human, sometimes as a male, sometimes as a female. In every incarnation, this soul has respected and honored our Earth Mother."

Sounds of approval rose from the elves. Grandfather Jekaht held up his hand to quiet them. "I will tell you tonight of a similar full moon eve thousands of years ago, a time when the great Yin energy dominated the earth and matriarchal societies ruled the lands. This soul was born to a priestess of the largest temple in existence at the time. She was conceived in a sacred ceremony, surrounded by stone caldrons of fire, witnessed by the Creator and the Earth Mother. She was named Jasmina after the intoxicating flower, and she was raised from birth to be a priestess. By the time eight summers had passed, she was assisting with ceremonies at the temple."

Eight years old, I mused silently. *Why—Angel just celebrated her eighth birthday.*

Jekaht eyed me as if he had read my thought, then went on. "As you may know, in those days men and women lived separately. They came together for various reasons, and when they did, the men always worked for and served the women. Naturally some men became restless and questioned this arrangement. After all, they were stronger than the women, but the women were smarter and therefore held the power.

"Jasmina's father was a strong, handsome man with golden skin and onyx-colored hair. The first time he saw the girl, he knew he had fathered her, for she had his ebony eyes and dark curled tresses. The young females were not allowed to fraternize with the men and boys, but this man wanted to know his beautiful daughter, so he made a daring and reckless plan.

"In those days, the climate was temperate, so no fires were needed for warmth. Women had control of the cook fires and the temple fires. In fact, fire was seen mainly as the gateway to connect with the goddess. Very late on this full moon night, Jasmina's father sneaked into the temple. He had been there many times to participate in ceremonies, so he knew how to conceal himself from the women guarding the sacred fires. In one hand he held a tree branch, in the other a stone. Once in position, he lobbed the stone down the temple steps, then darted to the closest cauldron to light the branch. The guards followed the sound of the falling rock and did not see him dash around the back and down the hill with the flame.

"Swift were his feet as he circled the temple to a patch of brush near the compound of the priestesses. With no hesitation he hurled the burning branch into the bushes, then hid from view. The brush exploded into flame! The sentries in the compound cried, 'Fire!' Soon the women were awake and battling the blaze with wet branches and bowls of water.

"The distraction he had created gave him the opportunity to creep stealthily into the area where no men were allowed. Several girls were watching the commotion through a window in the compound wall. He spied Jasmina and, faster than the strike of lightning, grabbed her and disappeared into the night. The child's cries were not heard above the din.

"Carrying her over his shoulder like a sack of grain, he did not stop until he reached a hill some distance from the temple. He was thoroughly spent and sat panting, holding tightly to Jasmina's wrist.

"The girl felt a strange mixture of terror and curiosity, for she had seen men only from a distance.

"He looked into her eyes, so like his own; they were wide with fear, her face, tear-streaked. 'It is all right,' he said, still breathing heavily. 'I will not harm you.'

"She squirmed away, but he grabbed her by the ankle. 'You stay with me now!' he told her brusquely.

"Our little Jasmina curled herself into a ball, arms around her knees, toes digging into the earth. She had been taught that the earth provides all needs, so she silently asked the Earth Mother for help.

"Her abductor pointed to his face. 'Do you see? You look like me! I am your father. Do you know what that is?'

"She stared at him, her ebony eyes reflecting the moonlight.

"'Don't be afraid. I took you because—I want to know you. You are a part of me.'

"'We are all a part of the Earth Mother.' She finally spoke.

"'Ah!' said he. 'You have learned your lessons well. You have not learned who I am—who any of the men are. I want to teach you.' He had become tired of restraining her. 'Can I let go? Will you run? I will catch you again if you try.'

"She sat as still as a stone and stared at him as he released his grip. He rubbed his dark, curly beard, wondering how to explain his part in her existence."

Tittering and chuckling came from some of the listening elves.

Jekaht nodded. "Yes, a delicate subject, especially for one so young. But this story is not so much about what Jasmina's father did as about what she did.

"As the unfamiliar man beside her began to talk of the sacred ceremony that led to her conception, she breathed a prayer into her hands. 'Dear Earth Mother, I am your devoted daughter. Please help me understand what is happening.' She then dug her fingers into the soil, as if she were holding on for life.

"Suddenly a vision came into her mind. She clearly saw the image of the man beside her stealing fire from the temple and torching the trees and bushes by her abode. Becoming both angry and afraid at the same moment, she took a breath. Then this little girl reached deep inside her for courage.

"'You set the fire!' She spoke in a strong, even tone.

"He was startled, losing his balance momentarily, then stepping toward her. 'You saw me?'

"She took a sharp breath. 'Admit that you burned the shrubs, the trees, the very ground!'

"For a second time, he was taken aback. 'It was for you—so I could reach you, spend time with you—know you.'

"She felt a pang of fear in her belly. Clamping her eyes shut, she prayed silently once more. 'Dear Goddess, dear Earth Mother, protect me. Show me what to do.'

"Again an image came to her. This time she saw the man on his hands and knees, forehead pressed against the ground. Radiant emerald light flowed from the earth encircling him. She felt power surge within her and strength she had never known before.

"Kneeling in front of her, his eyes searched hers. 'You are a part of me,' he said softly.

"She stood abruptly and sprinkled the soil clutched in her hands over his head. 'No matter what your reason, you have no cause to injure the Earth Mother or anything upon her. You must ask to be pardoned.'

"He did not expect this. 'Ask who? The priestesses?'

"Her dark eyes softened. 'We are all children of the earth. Ask the Great Mother, for it is she you have burned.'

"He stared at her.

"'I have seen that you will be forgiven if you are truly sorry.' There was no question: she was in control now.

"He held her gaze and saw her power, then exhaled and lay his head on the ground. 'I did not mean to harm anything,' he began.

"Jasmina spoke with authority. 'Address the Great Mother.'

"'Great Mother, I am truly sorry that I injured you—your plants, your trees. Please forgive my impulsiveness. I wished only to see …'

"The child raised her arms. 'Emerald light engulfs you. Great Mother pardons you. Now you must return me to my home, for there is healing to be done and I am learning this art.'

"Overcome with awe, he escorted her back to the compound. At first light he quietly joined the men who were helping clean up the burned area, while Jasmina added her young voice to the group of priestesses, women, and girls who were singing a healing chant for the trees and plants."

The elves, especially the children, applauded the old storyteller. He bowed his head in appreciation.

"Now tell me. What attribute did this blessed soul practice? What did Jasmina learn?"

"Prayer to the Earth Mother!" one voice called out.

"Yes," Jekaht responded, "though she was taught this by the priestesses."

"Receiving help in the form of visions?" speculated another elf.

"Most females in that time experienced this. What did she learn on her own?"

"Courage." I spoke up.

"Correct, Spirit Guide! All enlightened leaders must have courage." The elder waved his hand above his head. "Now let's have a song! Let the celebration continue!"

As the elves began to sing, some moving into the circle to dance, Nyna placed her hand on my arm. "Time to return to Angel."

We slipped quietly away and soon I was again by the bedside of my charge. As soon as I thanked Orillo, the two elves were gone.

"My dear Angel." I caressed her with golden light. "The Rose Moon is smiling through the window—and I just heard the most marvelous story— about a girl just your age."

CHAPTER THREE
CONCLAVE BY THE SEA

The briny air and the sound of breaking waves lulled Angel into a peaceful sleep. For her tenth summer, the extended family had rented a large cottage on the ocean. My young charge came alive in the sun and waves and had played all day to the point of sunburn and exhaustion.

Sitting by her cot on the upstairs porch, I let my gaze wander over the beach and seascape. Lights from cottages along the cove created a string of pearls, which led to the dark expanse of ocean.

As I was reviewing the day, a busy one for Angel filled with sun, sand, sea, and dozens of relatives, I felt a tap on my shoulder. Surprised, I turned to see Prince Orillo standing beside me, smiling, his violet cloak shimmering in the breeze.

"Greetings, Mr. Stillwater."

"Hello. You startled me, Orillo—and please call me Darci."

He peered over at Angel. "She seems to be in a very sound sleep."

"Yes. She's exhausted," I replied.

He then leaned back against the railing, the sea breeze ruffling his hair. "Has she been writing stories?"

"Yes."

"Good. Encourage her. She will have many tales to tell."

"What kinds of tales?" I asked, thinking about her last homemade book about a pony.

"Spirit stories. She will come to know the elves—to know me—perhaps even the avatar."

"This avatar you speak of every time I see you, who is she?"

"You mean: who has she been? She is not currently on Earth."

"Tell me about her, Orillo. When will she arrive?"

"That I cannot say. The timing depends on how events unfold on this planet." The nearly full moon emerged from a bank of clouds sending a path of glitter across the waves and illuminating the white-blond hair of the elfin prince. Orillo nodded at the reflections, his eyes dancing with lunar light. "Time for you to know more. There is a conclave of elves close by. Take yourself west along the shore until you reach the rocky crags. You'll see the glow of their circle."

Making certain Angel was asleep, I entrusted Orillo with her care. As I floated from the second-story porch, a tiny brilliant sphere of light appeared by my side.

"Beautiful evening by the sea." The high, sweet voice came from the glowing globe. I peered at it and, to my amazement, saw a small luminous being. She shone too brightly for me to make out her features, though I could see tiny wings that moved rapidly like those of a hummingbird. Her form seemed fluid.

She flew nearer. "Follow me, Spirit Guide."

West along the beach we glided. My companion seemed to enjoy floating about six inches above where the waves lapped the shore. Soon we were at the end of the sand where giant rocks rose to form a great hill of stone. To my surprise, my phosphorescent friend led me out over the water and along the base of this outcropping. A moment later I saw the glow Orillo had mentioned. A shallow cave about ten feet above the waves was illuminated, though I could not tell if the beings gathered there imparted the golden light or if the rocks themselves radiated the glow. As we drew closer, I saw a circle of elves seated on the stone floor with dozens of tiny lighted spheres floating around them.

"Greetings, Spirit Guide!" I heard a voice call out. "Come join us!" A jolly fellow with a short beard and bright blue jacket waved for me to sit by him. I thought I recognized him from the gathering in the woods three summers before.

As I seated myself, one of the tiny glowing spheres settled on my shoulder, providing me with the opportunity to examine her more closely. I could discern her translucent wings, and her deep blue garment seemed to lap and surge around her like the ocean waves.

"She likes you," chuckled the elf who had greeted me. "I am Feman Foreste at your service, Spirit Guide. Welcome to our gathering."

"Thank you," I replied, gazing around the circle at the radiant elfin faces. "I am Darci Stillwater. Prince Orillo sent me."

An excited buzz rose from the group.

"The prince is here?" asked the elf next to Feman.

"He is just down the beach on the porch of a cottage—watching my charge so that I might join you."

"Then we are very honored to have you amongst us, Darci," said Feman. "The prince must wish you to hear the story. Preparations for the arrival of our avatar have begun. Telling her soul story is one of the ways we draw her to us and welcome her."

At that moment, another tiny being darted in front of me and hovered. The rapid flutter of wings tickled my nose, and Feman laughed as I wrinkled it.

"Oh, forgive me, Radnuton. Mr. Stillwater, the faeries wish to be introduced. I did not know this is your first experience with these elementals."

"Yes, sir. It is. They seem to know."

The little creature lit on my knee and bowed. His striped cape looked as if it were made of rain, and his hat appeared to be fashioned from a fresh leaf, though he appeared so luminous I caught only a glimpse of his likeness.

Feman laughed again in his jolly way. "Meet Radnuton Rainbee. The faery perched on your shoulder, the one who led you here, is Myna Sealong."

"Pleased to meet you," I managed, still amazed.

"We're here because we have an avatar arriving too!" Radnuton informed me.

"There are many such gatherings all over the planet." Feman gestured, sweeping his hand. "It is our way of welcoming these highly evolved beings."

Radnuton jigged around joyfully. "We're preparing an energetic path for them to enter."

Feman smiled. "By telling their stories, we draw them to their destiny on Earth."

"I see." I wasn't sure I did.

"Let's begin!" The elfin voice came from the other side of the circle.

"Very well," responded Feman, rubbing his hands in anticipation of the telling. "Since Mr. Stillwater has other duties, we will start with the tale of another lifetime lived by the precious soul who is to be the elfin avatar."

Faeries who were airborne settled on the knees, shoulders, and caps of the elves, and all turned their attention to Feman.

"We journey now to India in a time of magic and mystery. In those days even more than today, elephants were coveted beasts of burden. Not only did they carry people and goods, they could also move fallen trees and spray water with their trunks. In that lifetime, our avatar lived as a boy named Rahid. Because his father was an elephant trainer, he grew up around the giant beasts and helped with feeding and bathing them. His rapport with the elephants grew until he could understand their expressions, movements, and sounds. He loved all those in his father's care, though his favorite was a female named Rana. They had been constant companions since her birth. When she was old enough, Rahid trained her. So devoted were they to each other that Rana would allow no one to ride her except the boy.

"When Rahid was ten, a gang of men raided his father's land and stole the valued pachyderms, all but Rana, who refused to go. The thieves had beaten her, trying to force her out of the yard. When Rahid arrived early the next morning to feed the herd, he found his beloved beast injured but alive. He wept bitterly as he inspected her wounds and saw how she had been abused. 'Oh, Rana, dear Rana!' he cried. 'How could anyone hurt you so?'

"The theft was devastating to his father and, indeed, to the entire extended family for the elephants provided their sole living. In those days, there were no laws or policemen, only a generally understood creed of integrity. Rahid's father called on his relatives, his neighbors, his friends, and his customers to help him find the stolen animals.

"As much as the boy wished to help with the search, he could not leave his beloved Rana. He brought her close to their home, which was at a distance from the elephant yard. Camping by her side, he tended her injuries, all the while talking to her, stroking her forehead or her trunk. Several lacerations were deep and needed special attention.

"On the third night after the theft as Rahid slept in the grass by Rana's side, he had a nightmare. Scowling and thrashing in his sleep, he saw the thugs beating Rana as they tried to drive her away with the others. In the dream Rana turned to him and clearly cried his name. Still asleep, he screamed. Feeling her trunk tousle his hair, he heard her say, 'I can show you where the others are. Climb up on me.'

"'But, Rana,' the boy replied, still dreaming, 'are you well enough to travel?'

"'Of course,' the pachyderm responded. 'You'll see for yourself.'

"As soon as Rahid scrambled onto his beloved elephant, she immediately traveled in a different direction from the one taken by the search party. Moonlight made flickering, dappled patterns on her back as her giant feet seemed to hover above the ground. She moved noiselessly through brush, under trees, and along a river.

"Rana's voice seemed to float into his head. 'We must be very quiet,' she told him. 'The robbers are close by.'

"Only moments later, Rahid saw the glow of a campfire in the distance. From his vantage point, he spied the stolen elephants on a flat plain by the river.

"'How did they get there?' he wondered. 'Their tracks went in the other direction.'

"To his surprise, Rana read his thoughts and replied, 'The clever thieves drove them south, then, upon reaching the river, forced them to wade north. The moving water obscured their tracks.' She seemed to gesture with her trunk. 'There are too many robbers. We must get help.'

Turning and gliding back along the way she had come, she seemed to sail effortlessly, almost as if she were flying.

"Again Rahid felt her trunk touching his head, this time waking him from the dream. The boy jumped up and ran to the house where the searchers were preparing to set out again.

"His father appeared tired and worried. 'Is Rana better? Do you wish to come with us today?'

"Rahid hopped from one foot to the other with excitement. 'I know where they are!'

"His uncle raised an eyebrow in amazement. 'Our stolen animals? But how?'

"The boy grinned. 'Rana showed me in a dream—though it seemed so real. We must go north.'

"A neighbor waved his hand. 'But their tracks go south.'

"Rahid's father reminded the group that they had lost the trail. The boy quickly told them that the robbers had driven the animals south to the river, then north through the current so they would not be followed. 'Rana told me,' he said.

"Shaking his head in disbelief, an uncle asked, 'Your elephant talks?'

"'I hear her—inside my head,' he told them.

"His father smiled. 'Elephants communicate with each other over many, many miles: this much we know. All right, son. Show us the way.'

"'Bring many with you, Father. The robbers are numerous and strong.'

"Adding more men, the searchers moved quickly and surrounded the camp of thieves. The element of surprise gave them the advantage. They successfully captured the robbers and rounded up the elephants. After herding them home, Rahid and his father thanked Rana. As the boy was stroking and hugging his elephant, he was surprised to hear her say, 'Thank you. There is much love between us.' From that day on, the boy and beast conversed mind-to-mind and remained friends for life."

The group of elves applauded as the faeries rose from their perches cheering in high voices.

Feman bowed slightly, then gestured to quiet the crowd.

"I told you this story because our avatar learned something important in that lifetime. Does anyone know what it was?"

As the storyteller looked from face to face, a voice came from across the circle. "Love of animals?"

Feman raised his index finger. "Yes, but that wasn't the most significant skill."

I ventured a response. "Telepathy?"

"Yes, Spirit Guide!" The elf grinned and nodded. "Mind-to-mind communication is an indispensable ability. We all need strong telepathic skills when dealing with humans and their world."

"Will our avatar have to deal with humans?" The question came from an elder female elf not far from me.

"Oh yes," the storyteller responded. "Her ultimate goal is to appear to humans and make them aware of us and our place on Earth. She will use telepathy to communicate to humankind." He nodded to me. "Pay attention, Mr. Stillwater. You can choose to be involved with our beloved avatar in a most important way."

I was taken aback. "What way is that?"

Feman winked at me. "You shall learn the possibilities—but now you must return to your charge and relieve Orillo, for we wish him to join us."

Radnuton landed on my knee. "Can you find your way back, Spirit Guide? I'll be glad to show you."

"Thank you but I know my way." I looked around at the unusual gathering. "And thank you for your company and that fine story."

A chorus of voices, low and high, bid me good-bye as I bowed and took my leave. Drifting from the illuminated rocks, I floated over the waves to the beach. The tide had receded; sand and stones glistened in the moonlight; a gentle breeze wafted off the ocean. The beautiful, tranquil scene reminded me again of how much I loved the earth and how happy I was to be here watching over my dear Angel.

Chapter Four
The Great Willow

The great willow outside Angel's home stood twice as high as the house and could be seen for miles. Its long graceful branches swayed in the wind, occasionally fingering the windowpane of the bedroom she shared with her sister.

Each summer their father would trim the branches, which often reached to the ground. The girls, who liked to play under the tree, sometimes gathered the cut branches and fashioned them into hula skirts.

In August of the summer I met Feman, a family reunion of their father's Scottish clan was held at their modest home. The relatives were too numerous for the small house, so the parents set up a long table under the willow. The group was boisterous, laughing and chatting in thick Scottish accents. Angel marveled at their speech, which was supposed to be English like hers, but she couldn't understand a word the adults were saying. She felt left out, often the case for my charge. Her self-esteem had not improved even though she was doing well in school and had developed her talent for drawing.

That day she had a disagreement with one of her cousins over the sketch she had done of a fairy from a cartoon movie. I stood close to the arguing children, wishing I could introduce Angel to the faeries I had met, showing her how they were far more splendid than the animated two-dimensional ones. Indeed, there was so much I wanted to tell her but she was unaware of my existence, at least consciously.

The party continued into the night, loud voices and laughter rising through the branches of the willow into Angel's bedroom. Finally, all was quiet and my dear charge drifted into deep sleep. Seizing the opportunity, I fashioned a dream about Radnuton Rainbee, Myna Sealong, and the other faeries I had met, then slid the sparkling images into her mind.

The next day was humid. Thunderstorms approached from the north. The sisters and their mother watched from the front porch as the sky darkened over the farm and silos in the distance. When thunder boomed loudly overhead, Angel ran up the stairs to her room and sat on the bed hugging her knees. Willow branches whipped the window as lightning flashed and rain drenched the landscape.

Late that evening when I was balancing Angel's energy, I heard a tap on the window. The night was quiet with only a very light breeze, so I knew it wasn't a branch making the sound. Once by the sill, I saw Radnuton hovering among the slender leaves of the willow.

"Ho! Darci Stillwater!" he called in his high, ethereal voice. "Come join us!"

I was surprised. "Where?"

The petite being pointed to the base of the willow and disappeared. Looking down, I saw the trunk of the great tree and the ground under it glowing as elves and faeries gathered.

"You may join them." Nyna's voice came from behind me. "I know you wish never to leave your charge, so I will sit with Angel."

"Nyna! How good to see you."

"And I, you, Darci." The grandmother elf curtsied gracefully. As she glided to Angel's bedside, her emerald dress shimmered with a luminescence all its own. Her white hair was braided and wound upon her head like a crown. She nodded in my direction. "She will be fine. You go. There is a great storyteller here tonight."

After thanking Nyna, I floated out of the second-story window and joined the group coming together under the giant umbrella of willow branches. Glancing up, I marveled at how the underside of the leaves and limbs were illuminated by the strange glow that seemed to accompany these elfin gatherings.

As I glanced around, I recognized Orillo and moved to his side. "Prince Orillo, hello."

"Greetings, Darci." When he smiled, his eyes glistened with either merriment or mischievousness; I couldn't tell which. "Come. You shall have the seat of honor by the trunk of the tree." He motioned for me to make myself comfortable. "After all, this is your home."

As soon as I sat, the elves did the same, forming a circle. The dozen or so faeries present lit in the branches above us. Only the prince remained standing.

"Welcome all," he began. "As our avatars prepare for their entrance onto the earth plane, we prepare also. We make way for them by telling their stories, by singing their praises, for they have traveled many roads and learned many things." Standing, hands on hips surveying those present, he paused, his burgundy cape fluttering in the summer breeze.

I, too, looked at the elfin faces, radiant in the rarefied light, recognizing several from other gatherings I had attended. Since this was my third, I was starting to feel more comfortable around these elementals.

The prince held up his hand. "Tonight I welcome an old friend and storyteller from the great continent south of this one."

"South America!" An elf near me spoke up.

Orillo nodded. "Please welcome Sarlia Contoza."

As the elves applauded and faeries cheered, an iridescent being twirled from behind the trunk of the willow to the prince's side. She was magnificent with sparkling rose veils fluttering around her. Her dress seemed to be lavender lace; her black and silver hair was plaited in a thick braid that hung over her shoulder, and she wore a fresh pink rose tucked above her elfin ear.

Kissing her hand, Orillo led her into the circle. She nodded her thanks, then elegantly walked around looking from face to face. She stopped when she reached me.

The prince appeared at my side. "Madame Contoza, may I introduce Darci Stillwater?"

When she fixed her dark eyes upon me, her penetrating stare transformed into a smile. "Ah, Mr. Stillwater." She finally spoke, her voice deep and resonant. "There is much said about your participation."

"Participation? Participation in what?"

Before I had finished speaking those few words, Sarlia spun away and clapped with authority. "Come, come. You wish a story, si?"

Affirmative cries rose through the branches of the now luminous willow.

"All right, then. This is a tale of our elfin avatar when she lived long ago on the continent of South America. She was born the daughter of an influential man who was a designer of pyramids. This was during the time of an advanced civilization, which had medicine, domesticated animals, impressive construction, and more. Schooling was done by the extended family.

"Our avatar, named Leijasa in that lifetime, was a beautiful female with golden-colored skin, onyx eyes, and hair as dark as a moonless night. Of the four children, she was the one most interested in her father's work. Her mother taught the children basic skills such as language and household management, but Leijasa longed to be tutored by her father.

"One stormy day, she followed him to work, to the future site of a great pyramid. He had designed the temple and had been working with the head of construction to assemble a team of builders. Eyes wide, Leijasa watched from behind a tree at the edge of the field as a high priest in ceremonial garb approached her father and the head builder.

"The holy man was scowling and spoke loudly. 'Change your plans! The temple must be twice as big and further in that direction.' He gestured toward the woods. 'I must have the main entrance facing the rising sun. This will be an immense structure, one that will stand for centuries as the sacred center of the universe, if the deities are willing. Angering them will not do!'

"Leijasa's father scanned the site while the man in charge of construction responded to the priest's demands.

"'What you're asking will require felling many trees. This will delay the placing of the first stones.'

"'So the stonework will begin on the next moon cycle. That is not important. I have had a dream and saw that this is how it must be!' the priest declared.

"Leijasa's father nodded to him. 'We must be certain of the placement and orientation. Walk with us, your holiness, and together let us mark the new parameters.'

"The priest seemed relieved and told the men, 'I know I shall receive another sign that the deities approve of these changes.'

"Her father turned and began to move in her direction, so she quickly retreated, though she was fascinated by what she had seen and heard.

"Although Leijasa had lived fifteen years in Mayan society, she had been well protected by her family. However, our avatar was both strong willed and curious. The next day, the sky still filled with storm clouds, she dressed in her brother's clothes, tied her hair up with vine, and again followed her father. Approaching the area, she heard a strange, sad moaning, then another similar sound overlapping the first. A few steps closer, the clamor of cracking branches and the thud of a freshly hewn tree cut through the forest. As the noise of stone tools hacking wood became clear, more groans and deep cries reached her ears. She not only heard these strange outcries, she felt them in her heart and belly.

"Skirting the site, she quietly joined the young men and boys who were clearing the area. The closer she got to the crew, the louder the moaning became. Mystified, she tried to blend in by pulling a severed branch to a pile. A boy about her age noticed her.

"'You're new,' he remarked.

"'I started today,' she responded attempting to deepen her voice.

"He raised an eyebrow while wiping perspiration from his cheek. 'This is hard work. You're a bit skinny to be on this crew.'

"'I can do the job,' she retorted defensively. She grabbed his arm. 'Doesn't that sound bother you?'

31

"The boy raised an eyebrow. 'What sound?'

"'All the moaning and groaning. Don't you hear it?'

"He shrugged. 'Juarto hurt his back yesterday and he groaned a bit, but he's not here today.'

"Deciding not to pursue the conversation, she shrugged as well and continued to drag branches, but the longer she stayed, the harder it was to listen to the overlapping waves of despair. As the crew took a break for water and food, she walked among the stumps. When she reached the line of trees that were next to be cut down, the largest touched her with a branch and released a quiet moan.

"'It's you!' she exclaimed. 'The sounds are coming from you trees!'

"Concealing herself behind the trunk of the great tree, she lay her hands and forehead on the bark. Feeling a subtle vibration, words floated into her mind.

"'Dear one, you hear us, you hear our distress as we are chopped in half and destroyed.'

"'Chopped in half? What do you mean?' the girl asked.

"'When the men cut us down,' the tree replied, 'they take away the half that reaches to the sky but leave the other half, our roots that reach into the earth.'

"'I'm so sorry.' She sent the thought back to the tree as her heart swelled with compassion. 'Why don't the others hear you?'

"'Dear one, you are sensitive and far more tuned to the subtle vibrations of the flora than are others of your species.'

"'What can I do?' she whispered. 'I am just a girl. I cannot stop them. You are all being felled to make way for a great temple.'

"'You needn't stop them,' the tree responded telepathically. 'But there is something you can do.'

"'I'll help however I can,' she promised.

"As the tree replied, a picture entered her mind, an image of the elder high priest, hand raised, standing before this very tree. 'We are not respected as wise and generous beings. If we are approached with reverence and asked to give ourselves, we do so joyfully.' In her mind she saw every man on the crew place an offering at the base of each tree before cutting it. A branch of the great tree gently touched her shoulder. 'Tell the others what I have told you, for this site will not be sacred and fit for a temple unless you do. The deities ask that this be done.'

"She kissed the rough bark, took a deep breath, and marched toward the man in charge of the cutters. Approaching, she prayed for the words to convince him. He stood and was about to order his crew back to work when she stepped in front of him. Staring down at her, he observed that this odd-looking young person was small and delicate like a girl but dressed as a boy. Looking up, she met his gaze, fixing her eyes on his. In a bold voice she stated, 'No more trees can be cut today. They do not want it.'

"'What?' He appeared surprised and amused. 'Who doesn't want it? We're already behind schedule.'

"She thought fast. 'The deities. I received a sign.'

"He was taken aback by her reply, then frowned at her, doubt on his face. 'Why should I believe you?'

"Our avatar was ready. 'Take me to the high priest,' she told him. 'But you must cut no trees until I have told his holiness what I have heard.'

"He waved at her dismissively. 'You go to the priest. We must get back to work.'

"Leijasa knew she had to stop the men from hacking down any more trees. Although she felt fear rising in her, she could think of only one way. Turning on her heel, she strode not toward the village and the priest's abode, but in the opposite direction to the trees. She used her flexibility and strength to climb up into the large tree that had spoken to her, coming to rest near the trunk on a limb facing the man and his crew.

"He was not pleased. 'Come down now!' he yelled.

"'No!' she shouted back stubbornly with more courage than she felt. 'I will climb down once you bring the high priest here to me!'

"There was nothing the man could do. He directed his crew to continue to clean up the site, but to cut no trees. The men and boys stared up at her from time to time as they went about dragging and piling the remaining branches.

"The boy who had spoken to her earlier walked to the base of the tree and called up. 'You're crazy! You're going to get into trouble. You'll get us all into trouble!'

"She shook her head defiantly. 'I'll be in trouble if I don't do this!'

"At that moment her father walked over to see what was happening. He had been talking with the men who were going to lay the cornerstones. When he gazed up into the tree, at first he did not recognize his daughter, but when he heard her voice, he knew it was Leijasa.

"'My daughter! What are you doing?' he cried. 'You disgrace us here at this sacred site!'

"'No, Father,' she called down, 'for I have had a sign from the deities. I must tell the priest.'

"'Climb down now, Leijasa! If you insist on seeing the priest, let us go together, but first you must wash and change your clothes. You are not presentable.'

"Glancing at her bare arms and legs, she saw how dirty and scratched they were. 'I cannot, Father,' she replied holding tightly to the trunk. 'These men will cut this tree down if I leave here.'

"Shaking his head, he mumbled, 'You are the most stubborn of my children.' Raising his voice to reach her high above him, he called, 'I will ask them to delay the cutting. Now come down!'

"Leijasa was undecided. She trusted her father, but didn't know if the other men would heed his request.

"Once again she heard the tree speaking, its words reverberating in her heart and mind. 'Stay and protect us, compassionate one. Inform the others of our wishes.'

"She answered her father in a strong voice. 'I must do this. You will soon learn why. If you bring the high priest to this tree, I will tell him and all of you about the sign I have received.'

"Her frustrated parent tried one more time to convince the girl to climb down. 'I love you, my daughter, but this madness will not turn out well. Come down now or I shall have to punish you!'

"Her body trembled as she replied, 'This will end well, Father. You'll see. But you must fetch the priest. I'll stay here as long as it takes. I will not move!'

"Though upset and anxious, her father realized his only action was to find the priest. A crowd began to gather as word spread about the girl in the tree. By the time he returned with the holy man, many people were standing in the clearing, all eyes on Leijasa.

"The priest appeared annoyed. 'What is this nonsense, girl? Come down now! You have interrupted my day.'

"Having thought about the situation, our avatar decided that she had the advantage from her perch. From that height her words could reach the crowd, so she stayed where she was. Taking a deep breath, she bravely addressed the elder. 'Thank you for coming, your holiness. Hear what I have to say, then I shall come down.'

"'Go on. Go on,' the old priest sputtered.

"She tightened her grip on the tree whom she now felt was her friend. 'This is to be a sacred site, is it not?'

"'Yes, yes,' replied the elder in exasperation.

"'The deities have told me that they wish the trees to be acknowledged and appreciated before they are cut.'

"The elder glared at her skeptically as her father shook his head.

"She ventured more. 'There will be sadness and trouble here if this is not done.' Her voice was stronger now. 'The trees give themselves willingly, joyfully, if they are appreciated and respected as wise and generous beings.'

"Her father looked at her as if he were seeing his daughter for the first time, for her words had stirred his heart.

"The priest, however, was not convinced. 'Why do the deities tell you such things? Is it not my place to communicate with them?'

"She heard the great tree moan then say, 'He is too busy, too preoccupied. Stay strong and help us. Repeat what I have told you until you are believed.'

"Leijasa sighed. 'They say you have been too busy. What they ask is not so difficult: offerings at the base of each tree, thanks to each tree that is to be sacrificed. Oh, if only you could hear the terrible moaning because this has not been done!'

"The elder coughed. 'Moaning? Who is moaning? There is no sign from the deities. Come down!'

"She sat silent, not knowing what to say. The great tree sent her powerful words. 'Tell them the deities wish this and they send a sign now!'

"Inhaling, she stated those exact words, projecting to the priest and the crowd. As soon as the last word was spoken, a brilliant flash of lightning sliced the sky, striking the pile of brush and setting it afire. Clamorous peals of thunder followed, and all who had gathered scattered in fear. Even the priest ducked and covered his ears. As rain began to pour, Leijasa's father addressed the elder. 'That truly is a sign, your holiness. Let us do as she asks.'

"She saw the priest nod in agreement, and when he did, she heard the trees sigh happily. 'Thank you, blessed one,' said the great tree. 'May this custom continue for centuries to come.'

"That is the end of my story, which reminds us to respect and appreciate the trees and shows the amazing ability of our avatar to communicate with nature.'"

Sarlia smiled, bowed, and danced in the circle to applause and cheers. She raised her eyes to gaze at the illuminated branches and leaves of the willow. "Thank you, great tree, for your presence, your protection, your grace, and your beauty."

As those gathered continued their applause, thanking the storyteller, I heard what most of the others did not. Since I was sitting by the base of the great willow, leaning on the trunk, I felt a low rumbling vibration and heard a deep, jolly laugh. By the expression on Orillo's face, I knew he had also felt the tree's joy.

Stepping nimbly to Sarlia's side, the prince clasped her hand. "Wonderful storytelling—and it shows how our avatar developed a rapport with the flora."

"Especially trees!" interjected a young elf.

"After that incident," Sarlia added, "Leijasa was considered blessed. She eventually told others about her gift of telepathically communicating with the forest. From then on the Maya included new practices in their rituals especially to honor the trees."

The elves and faeries cheered anew. Orillo winked at me and I knew it was time for me to return to Angel's side.

As I relieved Nyna and settled close to my sleeping charge, I yearned to tell her what I had experienced under the great tree that tapped on her bedroom window. If only I could communicate with her as the trees had done with Leijasa. Sighing, I held in my heart the possibility that this might manifest for us in the future. I decided the very least I could do was fashion a magical dream about the great willow in her yard, the tree she knew so well but didn't really know at all.

CHAPTER FIVE
BLUE SKY BREATHING

Only a few years later, my charge was quickly becoming a beautiful young woman. However, she did not see herself that way. Angel's lack of self-esteem led her to be shy in social situations, especially at school. To compensate, she focused on her studies and achieved excellent grades.

Her life was not easy. Financial hardships kept her parents on edge. By the time she was a teen, her father had become a full-blown alcoholic, visiting a local bar every night after work. More often than not, Angel, her mother, and her younger sister and brother ate dinner without him. I watched her scramble to hide when her father's car pulled into the drive. She was terrified of the man, and my heart ached every time I saw her cringe in fear.

Music made her happy. Her mother usually had the radio on, playing the popular songs of the day. At sixteen she fell in love with a band from England, my last home when I was a human in the eighteenth century. She and her sister pasted pictures of the four young musicians on the ceiling of their shared bedroom. I cannot count the number of nights I looked into their faces as I hovered over Angel's bed. The styles in Liverpool were certainly different in my day.

Late one evening as I was helping to balance Angel's energy, I noticed a wavering glow outside the window. Floating over and looking out, I saw Nyna, Prince Orillo, and a Spirit Guide who appeared to be a Native American elder. I knew that the feather bonnet encircling his head and trailing down his back indicated his status as tribal chief.

Nyna saw me at the window and waved. After descending slowly and landing near the elfin grandmother, I bowed to all three.

"Darci Stillwater." Nyna extended a hand in my direction, then gestured toward the native man. "Meet Chief Blue Sky Breathing."

"My pleasure, Chief."

"The pleasure is mine, Mr. Stillwater. I have heard much about you."

Before I could ask what he had heard and from whom, Orillo stepped closer to me, his eyes dancing with excitement. "Darci, Chief Blue Sky Breathing has much to tell us. Nyna will stay with Angel while we accompany the chief."

"Where to?" I asked, remembering that Angel had had a rough day and needed my attention.

Nyna patted my arm as she read my mind. "Don't concern yourself. I will attend to Angel's needs. I'll give her an excellent elfin healing."

I nodded, for I had grown to trust both her and the prince.

"The chief will show us where," Orillo interjected. "And I, for one, cannot wait to hear his stories of our avatar." He grinned. "And you, Darci, you shall begin to learn about your connection."

"My connection?" I asked, but the words vaporized into the misty summer night. We were suddenly moving, flying through the glen behind the house, Chief Blue Sky Breathing in the lead, the elfin prince close behind, and me doing my best to keep up with them. After traveling for about two miles, we entered a thick wood. The others slowed when we reached a stream, then halted at the base of a small waterfall.

Orillo and I watched as the chief removed bundles of small sticks from one of the bags he carried. How strange; I hadn't noticed them before. We stood in respectful silence as the Native American Spirit Guide chanted and sang while planting each stick in the center of a stone circle. Once he had built a teepee of twigs, he moved his hand over it in blessing, and the sticks burst into flame. Then he removed a pinch of tobacco from another pouch, spoke some words, circled his hand three times through the flames, and dropped the offering into the fire. Sparks rose toward heaven. Only then did he motion for us to sit, lowering himself into a cross-legged position beside a pile of branches, something else I hadn't noticed before.

For a while, the chief broke branches and fed sticks into the fire without uttering a word. When the blaze was to his liking, he turned to us and nodded.

"This soul's stories must be told," he began, his deep voice rough with urgency. "There is currently no record of his deeds when he walked the earth as an American Indian man."

I bravely spoke up. "Yours was an oral tradition."

The chief nodded, his face ancient in the flickering firelight. "It saddens me that, as our people turn to modern ways, our traditions are being lost." He stared into my eyes. "You and your charge can help change this."

I was stunned. "How?"

Orillo jumped in. "By telling the stories, of course! That's why I'm here tonight. I want to learn all I can about our avatar."

Blue Sky Breathing poked the fire and sparks flew skyward. "You know the soul of whom we speak will enter in a female form this time."

"An elfin form!" Orillo sounded excited and proud.

"Back when I walked the earth as a human and knew this soul, he was born a boy. But that is not where to start. The place to begin is with you, Darci Stillwater, with you and your beautiful young charge."

Orillo and I exchanged glances, then settled back to absorb every word.

"Long before Europeans came here, the red race populated this land from shore to shore."

I nodded. I knew that much.

Blue Sky Breathing added a thick branch to the fire, then looked me over. "I know you have learned about many of the incarnations you have had on Earth."

"Yes," I responded. "I read about them in *The Great Book of Lifetimes* when I was training to become a Spirit Guide."

The native elder's face wore a wise expression. "Did you know that some of that knowledge was purposefully withheld? That not all your Earth lifetimes were shown to you?"

Surprised, I uttered, "I did not."

No words were exchanged for what seemed like a long time while sounds of the summer night encircled us.

At length, the elder spoke. "You, Darci, lived several lifetimes as an American Indian. The one I am about to relate is important, and now is the time for you to learn of it."

I almost asked why, but knew I would discover the reason if I listened carefully.

"Before Europeans populated this continent, you, Darci Stillwater, were born into a tribe that inhabited what is now called the Qu'appelle Valley. You had many brothers—older brothers—who taught you how to hunt and fight. You became agile and strong, true with your spear when fishing and with your arrow when hunting.

"When hunting with one of your brothers, you happened onto a clearing where elk were mating. Your brother who had a son and a daughter teased you. "'Losath, when will you take a woman as the elk takes a mate?' He slapped you on the back saying, 'You are strong, healthy, and ready to provide for a family. Who of the young women draws your eye?'

"You smiled but did not answer. What your brother did not know was that since you were a boy, you looked upon the chief's daughter as the most beautiful of all the females. When you were ten and she was five, and you found her playing with pebbles in a stream making circular designs with stones, you asked her, 'Amisimma, why do you place the stones in that way?'

"Shy in the presence of a boy twice her age, she looked up at you, then down at her feet as she replied, 'I am sorting the stones by color. Do you not see?'

"In truth, you could not see the subtle differences and thought it quite magical that she could."

41

As Blue Sky Breathing spoke, scenes of this incarnation began to flash before me. I saw myself as a young man hunting and fishing in this lush Canadian valley with its chain of lakes. The elder's eyes held a wise look as if he could see the images surfacing in my mind.

He continued, "You watched Amisimma grow into a beautiful young woman. You knew many men in the tribe would want her for a wife, so you quietly began negotiations with her father long before she was old enough to take a husband. When you were seventeen and she was twelve, without telling any of your brothers, you brought the chief a fine buffalo hide and asked for her hand. Her father, Chief Lakimasa, a big man, smiled, accepted the hide, but waved you away. Each year thereafter, you secretly brought him a gift and asked again. Each year he would accept the offering but claim she was too young to leave his teepee. So when you watched the elk mating and your brother teased you about starting a family, you knew whom you wished to partner, and you took the elk sighting as a sign that it was time to declare your love and admiration openly, for Amisimma was about to turn sixteen."

I suddenly remembered what happened. "I b-brought horses," I stammered. "Many horses."

The old one smiled. "That you did—and you made a big show of it, too. As Amisimma peered out of her father's teepee, you rode into the camp with a dozen fine horses kicking up dust and causing a ruckus. You stood tall and strong declaring your intention before the chief."

The memories were clear. "I saw her peeking out from behind the flap, her brown eyes so beautiful. My heart was afire!"

"Your soul recognized hers," Orillo interjected.

They both stared at me as realization struck. "My dear Angel!" I exclaimed. "Angel was Amisimma!"

Blue Sky Breathing took a pinch of tobacco, spoke a prayer into it, then tossed the offering into the fire. "A prayer for you and Angel," he said quietly. "The smoke takes it to the Creator."

I nodded. I knew that somehow.

We sat for a few moments listening to the waterfall, the breeze through the leaves, and the croak of a nearby frog, then the elder continued the story, though at this point, I could have told it. I was quickly remembering my life as a Cree Indian.

"Chief Lakimasa gave his consent, and a bonding ceremony was planned." Blue Sky Breathing nodded in my direction. "Yes, Darci, you could tell the tale from your point of view, but I can relate it from both sides."

"Both sides?" I wasn't sure what he meant.

"You gathered ceremonial regalia from your father and brothers, but do you know how Amisimma prepared?"

I thought I remembered something, but my mind was foggy about that. "I guess not," I replied.

"Like all Cree girls, she had already learned cooking, locating and transporting water, gathering and storing wild plants, preserving food, building and maintaining fires, cleaning hides, and sewing clothing. Now, however, the elder women tutored her daily on becoming a wife, mainly about the first nights of marital experience.

"The day of the bonding ceremony arrived, a fine crisp autumn day. You donned your finest regalia and entered the circle."

"I was very excited!" I added as my heart beat faster in remembrance. "I was filled with joy at the thought of holding Amisimma close, feeling her warmth as we shared a pallet during the cold winter months to come."

"Amisimma was excited, too, but so nervous she trembled as the women prepared her. To help calm her, Jokhoja, her mother, offered some herbal tea. The young bride tried to steady herself and finally ceased shaking as drums heralded the start of the ceremony. All the women left the teepee to take their places in the circle, all but one of the oldest grandmothers. She motioned for the bride to come stand by her. With a toothless grin, she shoved her fingers into a gourd that appeared to hold grease of some kind. In a swift motion, she scooped some of the contents, then reached under the girl's bridal tunic applying the ointment to the bride's private areas in an invasive manner. Amisimma gasped, but had no time to react further as the old woman pushed her from the teepee. The girl's parents were waiting to escort her. The bride felt the ointment tingling and burning between her legs, but tried not to cry, though her eyes watered with discomfort."

Feeling my heart twinge with compassion, I spoke softly. "I remember her tears."

"During the ceremony when you stood back-to-back and all the tribe members around you were singing and chanting, she cried as the stinging grease began to dribble down her legs. Most who saw her tears thought she was sad to leave her family."

As we sat quietly watching the fire, I began to have my own vivid memories of the marriage ceremony. Seeing myself clearly as Losath, the Cree warrior, I recalled that my brothers painted me in preparation. I was wearing very little. Bands of wolf and bear fur cuffed my wrists, arms, thighs, and ankles. I, too, was smeared with grease, but it did not sting. It was applied for warmth and perhaps for the sheen it gave my muscular body. I didn't notice the nip in the autumn air as my heart raced in anticipation.

Staring at me with a knowing look, Blue Sky Breathing nodded. "You were a handsome native man in that lifetime, Darci, strong, confident, and courageous. The one thing you had yet to experience was marriage. As Amisimma was schooled, so did your brothers teach you about the art of copulation. Each had enticing suggestions for your wedding night."

"One of my brothers drew a diagram in the dirt with a stick, a map of a woman." I laughed and the others smiled. "I was not concerned. I knew my heart would guide me."

"Yes, Darci." The elder storyteller tossed a log onto the blaze. "You loved and desired Amisimma for years before you were allowed to touch her."

"No wonder you were so excited at the ceremony," Orillo added.

"I remember it went on far too long, way into the night. When Amisimma and I were back-to-back in the center and the people were dancing around us, I touched her for the first time and felt her tremble.'

"When were you allowed to be alone?" Orillo queried.

The memory flashed clearly in my mind. "Everything had to be done in a certain way because the tribe was celebrating the wedding of the chief's daughter. Singing, chanting, and dancing us to our new teepee was part of the ritual."

The elder continued where I left off. "It was customary for the teepee of newlyweds to be placed at a distance from the others for privacy."

Sighing as I recalled the moment we were finally alone, I saw us standing on opposite sides of the conical tent, staring at each other as tribal members continued to dance and chant outside. Once they returned to the central fire, all we could hear was the nearby brook. I sat on a bearskin and motioned for my bride to join me. Her eyes were wide as she moved slowly in my direction. Once she lowered herself next to me, I took her hand and told her I was honored to be her mate. We sat silently for a long time until I noticed a fat tear trickling down her cheek and dripping into her long dark hair.

I remember my heart aching as I spoke softly into her ear. "You must tell me why you cry."

She looked down and shook her head.

"I am your husband, your protector, your family now," I told her. "You must trust me."

More tears followed the wet paths that streaked her cheeks. My heart filled with compassion as I recalled how I ached for this beautiful young woman. "This is your first night away from your family," I whispered as I squeezed her hand. "You must miss them."

"Oh, yes!" she blurted. "Mother—Mother didn't tell me ..." She withdrew her hand from mine, covering her face as she broke into loud sobs.

Both Orillo and Blue Sky Breathing were watching me, reading the memories as they flooded my heart and mind.

The elder smiled wryly. "It was not how you had pictured your wedding night."

"No, no, it wasn't," I admitted. "But I loved her so. I recall stroking her hair and rubbing her back to comfort her. Then—then I saw the grease on the inside of her leg and her red and irritated skin. I touched it lightly and she threw her arms around my neck, burying her face in my chest to muffle her cries." I sighed deeply. "I held her close, something I'd dreamed of for years, but instead of uniting in desire, I felt her body shake in my arms."

Suddenly transported to the very scene I was recalling, I had my arms entwined tightly around my lovely young bride. Gently pushing her away from me, I gazed into her eyes.

"Come, Amisimma," I coaxed. "Tell me what is wrong?"

Shyly she lifted her deerskin dress. I could not believe what I saw. The inside of her legs and thighs were red and coated with grease. I could only imagine how extensively the invasive ointment was applied.

"What has been done to you?"

Quickly lifting her in my arms, I carried her to the creek, wading into the pool where the water was chest-high. The chill of the cold water seemed to relieve her pain, and I was soon able to lay her on the mossy bank. Very slowly I pushed back her wet dress and, taking small soft tufts of moss, gently washed her legs, thighs, and finally her womanliness. She shivered in the chill night air, so I carried her back to our new teepee placing her near the fire. Once I had rekindled the blaze, I removed her wet clothes. The flickering light revealed that the redness on her skin was abating. Then I stripped off my ceremonial garb. The expression on her face informed me that I was the first man she had seen unclothed. Wrapping us in a warm blanket, I kissed her tenderly and told her we were together now. There was no need to force the consummation. There would be time enough.

"You were kind and compassionate," said Blue Sky Breathing.

"You really loved her," added Orillo.

"I love her still," I murmured, as I thought of Angel back in bed asleep. "But I have a question."

Chief Blue Sky Breathing nodded.

"What does this Cree lifetime that Angel and I lived so long ago—what does this have to do with the elfin avatar?"

The elder smiled, the corners of his eyes crinkling. "I've been waiting for you to ask."

Orillo came to my side and knelt beside me, patting my shoulder. "The stories you have heard about the soul who is to come to Earth as one of the seven, the soul who is to serve the earth as the avatar for the elves …" Moving in front of me, he stared into my eyes. "That extraordinary soul was the first-born child of Losath and Amisimma."

Chapter Six

The Birth of Influence

Orillo's words stunned me. I had fathered the extraordinary soul, the one who generated so many stories, the one who was to come again to Earth.

The old chief stared at me. "We have been here for some time. Perhaps you wish to return to Angel."

"But—but—I have so many questions," I stammered. "Was the child a girl or a boy? What was our life like? What did the avatar learn when I was his or her father? Did I ... ?"

Blue Sky Breathing raised his hand. "Hush now, Darci. Your questions will be answered fully. You will learn all you wish about your days in what is today known as Qu'appelle Valley, Saskatchewan."

"Shall we gather again tomorrow evening?" Orillo suggested. "Darci, do you wish more time than that to process what you have learned?"

"Let's meet tomorrow," I replied eagerly.

Leaving the elder by the magical fire, Orillo and I flew through the night. Even before we reached the little red house where Angel lay sleeping, I was mulling over all I had heard and experienced. Up until now, I wondered why the elves insisted on involving me with preparations for the arrival of their avatar. Now I saw why I was included. This soul had at one time been my child.

The next day I attempted to focus on Angel at her summer job as a playground instructor providing activities for local children. She was teaching the older ones to play chess while the younger were drawing with chalk on the blacktop. Watching over Angel was always enjoyable for me, especially because I could see the colors in her energy field flux and change as she interacted with the children. I could tell they liked her and she liked them. I thought again and again about the fact that she had birthed the soul who was to return as the elfin avatar. What had her experience been? I thought perhaps my memories would return as they had the night before, but recalled nothing further. Perhaps the presence of the magnificent American Indian Spirit Guide made the difference, or maybe it was the mystical fire. I did not know, though I looked forward to what I would learn that evening.

As before, Nyna arrived to tend Angel, who slept soundly even with curlers in her hair. The elfin grandmother gestured at the photos on the ceiling and shrugged. "They look a little like elves." She smiled. "Except for their ears, of course."

Prince Orillo was waiting outside by the Rose of Sharon bush, but Blue Sky Breathing was not with him.

"Where's the chief?" I asked, glancing around.

"He stayed at the spot by the waterfall," Orillo answered. He says he's holding the energy there and that it's a sacred space, especially while we tell these important stories."

"Then let's join him." I began the journey instantly with the elfin prince close behind.

The chief was as we had left him the night before except there was an addition: beside the fire on the ground was a design made of small stones. The pebbles formed an arc with a line through it, the line at an angle. Orillo bowed to the elder and I did the same. The old one smiled and nodded as he poked the fire. Picking up a deerskin pouch, he held it out for us to take.

"Tobacco," he told us. "Make prayers."

The prince and I knelt by the blaze and took pinches. Speaking a prayer into the soft, stringy, brown substance, I smelled the familiar fragrance and realized I must have done this hundreds of times when living as an Indian.

After handing back the pouch and settling down, we waited for the old one to begin. Remembering the long silences of the night before, I asked a question to get things started.

"Blue Sky Breathing, last night I remembered so much about what you were describing, yet today no more memories came."

The elder added a log to the blaze. Rising sparks seemed to take flight as soon as they left the fire. He looked at me. "You have vivid recall in my presence, Darci Stillwater, for I am a shaman of the highest order." He offered his own tobacco prayer, then continued. "Tonight you will learn of the birth of your son, a man who became one of the most influential Indians of all time—Naquahris."

"Naquahris," I repeated and, as I spoke the name, it echoed with familiarity in my heart.

"Naquahris," I heard Orillo utter with respect.

The chief allowed the name to hang powerfully in the air, then began the tale. "Let us return to your wedding night as Losath, the Cree warrior. You adored your bride and held her close the night through. You both talked of many things: your childhood, your families, your dreams. By dawn a strong friendship had blossomed between you. Although you desired her, you controlled your passion out of respect and love."

"It was difficult," I added as the memories again began to flow. "But I so wanted her to be happy." In my mind I saw the two of us entwined as first light arrived. At my urging, we dressed quickly and I escorted her to her parents' teepee. I was determined to uncover the reason the painful ointment had been applied to my bride.

Chief Lakimasa was offering morning prayers with some of the braves and elders by the center fire where our bonding ceremony had taken place. Her mother was rekindling the cooking fire, but stopped when she saw us walking toward her.

Dropping the poker, she grasped her daughter's hands. "Why are you here? What is wrong?" Yohaya looked back and forth between my new wife and me.

Amisimma stared at the ground while I suggested we enter their teepee to talk privately. Once inside, I told Yohaya of my bride's suffering. "Who is this old medicine woman and what is this burning grease? Why was this done to my wife?"

Yohaya gently lifted her daughter's chin to look into her eyes. "This is the work of Quelela, is it not?"

Amisimma nodded, her eyes watering. "It happened so quickly, Mama. The old one grabbed my dress …"

Yohaya embraced and comforted her daughter. "Quelela was trained in the old medicine ways of another tribe. She married into the Cree nation long ago—before I was born—and is a widow now. Most of the time she keeps to herself. I have been told that Lakimasa's father forbade her to practice the old medicine when he was chief. Oh, my little one." She kissed her daughter's forehead. "I should never have left you alone with her, even for a moment. Because she is an elder, I allowed her to join us as we prepared you. I did not know she had her own scheme."

Stroking my wife's hair, I asked her to stay with her mother while I sought out the mysterious old medicine woman. Quelela was sitting in front of her teepee at the edge of camp as if she were waiting for me.

"Congratulations, Losath." She grinned showing her gums. "You married the chief's only daughter, a good catch!" she cackled. "How was your wedding night?"

Towering over her, I nearly shouted. "It should have been my hands on my bride, not yours!"

"Shhhhh!" Quelela placed a gnarled finger to her thin lips. "You can thank me later when you have a fine, healthy son."

Surprised at her words, I did not respond.

"The old medicine always works." She rocked to and fro grinning. "My special ointment aids in conception. You will see. The others will see."

Anger coursed through me. "You used my bride to prove something to the tribe? Do you know what your grease did? Her skin was so reddened, her maidenhood so swollen and irritated that she wept in my arms from the pain!"

Shaking her head, the old woman's wrinkled face became serious. "My conception ointment has never before caused this. Young Amisimma must be very sensitive. Yes—very sensitive." She turned away and would say no more.

Glancing at Orillo and Chief Blue Sky Breathing, I saw that they had been following the story as it unraveled in my mind. The elder offered a Spirit Guide's view.

"This odd circumstance tested Amisimma's courage and your compassion." Blue Sky Breathing stared at me to make sure I understood his point, then continued the tale. "You set about cheering up your bride," said the shaman. "The next day you carved a little bird out of wood and whistled its song when you presented it to her."

I smiled. "That whistle became a signal between us."

"The third night was the full harvest moon. As you sat together by the stream watching the moonlight flicker on the moving water, she told you of a dream she had been given by the Creator, the dream of a child."

My heart pounded as if I were there sitting beside her in that moment. "She said she was ready to become my wife in every way. We talked of having children."

"This child in particular," the elder continued. "Her dream was a powerful one. She saw the baby arriving on the back of a great heron. The babe held a fish in one hand and an arrow in the other. What puzzled her was that the arrow was broken."

"A sign of either peace or defeat," Orillo speculated.

Blue Sky Breathing rearranged the flaming wood. "She also knew she would conceive when the days were still cold and snowy but were becoming longer."

As if transported in a whirlwind, I was suddenly there beside my young wife in our teepee. Wind howled and snow pelted our abode, but we were snug under a heavy buffalo robe. Although we had made love often since that full moon night in the autumn when Amisimma had spoken of her dream, she was always passive, allowing me access, but participating very little. I understood that this was partly due to instructions she had received from other women of the tribe. But this stormy night was different. In the firelight I saw both magic and passion in her eyes as she climbed upon me kissing my face, my neck, my chest, my thighs, my manhood. Whispering that she was a sleek red mare ready to be mounted by the finest, strongest stallion, she tempted me almost to the point of no return, then pulled back, only to entice me again to the edge of release. Each time she would speak about us as animals, likening us to the elk, the deer, the buffalo. Each time I thought I would lose my mind and my self-control, but my young wife could read me well. It was as if she held magical control over me. When I was finally at the peak of excitement, delirious with desire, she took me within her, and the explosion of our union shook us both to our souls.

Lying in blissful afterglow, I saw an expression on her face that I had never before noticed. It was more than contentment, more than peace—it was fulfillment.

"Naquahris was conceived that night," the elder's voice interrupted my reverie. It was obvious that he and Orillo had again been following my memories as they surfaced.

"In the morning, snow surrounded our teepee," I spoke aloud. "The landscape was sparkling white, and rays of the rising sun made the snow crystals glitter with tiny flecks of red, blue, green, and gold. I thought I had never seen anything more beautiful except perhaps the smile on the face of my young wife."

"The spark of life was within her." Blue Sky Breathing took tobacco between his fingers and spoke a prayer. "For the one who walked as Naquahris so long ago and who is to come again to Earth."

He tossed the tobacco into the blaze as Orillo quietly said, "Aho."

"She was so young, not yet seventeen," I mused. "Just a child herself."

"By today's standards," said Blue Sky Breathing. "It was common to begin bearing children at a very young age back then." He added two white stones to the design on the ground beside him. I was about to ask what it signified when he continued. "The spring was a joyous one for the Cree tribe, for their chief's daughter was with child, perhaps carrying their future leader.

Amisimma's happiness overshadowed the discomfort of pregnancy. As was the custom, the tribe moved to the hills farther up the river for the summer. You hunted with your brothers, Darci. You brought home many fine pelts and hides."

"Rabbits." I smiled. "My young wife wanted to make things for the baby from soft rabbit pelts."

"She had been taught to sew well. You helped her make a fine cradleboard lined with soft fur." The elder paused and looked up at the sky as if he were checking to see if the stars were in the correct position for him to relate the tale of the birth. He looked at me. "You had an accident on your horse that summer. Your mare stepped too near a nest of hornets and was stung. She reared and threw you, then ran off. You landed hard, then the insects came after you. Luckily your brother was nearby. He pulled you up onto his steed and raced away, but you suffered a number of painful stings and three broken ribs."

I winced at the memory. My brother took me directly to the medicine teepee, then went to tell my wife. When she arrived at my side, the medicine man was applying paste to draw out the venom. The pain was acute.

Blue Sky Breathing saw the memory in my mind. "The wise healer put your wife's hand in yours and said, 'Pain brings you knowledge, Losath, for it helps you understand what Amisimma will face when it is time to birth your son.'"

Looking into my wife's tear-filled eyes, I remember a jumble of feelings and sensations. The medicine man said we were to have a son, which filled me with joy, but my dear Amisimma would have to suffer.

The chief poked the embers and added three large sticks, then again checked the sky. "It took weeks for you to recover, Darci. You missed hunting with your brothers, but you did not mind sharing the days with your wife, whose belly now bloomed. She taught you how to bead, so you decorated a tunic she had sewn for the child."

"For when he was older and walking," I recalled. "He wore it at his first ceremony."

"We get ahead of ourselves, Darci." Blue Sky Breathing looked up, then nodded. "We must first speak of the birth. The time is right to tell the tale."

Orillo and I both glanced up to see a bright star directly overhead.

"Jupiter," said the prince. "Jupiter smiles down upon us."

The chief added a stone to the design on the ground. "As it did the night Naquahris was born. But let me go back to a few days before the birth. The time had come for the tribe to move back to the valley for the winter. You did not want Amisimma to travel, for she was heavy with child and had difficulty doing her daily chores, let alone riding a horse all day. It was decided that the rest of the tribe would go ahead and set up the winter camp. Your brother, Hiubesa, and his wife, Emhia, who had helped with many births, stayed behind with you. But the baby did not come and did not come. Your brother surveyed the sky with a concerned expression. He did not want the four of you to be caught by a snowstorm in the higher terrain. After much discussion, it was decided that your small group would begin the journey. Amisimma insisted that if you could get her onto a horse, she could ride, so you packed your belongings, including the teepee you had been sharing, and left the summer camp. Each of you rode a horse, and a fifth pulled a travois with the lodge poles, hides, and other essentials. Dark, threatening clouds rolled overhead and an icy wind blew as you descended along steep trails. Although you had recovered fully from your accident, you felt twinges of pain as the four of you moved slowly from the high hills.

"Sympathetic pains?" I asked.

"Discomfort from worry," Orillo speculated.

"Both," replied Blue Sky Breathing. "Amisimma did not complain, though she was terribly uncomfortable on horseback as she felt the baby shift, then shift again. On the second day of the journey, snowflakes spit from the sky on a cold wind. Mid-morning as the group approached a pass with a roiling stream, she cried out at the first contraction. Emhia saw that your wife's leggings were wet and knew instantly that the baby was coming, so she insisted that you stop and quickly erect shelter. The three of you helped Amisimma from her pony and wrapped her in a buffalo robe, keeping her warm while you set up a makeshift hut using branches and hides. You had to work quickly and build what you could.

"We were by a waterfall," I remembered. "Much like this one."

The elder's eyes glistened as he saw realization on my face. "Yes, Darci. This story begged to be told by a beautiful waterfall."

"The snow came harder and faster," I told the others. "I feared our little shelter would be blown away."

Once again I was instantly back in the scene, kneeling by my laboring wife, holding her hand. With each contraction, she moaned as the wind wailed in sympathy. Snow was accumulating, filtering into our tiny shelter through gaps in the hides. My brother went out into the blizzard to add fir boughs to the outside, for now it was certain that this was where my son would take his first breath.

Amisimma lay glassy-eyed, though when a contraction surged through her, she squeezed her eyes tightly and moaned. It was as if she had become an unfamiliar creature. She was completely controlled by the birth process. My words, my touch, seemed to do nothing to comfort her. The circumstances were less than ideal, and I knew other tribal women had died in childbirth. I prayed over and over that my wife and son would be safe.

The daylight hours waned and darkness enveloped our camp. My brother brought us the last of the hides and blankets as we had no room for a fire inside, and blowing snow prevented one from being built outside. The wind increased as Amisimma's labor deepened. Emhia looked concerned. I asked her what I could do. I had never felt so completely helpless. She told me to sing a prayer, calling my son to come to me. My brother had a small drum, so he played while I chanted and sang. After a long while as I stopped to drink water, I touched my beloved's face, now damp with perspiration. As I did, I heard a distinct sound close by—the snort of a buffalo. Lifting the hide that covered the entrance, I peered into darkness. The storm had stopped, and the magnificent beast, covered in snow, stood only yards away. When it snorted again, frosty plumes rose from its nostrils. I took a deep breath. A white buffalo at our doorstep was certainly a good sign. At that very moment, Emhia cried, "He comes! The baby comes!" I heard the buffalo snort even louder as my son took his first breath.

My heart was so full, I cried tears of relief and joy. There was no more beautiful sight in the world than my new son in the arms of his brave, exhausted, but very happy mother.

Emhia shooed us from the enclosure so that she could clean the mother and child. My brother and I left to build a small fire near the entrance of the hut. The buffalo had gone, but we could see its tracks. Hiubesa marveled at how close it had come. We both looked up at the clearing sky and saw a large, very bright star overhead.

"Jupiter." Orillo's voice interrupted my memory. "Jupiter was high in the night sky when Naquahris was born, just as it is now."

The three of us gazed skyward at the giant planet.

"Your son was born a man of power and influence," said Blue Sky Breathing. "The buffalo's presence represented strength, power, and the ability to benefit your people. Jupiter smiling down indicated he would be a man of influence who would expand the thinking of the people and bring peace. The waterfall showed his sensitivity and flexibility, and snow that fell covering the ground when he was conceived and during his birth was a blessing from the Earth Mother herself. She knew in her infinite wisdom that this precious soul had come to honor and serve her."

Shaking my head in amazement, I uttered, "I never recalled any of this until now. Why did I not remember such important events?"

The elder threw a log onto the fire. "Because the time was not right. Now—now is the time for you to learn about this soul."

"You say this one returns as an avatar. Will I meet Naquahris again?"

Orillo responded, "Yes, but remember—all seven avatars come in female form."

"And, Darci ..." The elder's voice was deep and raspy. "... you can choose to participate in her arrival."

"I can? How?"

Blue Sky Breathing took his time making a tobacco prayer, then stared at me. "You will know this soon enough. First we shall tell stories of the life of Naquahris."

"I think we must save them for another night," Orillo offered. "Darci has been away from his charge for many hours." Looking at me, he paused.

"Besides, I imagine you would like time to assimilate what you have relived here tonight, am I right, Darci?"

As anxious as I was to hear more, I nodded in agreement with the prince. "Can we return tomorrow night?"

The elder's face wrinkled into a smile. "Yes, yes. Come tomorrow. I will stay here and hold the energy. Once we speak of Naquahris and his deeds, this spot is blessed and sacred for all time."

We thanked Blue Sky Breathing and headed swiftly to Angel's home. The sounds and especially the smells of the summer night filled me as we flew. How interesting that during this, the warmest month, we were hearing of a child both conceived and born in the snow.

After expressing my appreciation to Nyna, I took over by Angel's bedside. As I was blessing her and balancing her energy, I thought about how brave she had been as Amisimma. Now, at the same age, she had other challenges to face. I wondered if one day she, too, would come to know Naquahris again.

CHAPTER SEVEN
BELOVED OF THE EARTH

The summer day dawned misty and humid. Angel and her sister helped their mother with housework. Dusting the furniture was a regular Saturday chore for the girls. Grumbling a bit, they hurried through the task so that they could meet friends at a swimming area a couple of miles from their home.

The acreage, which included the waterfall I had been visiting as well as a man-made pond for swimming, had been designated as a state park years before. Staying near Angel as she swam and sunbathed, I wondered if Blue Sky Breathing knew we were nearby.

That evening Nyna once again arrived with Orillo, though this time the grandmother elf spent a few moments talking with me. "Dear Darci." She patted my hand. "You must listen carefully to all that Chief Blue Sky Breathing reveals. Soon you will have a decision to make."

"A decision concerning the avatar?" I asked.

"Yes, about your participation in her arrival and perhaps her life." She placed a finger to my lips before I could ask more. "Go, Darci. Do not worry about Angel. You know she is in good hands—mine!"

Flying through the misty summer night, Orillo and I reached the waterfall quickly for we now knew the way. The old chief was waiting beside the magical fire, which glowed warmly, and I noticed that more stones had been added to the design on the ground. A second arc of pebbles had been placed above the first, with the diagonal line continuing through both.

Without words, Blue Sky Breathing handed us the pouch of tobacco. The prince and I whispered our prayers into pinches of the pungent substance, then added them to the fire. The elder nodded approvingly.

Watching him stir the blaze and add wood, I noticed that he appeared brighter and more vital.

Orillo noticed too. "You're looking well, Chief," said the prince. "Telling these stories agrees with you."

"Yes, this is true. My essence is strengthened and my energy replenished by telling them. You see, it is my sacred duty to see that they are not forgotten. That is especially true of the tale I tell tonight. My sole purpose for being here on Earth at this time is to make sure this story is remembered and goes on."

"We are glad to hear it," I enthused.

The elder's eyes reflected the flickering fire. "You tell the tale too, Darci— with your memories. Your presence is essential to reviving and retelling the tale of Naquahris."

"It is only in your presence that I remember." I bowed my head humbly.

"The birth was certainly magical. Was the baby healthy?" Orillo asked, eager to begin.

"Yes, the babe was strong and vital." The chief said his own prayer and tossed the tobacco offering into the blaze. "Darci, you insisted that Amisimma rest for a day after the birth and she did not argue. Much of that time, you held her as she slept, the baby nestled between you. Your brother kept the fire going and roasted a partridge while his wife kept a close eye on mother and newborn. She made an herbal tea to support Amisimma's speedy recovery from childbirth.

"The weather held, and the day after, you continued the journey to the valley and the tribe's winter camp. Your group traveled slowly, stopping so that the new mother could nurse. In two days, you had joined the main Cree encampment."

It took telling only this much of the story to trigger my memories once again. "One of the young braves saw us in the distance and rode out to meet us. It was approaching nightfall and the setting sun edged the purple clouds with pink and gold."

"The boy raced back to tell the others that both the child and the chief's daughter had survived," Blue Sky Breathing continued. "Drums were sounded in celebration as you rode into camp. Much joy lived in the hearts of the people."

"The old woman who smeared the grease on Amisimma—was she still with the tribe?" Orillo asked.

"Oh yes." The chief nodded. "The elders were the first ones allowed to see the new babe, and Quelela was among them. That old grandmother pointed a crooked finger at the infant and grinned her toothless grin. 'My ointment works well, does it not?' she said in her raspy voice. As she tottered away, you took her arm and reminded her quietly of Amisimma's discomfort and reddened, irritated skin. 'Old medicine still works well. The tribe has its new leader,' was all she said as she continued on her way."

"Her ointment was to ensure conception," I clarified.

"To ensure conception and a healthy birth, but Amisimma was too sensitive for the strong concoction. Quelela chose to believe that her old-time medicine had worked, but it had proved a challenge for you and your bride. You warned the old woman about using it again and did not concern yourself further."

"In essence, you forgave her," said Orillo. "No wonder you are a Spirit Guide, Darci."

"You earned your place as a Guide during many Earth lifetimes," added Blue Sky Breathing as he tossed a large log onto the fire. "Tonight we shall speak of the childhood of Naquahris. He walked on sturdy legs by summer's end. At the harvest celebration, he stood at your side."

"I remember!" I exclaimed. "Not yet ten months old and he was able to take my hand and walk with me!"

"The baby's eyes were wide with excitement as he watched the dancing and singing," the elder continued. "His grandfather, Chief Lakimasa, gave the boy his first drum that night."

I couldn't help smiling. "I held his little hand and helped him strike it in time with the others."

"What does Naquahris mean?" Orillo asked.

"Beloved of the earth," responded Blue Sky Breathing. "And he was."

No one spoke as the elder offered more tobacco prayers and added another stone to the design. Rearranging the burning logs with a stick, he went on. "He loved many things as a child—trees, the animals, water, though he especially liked stories. Back in that time, telling stories was a part of daily life, and many in the tribe, especially the elders, took turns entertaining the children. But storytelling was more: it was the way we taught and remembered our history. In fact, there were those who chose to do only this."

"In other words, it was a vocation, a calling," I clarified.

"A highly respected one," said the chief.

"These storytellers traveled from tribe to tribe," I recalled. "They were messengers, too, carrying news."

The chief nodded. "They were known as twisted hairs because of the way they twisted their hair on top of their heads." The elder's face wrinkled into a wise smile. "It was always a great event when a twisted hair came into the Indian village. Children recognized him right away from his unusual hairstyle and ran to greet him. All made him welcome for it was an honor to have the traveling storyteller as a guest in your teepee. Naquahris was fascinated by this strange and magical man who spun tales all day and sometimes far into the night."

Memories of my handsome young son were rapidly returning. "At three, he told us he wished to become a twisted hair when he grew up. I remember sitting by his sleeping mat as we were settling him for the night and explaining that his destiny was to become chief of the Cree. He said, 'No, Papa. My brother will do that. I am to be a storyteller.' Surprised, Amisimma and I looked at each other. We had no other offspring at the time, though soon after my lovely wife discovered that she was with child."

Blue Sky Breathing laughed quietly. "Naquahris—so young and already so wise. He knew his destiny, and began collecting stories from that moment on.

"When he was seven years of age, he was walking by the lake on an autumn day. The tribe had returned to the valley floor to set up winter camp. The day was warm, so the boy waded in the water. He was delighted when he saw a turtle climb onto a nearby rock and turn slowly to face him.

"'Hello,' said the turtle.

"'Hello to you,' the boy responded, not at all surprised that he could hear the creature.

"'I hear you like stories.'

"'Oh yes! Tell me one, please.'

"'Come sit by me,' the turtle invited.

"So Naquahris sat on the large rock, his feet dangling in the water, the turtle by his side.

"'Once long ago,' began the reptile, 'this land was nothing but swirling stardust. At first, turbulence dominated but eventually quieted. Stardust collected into spheres and soon a beating heart, like yours and mine, lived within each orb. One of these hearts belongs to our Earth Mother and is beating beneath our feet, Naquahris.'

"'You know my name,' said the boy.

"'Do you think I would tell such an important story to just anyone? You see—I know you will remember every detail and retell it accurately. That is important for storytellers.'

"'You know I want to be a twisted hair?'

"'Earth Mother informs me of many things.' The turtle stared at Naquahris. 'She tells me of your destiny and the path to it. You will tell our stories—and there are many. But you must know that walking the earth as a twisted hair means you will travel far from your home.'

"'I know this,' replied the boy. 'I would like to travel as long as I can come home sometimes.'

"The turtle nodded. 'There is much more to becoming a twisted hair than only storytelling. You will learn.' And with that, it slid back into the lake."

After a moment of silence, I said, "Amisimma and I continued to suggest to our son that he was more suited to becoming a hunter, warrior, and leader of our people, but the boy held true to the decision he had announced when he was three."

"You didn't want him to leave home," offered Orillo.

Shaking my head, I sighed. "I knew it would break my wife's heart even though we had another healthy son. One never likes to see one's children leave, perhaps never to be seen again."

Blue Sky Breathing adjusted the blazing logs with his poker stick, then added another chunk of wood. "Naquahris learned skills along with the other Cree boys his age—fishing, hunting, riding—but he would do something the others did not. He often went by himself into the woods and stayed for extended periods of time."

My memories were returning as the elder talked. "When I asked my son why he took such long walks alone, he replied that he was collecting stories."

Blue Sky Breathing chuckled. "Yes, Naquahris was fascinated because he could converse with the trees, the plants, the animals."

"Of course!" Orillo jumped in. "He had already lived a lifetime as Rahid, who could communicate with his elephant, and as Leijasa, who talked with the trees! His soul knew these skills!"

"And still does," said the chief. Then, in a surprise move, Blue Sky Breathing stood, feathers in the headdress rustling down his back. His dark eyes reflected the flickering fire as he stared at Orillo then me. "It is time for me to reveal my part in this tale."

As he paused, my head spun. I hadn't considered that the elder might have been involved in more than just storytelling. Rolling the concept around in my mind, I realized it made sense. That's why he had been describing everything in such detail.

"I, too, was Cree," said Blue Sky Breathing. "I was Lakimasa, chief of the Cree. Amisimma was my daughter and Naquahris my grandson."

"Chief?" I murmured, stunned.

"We are doubly honored," added Orillo.

From a small pouch attached to his waist, Blue Sky Breathing took a pinch of a yellow substance, closed his eyes in prayer, then tossed the dust into the fire. It exploded into a thousand sparks that soared skyward. He followed them with his eyes, sat back down, and added a large log to the blaze.

"When you were my son by marriage, Darci, you came to me, concern on your face. You told me of your son's choice to become a twisted hair. It was the day Naquahris turned ten."

As before, the memory returned in a flash. There I sat, cross-legged, opposite my wife's father, the great chief. Lighting the bowl of a long-stemmed pipe, he nodded and smiled. "Go. Bring the boy to me."

I did so immediately. Soon I was facing the chief with my son sitting by my side.

"Naquahris, my grandson," spoke Chief Lakimasa. "This was a joyous day ten sun cycles ago when you were born. It is a special day." He puffed on his pipe. "Your father tells me that you do not wish to become chief of the Cree."

The boy looked down at mats on the floor of the teepee. "That is true, Grandfather."

"I can tell you the duties of being chief and can also help you understand the path of the twisted hair."

Naquahris nodded, eyes large with wonder. This was the first time his grandfather had spoken with him in such a serious way.

"As chief, I make decisions for the tribe, but do so with the help of those who converse with Spirit. A twisted hair is one who talks with Spirit, one who hears Spirit. A twisted hair is also a warrior, a shaman, and a medicine man. A twisted hair is a man or woman of power and knowledge."

I remember asking, "What makes a twisted hair different from a traditional medicine person?"

"A twisted hair has the desire and ability to seek knowledge from all sources."

"What do you mean 'all sources'?" I wanted everything to be very clear to my young son.

"Twisted hairs learn to use every available resource around them. If you walk this path, you will know what this means for it leads to enlightenment. Such beings learn to walk their talk and touch all they meet with kindness, compassion, understanding, and beauty."

Turning, I looked at my son, who was listening intently.

"This is my calling! I know it is!" the boy shouted. "My father wants me to be chief like you, Grandfather, but I must listen to what Spirit tells me."

"My boy," responded Lakimasa. "I wish you to follow your heart. What does Spirit tell you?"

An incredible tale unfolded. "Grandfather, Father, I must tell you what I have seen and heard. On the last full moon when the women were gathering and drying herbs for winter and the hunters were stalking elk and deer, Hiubesa was teaching a group of us how to make arrows. While I sat under a big pine watching and listening, the wind rustled the needles over my head. I heard the tree calling me to go into the forest. It was not difficult to slip away while all the other boys watched Hiubesa sharpen an arrowhead.

"Once in the woods, I heard a sweet song—not of a bird. No, it sounded like the song of a woman, but no woman I had ever met. I followed the sound to a grove of giant maple trees. Most of their leaves lay on the ground making a colorful mat. Seven deer stood grazing in a small clearing surrounded by these great trees. Suddenly I saw the singer, a beautiful woman standing among the deer. She wore white deerskin, her dark hair braided and wound around an antler headdress. Her eyes were closed as she sang, though she turned toward me as I approached. I thought the deer would scatter as they usually do when men come upon them in the woods, but these did not. It seemed as though they were guarding this wondrous maiden.

"The words of her song changed as she faced me. 'Naquahris, beloved of the earth, come nearer to me. The Earth Mother wishes me to bless you in her service.'"

Lakimasa and I stared at each other in astonishment. "Please go on," I encouraged.

The boy inhaled deeply, then continued. "I will admit—I was afraid. There was an intense white glow around the woman, and her voice seemed to have an echo in it. Suddenly she opened her eyes, and I saw they were brilliant purple! As she reached out to me, I felt a surge of love greater than anything I had before known. When I moved to her side, she embraced me. Once in her arms, I felt myself swirling around and around. I tried to see what was happening, but blinding white light engulfed us. Then the whirling stopped, which was good because I was getting dizzy."

Lakimasa and I chuckled.

The boy went on. "We were no longer in the woods, but in a field of white. I thought it might be snow, but before I could reach down to touch it, a buffalo stepped out of the mist. The great beast walked right up to me and said, 'Naquahris, beloved, the Earth Mother sends greetings. She asks you to walk in service to her. Tell stories of her beauty and abundance to all you meet. The animals, plants, trees, even the sky will share stories about her, and these you must then share with your fellow humans. Love and respect for our Earth Mother is important to all. You will help others hold this in their hearts.' The buffalo stepped back, disappearing into the misty white light.

"The woman again encircled me with her arms, and we whirled skyward, up, up, up, until darkness surrounded us. I squeezed my eyes tight, for fear of falling made my stomach quiver. Soon I felt as if we were floating. 'Open your eyes, young Naquahris,' said the woman. 'Look at our dear Earth Mother.' I did as she asked and must admit a little cry of amazement escaped my lips. Below us I saw a sphere of swirling white and blue. I remembered what a turtle had told me when I was seven—that sparkling stardust formed orbs with beating hearts. I saw this with my own eyes! I saw our Earth Mother from above, much as the Creator must see her!

"We floated for a while, then the woman hugged me close to her. I felt safe as we again were engulfed in a whirlpool of white light. Once all was calm, I opened my eyes to find that we were back in the clearing with the deer, great maple trees all around. My heart was beating so fast! The deer made a path for me, otherwise I would not have known which way to go. The woman guided me in that direction as she sang, 'Naquahris, beloved of the earth, you are blessed.' I stepped from the woods just as Hiubesa was concluding his instruction to the other boys."

After a silence, I asked, "Why did you not speak of this before, my son?"

"I held it in my heart," replied the boy. "I wanted to live with the experience for one moon before I shared it with you."

Chief Lakimasa nodded. "So wise for one so young. There is no doubt. Spirit has called my grandson, and we must help him follow his path."

Gazing across the fire at Blue Sky Breathing, I noticed the resemblance between him and the old Cree chief. I also realized that he and Orillo had again been following the story as I relived it in my mind.

"What an amazing youngster," offered Orillo. "To think—this soul is returning. What a joyous event for the earth!"

"We will speak of the life and work of Naquahris," said Blue Sky Breathing as he stirred the embers. "Return tomorrow."

Prince Orillo and I eagerly agreed. Soon I was back at Angel's bedside. Nyna and the elf prince sat with me for a while as we talked of what I had remembered. Once they left, I ached to share this incredible tale with Angel, for she was part of it, too.

CHAPTER EIGHT
EDUCATION OF NAQUAHRIS

Sunday morning meant Angel and her siblings went to church. Their father drove them, left them off, then drank coffee and read the paper while he waited. Angel was involved in the young people's group, the Pilgrim Fellowship, and during the upcoming winter was planning to join other members from around the state in a mission to Puerto Rico. Her team was to assist in completing a hospital in the jungle interior of the island. Observing her energy field, I could see how excited she was about the trip. Sparks of white and gold encircled her head like comets as the minister asked her to deliver a sermon about her experience when she returned.

During the warm August afternoon, she visited her neighbors, the family with whom she and her siblings spent their childhoods. The two oldest had been given guitars and were trying to learn the songs of a young folksinger and songwriter named Bob Dylan. To my ear, he wasn't much of a singer, though his lyrics were insightful.

That evening once the household was quiet and all were asleep, I awaited the arrival of the elves. Several hours elapsed, and I wondered if Orillo and Nyna had been detained or perhaps were not coming at all. Focusing on Angel, I occupied my time by clearing and energizing her solar plexus. Negative experiences seemed to affect her stomach and digestion.

Finally, the elves appeared beside me and Nyna explained their late arrival. "Chief Blue Sky Breathing has been fire keeper for the sacred blaze that he lit when you first visited the waterfall three nights ago. At dawn he will extinguish the ceremonial fire and be on his way. He requests that you and Orillo stay with him until the fire is out."

"We didn't think you would want to be away from Angel all night, so we waited until later than usual to fetch you," added the elfin prince.

"That's very considerate. Thank you," I replied. "So this is the last night of storytelling?"

"For now." Nyna's gaze was penetrating. "There is much for you to learn, Darci, as well as some surprises ahead."

"Surprises?"

Orillo tugged my sleeve. "The chief waits for us. We must go."

After informing Nyna of Angel's upset stomach, I left with the elfin prince. As we soared to our meeting spot at the base of the waterfall, I noticed Jupiter high in the sky.

Once we had offered tobacco prayers, the prince and I settled in our usual places near the fire. The design on the ground beside Blue Sky Breathing now had a third arc of stones over the first two.

Pointing to the pebbles, I asked, "Chief, what is the design you are making?"

"Every great leader has a spiritual symbol. As the story of Naquahris unfolds, so does his sacred symbol."

"I see," I said, not sure that I did.

"What we speak of here tonight does not take us to the end of the story." The elder added two logs to build up the blaze. "There are many tales of Naquahris traveling the land as a twisted hair, but we shall focus on the years he spent growing to manhood with the Cree."

"The years he spent with us," I interjected.

"Yes, Darci. The years he spent with you, me, and Angel. After the boy told us about his amazing experience with the deer woman, we set him on a shaman's course, for a true twisted hair is also a spiritual leader and medicine man. Once word was passed around the village about the boy's new path, Quelela came to me.

"'I am getting old, my chief,' she said. 'I wish to pass my medicine wisdom on to Naquahris.'

"As you might imagine, I hesitated to allow this because many in the tribe thought her ancient medicine ways suspect, but I had a dream that Quelela gifted my grandson with a clear white stone that shone brilliantly in the sunlight. I saw this as a sign that he must learn what he could from her."

In a flash, I was in a teepee, my son standing before me. He was older, perhaps fourteen. Over his shoulder he carried a satchel stuffed with roots and herbs, which he had gathered for the old medicine woman.

"What is Quelela teaching you?" I asked.

"Her knowledge of the plants is deep, Father. She says there is much she must teach me before she walks with the ancestors."

"Do you speak also with the tribe's medicine man and his apprentices?"

"I have not yet done so, for it would upset Quelela. Once she has passed over, I will study with them, perhaps share some of what I learned from the old one." Naquahris looked at me as though he were trying to decide whether to tell me something.

"Go on," I encouraged.

"Father, I think I have discovered why Quelela's ways are not easily accepted by our people." Pausing, he shuffled his feet. "She is an expert in toxic plants and poisons." He added quickly, "It is useful knowledge when applied for good."

After he left for his lesson, I realized that my son was spending more time with Quelela than anyone else in our tribe ever had.

"Naquahris absorbed the ancient knowledge as a plant soaks up rays of the sun." Blue Sky Breathing's voice brought me out of my reverie. "The day you were just remembering—that was the day you made a decision."

"Yes," I spoke up. "I decided that my son needed other teachers, too. I talked with you about it—when you were Lakimasa, chief of our people."

"And I agreed with you. We both knew the boy's path was sacred and very special. I sent a messenger to the Cree tribe camping south of us to request a visit from their shaman. My wife, Yohaya, was from that clan. She told me that their spiritual leader possessed much wisdom and magic. Word came that he would instruct the boy, but Naquahris must go to him. Nearly two years passed before this came about."

"I was uneasy about letting my son leave home," I recalled. "You told me to go with him."

Once again, the scene the chief spoke of filled my mind. Naquahris was riding his mare next to mine. Traces of winter snows remained in the shadows as early spring breezes tossed our long dark hair. Two days' journey by horseback would bring us to the neighboring tribe, so we camped overnight by the lake. Sitting by our small fire, I gazed across at my son. Flickering flames and shadows carved his young, muscular body. For the first time, I saw him as a man.

I smiled. "When I had lived for nearly sixteen suns like you, I killed my first elk," I told him, pride in my voice.

His dark eyes surveyed mine. "The elk speak to me, Father. I have no interest in killing them."

"You are gifted, my son," I replied, "though it is good that our hunters do not hear the elk speak as you do for their meat and hides help us survive. What do the elk tell you?"

"That all is sacred. That they gladly give themselves to us but that we must always pray and make offerings to them and to the Earth Mother before the hunt."

"The hunt is always blessed," I reminded him.

When he looked at me, I saw the wisdom of the ancients in his eyes. "The elk say that every hunter must hold gratitude in his heart and a prayer of thanks on his lips. Many hunters become caught up in the chase and the killing and forget respect for the animal."

Realizing that I barely knew the man my first-born was becoming, I asked, "Do other animals speak to you?"

"All Creation speaks to me, Father," he replied, "including the heavens."

The next day we were welcomed at our neighbors' encampment. Their chief and his daughter escorted us to the teepee of the shaman, Daekeriha. The elder was sitting with his eyes closed chanting words I did not understand. His conical tent was filled with bundles of herbs that hung in clusters from the lodge poles. The aroma was overwhelming. As was the custom, I presented Daekeriha with a gift of pelts and a carved pipe. He nodded his thanks, then made a shooing motion at me with one of his hands as he clasped the other around my son's arm.

Exactly what occurred in the shaman's teepee I cannot say. I spent the time talking with the chief and his daughter. With her husband away on a hunting trip, she seemed to enjoy our company. When night arrived, I was invited to stay in the chief's lodge. After the second day passed, I became concerned, as I had not seen Naquahris since leaving him with the shaman. Both the chief and his daughter assured me that, although Daekeriha had strange and mystical ways, he had never caused harm to anyone. Finally, on the third day I was summoned by a boy to go to the shaman's teepee. When I first entered the smoky atmosphere, I saw only Daekeriha puffing on his pipe. As my eyes adjusted to the darkness, I began to make out the form of another being. My son stepped toward me. I gaped at the transformation. His naked body was oiled and painted with symbols unknown to me. His legs were dusted with pollen, arms with pulverized leaves. Reeds were braided in his long hair, and the look in his eyes was otherworldly.

The old shaman nodded as he puffed. Removing the pipe, he told me, "We have been on a spirit journey."

"Are you all right?" I asked, stepping closer to my son.

"Yes, Father." His voice seemed deeper. "Sit with us. I will tell you of my experience."

Daekeriha pointed to a seat on the bearskin and offered me the pipe. Out of courtesy and respect, I accepted and took a puff. The old one then indicated that I should pass it on to my son. At that moment, I saw Naquahris as my equal.

With fire in his eyes, my son began to relate the tale. "My teacher, Daekeriha, knows many things. He told me of invisible beings who inhabit the Earth Mother along with the rest of us. Most humans do not see them or know of their existence. To make the journey to their world, I had to be protected. The first night was spent in preparation as Daekeriha covered my body in oil, pollen, herbs, and sacred symbols."

Refilling his pipe, the shaman added, "One cannot walk this path without protection."

Naquahris resumed the story. "I was very tired from our long ride, so my teacher brewed strong tea from herbs I had never used before. At first this tea melted away my fatigue but soon after brought dizziness. Daekeriha sat behind holding me as the teepee spun around and around."

The old shaman cackled. "He did well. The potion I gave him is strong and would make a weaker man ill."

When Naquahris moved his head, the reeds in his hair rustled. "Although I do not remember moving, we were suddenly at the entrance of a cave. My teacher encouraged me to enter, so I did."

"The Earth Mother called him to her bosom." The old one's voice was low and raspy.

"Once inside the cave, the trail was steep and rocky, descending sharply with unexpected turns. I had no torch, but the pollen on my legs glowed with enough light for me to see the path. As I traveled down for a long while, I must admit to thinking about retracing my steps on the climb back to the entrance.

"After crawling through a narrow opening, I found myself in a cavern completely lined with beautiful stones of all sizes, some as giant as our largest lodge."

"Crystals," Daekeriha nodded. "The highest life forms on Earth."

"It was wondrous, Father, like nothing I had ever before witnessed. The luminescence that shone from these amazing stones was spellbinding. I was on my knees in awe."

"An appropriate position at the throne of the Earth Mother," the old shaman added. "Your boy shows respect, Losath. You have taught him well."

After a pause, Naquahris continued. "As I knelt, humbled by the sight, not knowing what to do, I offered a simple prayer of thanks for the beauty that surrounded me."

"Good instincts, too," Daekeriha chuckled.

Fire still blazed in my son's eyes. "I stayed very still, for I felt I must be shown what was next. Soon I noticed that the radiance coming from the stones was changing. Some crystals glowed brighter for a moment, then others did the same. The play of light reminded me of the great glowing dance we sometimes see in the northern night sky. Then faint sounds reached my ears—tones, some high, some low, some in between. They became louder as the stones flashed more brightly. Never before have I experienced such majesty! And there amongst the sounds, I heard someone singing my name! 'Naquahris, Naquahris.' By the time the changing tones filled the cavern, the lights from the crystals were flashing so rapidly, so brilliantly that I was blinded. I do not remember anything more."

"He was overwhelmed and became unconscious," the shaman explained.

"Were you there?" I asked the old one.

He nodded. "I have been with your son day and night since you left us. Our physical bodies have remained here, safe in my lodge. Our spirit bodies traveled deep into the heart of the Earth Mother."

"What else do you recall?" I asked my son.

"When I awoke, I was in a lush green meadow. I remember thinking this odd because our valley is not yet warm enough to support such vegetation. Suddenly I realized I was not alone. Two incandescent beings sat not far from me, watching as I regained consciousness. Confused, I greeted them. As they smiled and introduced themselves, I noticed that their ears were different from mine—they were pointed."

My reverie was temporarily interrupted as I exclaimed, "Elves!"

Orillo responded with a grin. "As Losath, you didn't possess knowledge of elves."

"Let the memory flow on, Darci," Blue Sky Breathing directed.

Staring into the fire, I easily traveled back to the shaman's teepee. My son accepted the pipe from Daekeriha. Once he took a puff, he went on with the tale. "The young man told me his name was Hakrodt; the woman introduced herself as Nyna."

"Nyna!" I nearly shouted, once again shifting my focus to the present. "Nyna! Here on Earth—over four hundred years ago!"

Orillo placed his hand on my shoulder. "Darci, you know we elves come to Earth but once in this form, so we stay for hundreds of years."

"Yes," I responded, still shocked. "I had forgotten. I guess I never considered that Nyna has been here for so long!"

"Nyna Serahn is one of the elfin leaders on this continent," Blue Sky Breathing reminded me. "She is a highly respected elder."

"I am honored she has taken such an interest in me and Angel."

The chief and Orillo waited patiently for me to return to the scene in my mind. It took a while, for I was processing the fact that Naquahris, a human teenager, had met and communicated with elves.

Following my thoughts telepathically, Orillo said, "He was truly gifted."

"Your memories are telling this story, Darci," said Blue Sky Breathing. "Go back. Let Naquahris relate his experiences."

Closing my eyes, I took a deep breath and visualized the scene. My handsome son was staring straight at me. "I know what I say is unusual," he spoke softly, "but I saw these beings and conversed with them. Once I introduced myself, Hakrodt said they had been waiting for me. When I asked why, they came closer and sat with me in the soft grass. Everything about them was radiant—their eyes, their skin, their clothing. They informed me that they were two of the invisible beings who had been described to me before my journey, and that I was gifted with the ability to interact with them. Nyna then told me of my special calling. She said I was to walk in such a way that every step would kiss the Earth Mother and every word would honor her. Hakrodt then told me that I already knew this calling deep in my heart—to travel and retell stories given to me by the trees, the plants, the animals, and by the Earth Mother herself. Nyna must have noticed my surprised look, for she then said that I could hear the Earth Mother speak and that it was her voice singing my name in the crystal cave. I suddenly became very sleepy. As I lay on the grass, Nyna whispered that I could return to the crystal cavern whenever I wished to be healed. Heavenly songs filled my head as I drifted into slumber."

"Your son slept for nearly a day," said Daekeriha. "His body and spirit are not accustomed to such travel." He puffed on his pipe, then added, "The boy is fine now, though it will be best to allow him another night's rest."

"I will be glad of it," my son confirmed. "What I have told you must remain between the three of us for now, Father."

"Others will ask what you learned from the shaman. What shall I say?"

Daekeriha chuckled. "Tell those who ask that the boy was schooled in those things which cannot be spoken of by humans."

"The mysteries," I said in an attempt at clarification.

"One day this story shall be told," concluded Naquahris as the images faded from my mind.

"That day is today." Blue Sky Breathing's voice was deep and resonant.

At that moment, the three of us noticed that the sky was becoming brighter in the east. "When the first bird sings," said the chief, "we will extinguish the sacred fire."

"But what about the life of Naquahris? Did he follow his calling?" I asked. "I want to know what he did as a man."

"I, too, wish to know," echoed Orillo.

Blue Sky Breathing gazed over the fire at us. "This is part of our history that has been lost. I shall arrange for you to have access to it, for all that Naquahris accomplished is written in *The Great Book of Lifetimes*."

"Of course!" I exclaimed. "I have read my own incarnations in this book!"

"You shall make certain that your son's story is told," said the chief, "though this will have to wait. Angel is facing tumultuous times, Darci. You must focus on her."

"I shall."

Blue Sky Breathing nodded. "Do not forget what you have remembered and relived here at this waterfall, for this knowledge will help you make decisions in the future."

A bird in a tree high overheard sang the first notes, heralding a new day. The chief spoke solemnly. "We thank this fire for its sacred light, for protecting us, and for taking our prayers to the Creator."

"Aho," said Orillo as Blue Sky Breathing stirred the embers, moving them apart to cool. "All is well."

"Aho," I repeated.

Once back at Angel's side in the quiet moments of sunrise, I wondered what challenges lay ahead for us. My dear charge was the same age as Naquahris when he experienced the shaman's journey. How different her present life was from his in that long-ago time.

CHAPTER NINE
A QUESTION OF PROTECTION

Since entering high school, Angel was consistently placed in college preparatory classes. Her grades remained high and teachers encouraged looking at certain schools to continue her education. I was not surprised that she wished to study art, as it was her favorite subject. In the autumn of her senior year, she applied to several colleges, requesting scholarships. I rejoiced in her success, for not only was she academically at the top of her class, she was also socially more confident.

We Spirit Guides who watched over the individuals in Angel's family were well acquainted with one another. On an evening during Angel's senior year, I was balancing her energy as she slept when I found Garth, her father's Life Guide, at my shoulder.

"Darci," the big guide rumbled, "we must work together, for I fear there is trouble brewing."

Remembering what Chief Blue Sky Breathing had said about Angel experiencing tumultuous times, I asked Garth what he meant.

"My charge is a troubled man. I help him all I can, but he frets constantly about his first-born."

"About Angel?" Taken aback, I had to admit that I had been so preoccupied with Angel that I hadn't been observing her father. "What troubles him?"

"You know how Jim was raised, Darci. His upbringing in Scotland was strict and the family did not have many resources, especially once they moved to the United States."

Unsure where he was going with his statement, I observed, "He does much better now as far as providing for his wife and children is concerned."

With a troubled expression, Garth shook his head. "He worries constantly about money. He hoards it, never letting his wife know exactly how much he earns. Resentment toward his first daughter grows."

"Resentment? What has she done to warrant his resentment?"

"She chooses to continue her education past high school."

"Why does that concern him? He ought to be proud of her."

"College costs money. Remember, Darci, in the old country, men were rarely schooled past the age of sixteen. It was unheard of for girls to attend university."

"He doesn't want her to attend college? That's incredible!"

"Think about it." Garth placed his hand on my shoulder. "Jim has slaved in toxic, dead-end jobs since he returned from the war. He considers his paycheck as *his* to dispense as he sees fit. He thinks his family deserves to purchase only essentials with his hard-earned pay."

I sighed. "And college is not essential."

"That's how he sees it."

"But Angel has already been accepted to three schools. There is no stopping her now."

"Jim may try," said Garth grimly. "He feels the situation is out of his control. It angers and frustrates him. I want you to be aware that this is a very combustible situation."

Thanking Garth, I continued my energy work on Angel. When finished, I surrounded her with an extra layer of protective light.

Over the next several weeks, I observed Angel and her father. He was very closed, emotions shrouded in a cloak of gray. Garth had been watching over Jim since before the man was born, so the Spirit Guide had the advantage of knowing how to read his thoughts and moods. All I noticed was that Angel and her father did not interact a great deal. This was not surprising. She had been avoiding him since childhood when he began backhanding her at the dinner table.

One evening only days later, Angel was on the telephone with a girlfriend chatting about choosing between the three colleges that had accepted her. Jim was drunk and, as he came down the stairs clad only in his boxer shorts, I could see from the red in his aura that he was filled with rage.

"Get off the phone!" he bellowed.

Angel glanced up at him, fear in her eyes. She attempted to say good-bye to her friend, but her father tore the receiver from her hand and slammed it down. My poor charge was cornered as the angry, drunken man swore at her, slurring words. It was difficult even for me to make out what he was saying, though I understood enough to know that he was ranting about his hard-earned money and college expenses. Angel remained silent as she looked for an escape route.

To my dismay, he grabbed her, pulled her out of the chair, and hit her. Hearing the racket, her mother ran in from the kitchen, pleading with Jim to stop, and clutched her husband's arm, but he threw her off. Jim was out of control, hitting Angel again and again, tearing her blouse. Knowing that he was too strong for her, she did not attempt to fight back. How I wished at that moment to be in human form so I could force myself between them and protect her. What could I do? I had seen her father slap her many times, but this was different. This was a beating. I was horrified. Out of sheer desperation, I wrapped my spirit body around her. I felt her go limp as Jim shook her. When he grasped her hair and slammed her head on the floor, I cried for help. Looking for Garth, I did not see him anywhere. How could I stop this? How could I change what was happening?

As quickly as I sent my plea, I received an image. Back when I was training to be a Spirit Guide, I had learned how to pull the soul up through the crown of the head. As Jim slammed his daughter against the wall, I wasted no time. Running my thumb up her back, I loosened her spirit body and gently eased it up. It was a sight to see: the head, neck, and shoulders of her spirit body above her physical being. I immediately flooded her with love and compassion and, as I did so, felt her detach from the horrendous scene and view her father with much pity. Pouring more love into her, I saw the pity transform into compassion.

As soon as her energy changed from fear and resignation to compassion, Jim stopped. Releasing her, he flopped into a dining room chair and began to weep.

His wife pointed an accusing finger. "Look what you've done to my daughter!"

He needed no reprimand. He saw.

That night by Angel's bedside, I read her thoughts. "Once I leave home, I am never coming back." After the events of that day, I understood completely. Giving her a shower of love energy, I eased her into sleep and began to heal her injuries. Her emotional wounds, however, had become much deeper. Completing one love bath, I gave another. Just as I was radiating a third round of energy to my charge, Sottrol appeared at my elbow.

"After all your fine work, Darci, Angel will surely feel that someone loves her," my mentor smiled.

"Sottrol!" I was so glad to see the elder that I hugged him. Leaning back, looking into his sparkling eyes, I grinned. "That's the idea," I said. "But why are you here?"

My friend and teacher sat on the edge of Angel's bed and I joined him. "It is true. I rarely visit Earth, but word came to me that you and Angel have had an especially traumatic day."

"Oh, yes! Her father beat her! He was so drunk and angry and out of control—I thought he might kill her!"

Sottrol patted my hand. "Your quick thinking shifted the energy. Good job."

"Then why does my heart feel so heavy? I'm afraid she is scarred for life!"

"No, Darci, do not grieve. She is in the process of balancing her karma."

My mind flashed back to a reading in *The Great Book of Lifetimes*, an incarnation that Angel and I had shared. She was Gabriel, husband and father of eight, frustrated by losing employment, then outraged by his taunting oldest son. In anger, he had kicked the boy and the child had died from internal injuries. Horrified and distraught, Gabriel had closed himself off from the community, the church, his family, even from me, his wife at the time.

Reading my thoughts, the elder commented, "I see you remember that lifetime well."

I exhaled sharply, then replied, "I'm glad Angel was not fatally injured today."

"She will learn from this, Darci. You will see."

"I'm glad you are so confident."

We sat silently for a while listening to Angel's soft, sleeping breaths.

At length, Sottrol spoke. "I understand you have been learning from the elves."

"Yes," I responded, "though I have not had a visit from them for some time."

"Blue Sky Breathing is one of my cohorts. He told you about Naquahris."

"He did, though we reached a certain point and the story stopped. The chief said I must read the rest in *The Great Book of Lifetimes*."

The elder winked. "Can you guess what I have brought you?"

"The book! *The Great Book*!" I exclaimed excitedly.

Sottrol laughed. "I knew this would cheer you." With that, he raised his arms and wiggled his fingers. The great book appeared above us in a cloud of twinkling mist, then lowered into the elder's lap. "Would you enjoy some company while you read?"

"Yes. Please stay."

The elder chuckled. "Not me, Darci. I am called to be elsewhere."

"Then, who … ?"

At that moment, I saw a familiar glow in the window. Seconds later, Orillo stood beside me smiling.

"Orillo!" I returned his smile. "This has turned out to be quite a night."

"Greetings, Darci." The elf prince nodded to me.

Sottrol stood. "I will leave you to it." He handed over the giant tome. "When the words disappear, simply ask the book to return to its place in the library at the Spirit Guide University." The elder turned, climbed two invisible stairs, then vanished in glittering vapor leaving behind the fragrance of sweetgrass.

Orillo's eyes showed his excitement as he clasped my arm. "Many months have I waited for this moment. I have often thought of Naquahris and his story."

"I, too, have wondered about his life." Smiling, I patted the bed. "Sit beside me. We'll read together."

The Great Book of Lifetimes then opened on my lap. The pages were luminous, the text large and easy to read. The story began exactly where we had left it.

When Naquahris and Losath returned home from their visit with the shaman, Daekeriha, they learned that in their absence the old medicine woman, Quelela, had fallen ill. After Naquahris greeted his mother, his grandparents, and his siblings, he went to the old woman's teepee. The tribe's medicine healer and one of his apprentices were with her. Quelela lay with her eyes closed looking small and pale. As if she sensed his presence, she opened her eyes when Naquahris entered her abode.

Weakly waving him to her, she spoke barely above a whisper. "My student, my star."

The young man knelt by her side clasping her withered hand. "Quelela, my teacher."

"You will have many teachers and you will teach many," she told him, her voice wavering. "It is my time, young Naquahris. It is your time, too."

"What do you mean?"

"Hear me. You must pack and leave here. You are ready to begin your Earth walk. You have many, many miles to go."

"But, Quelela, I have only just returned."

"As I journey to join the ancestors, you must journey to your destiny." She coughed. Speaking was consuming what little strength remained within her.

"Hush, my teacher." Naquahris motioned for a gourd of water.

When the apprentice handed him the drink, Quelela shook her head ever so slightly. "Waste no water on me. My time here is over. You now carry my knowledge and the wisdom of many who came before us."

As she closed her eyes, radiance appeared around her head, most brightly at the crown. The light flamed upward as she ceased to breathe.

Naquahris remained in his home village for several weeks teaching the medicine healer and his apprentices what he could of Quelela's knowledge. This allowed him time to find the words to explain his upcoming departure to his family and, indeed, to the entire tribe. In truth, the young man did not know exactly why he was leaving. The old woman's admonition echoed constantly in his head, and he felt restlessness grow within him. After helping the tribe pack for the seasonal move to their summer campgrounds, he told his parents that he was not coming with them.

"I remember the day," I spoke aloud to Orillo. "My son embraced first his mother, then me. He said he was called to a new path, one that was different from ours."

"As Losath, you knew this was coming," Orillo responded. "Your son chose the path of the twisted hair, a life of constant travel."

"Knowing this did not make it easier when the time came. My heart was heavy and Amisimma wept."

"Now we learn what happened to your son once he left the Cree."

We looked at the page. Indeed, the scene had changed.

Naquahris was camped by the side of a lake so great he could not see the far shore. He was now at some distance from his home and family. Sitting by a small campfire, he listened to the wind through the trees. Rustling leaves whispered, "Beware, Naquahris, beware." He felt an uneasy churning in the pit of his stomach, so he gathered small branches and bunched them beneath his buffalo robe until it resembled a sleeping form. Climbing a nearby tree, he sat silently, watching. "Danger," said the tree as it swayed in gusts off the lake.

A few minutes later, Naquahris looked down to see a canoe slide quietly up to the beach near his dying campfire. Hopping quickly from the craft, two warriors threw their spears at the buffalo hide, piercing it. When they pulled back the hide to see the carefully arranged branches, they looked at each other, fear on their faces.

"A trap!" one growled.

Naquahris then cried out, making loud, unearthly noises. The two warriors craned their necks this way and that, but could see nothing as the wind carried the young man's sounds first in one direction then another. Afraid they were outnumbered, the warriors leapt into their canoe and paddled furiously away.

As the young Cree climbed down from the tree, he heard it say, "Naquahris, beloved, the Earth Mother will always protect you."

"Thank you," he whispered reverently. "I will always listen to Earth Mother and heed her words." Making an offer of precious pollen from one of his medicine pouches, he thanked the tree, the wind, and the Earth Mother for their ever-present protection.

At this point in the story, the writing disappeared from the page.

"I guess that's all for tonight," said Orillo.

Sighing, I closed the great book and telepathically asked that it return to its rightful place in the library at the Spirit Guide University. It slowly levitated, rotated, and disappeared.

"It is best that tonight's story was short." Orillo placed his hand on my shoulder. "You and Angel have undergone great trauma today. We will read more next time."

I nodded as the elf prince bowed and took his leave.

Gazing at my sleeping charge, I felt my heart fill with compassion. The bruises on her cheek and neck were clearly visible. I prayed for her and her father silently, then spoke aloud. "Great Spirit, if only I could protect Angel as the Earth Mother protected Naquahris."

CHAPTER TEN
INITIAL EXCURSION

Despite her father's objections, Angel planned to attend college the following fall. During the summer before her departure, she again held the job of playground instructor at the small local school. She was becoming a beautiful young woman, but as her Spirit Guide, I could see into her heart. I could tell that she feared her father and lacked respect for her mother, who, in Angel's eyes, was dependent and subservient. Her own self-image ricocheted between egotistically high and cripplingly low. I knew that one of her challenges in this lifetime was to find balanced and healthy self-regard.

During that summer before college, she went out after dinner with some friends. They decided to drive to the seashore and did not pay attention to Angel's curfew. When she returned well past the expected time, her parents yelled at her and meted a harsh punishment: no social interactions for a month. My charge was very upset, mostly because her parents had not listened to her side of the story. She was not driving and felt that she had no control of the situation. In her opinion, it was her friends who had ignored her curfew, not her. After being sent to her room, she fumed and cried. Once her parents and siblings had retired for the night, she packed a few things and left.

I knew where my charge was headed and stayed nearby as she walked five miles to the school. As playground instructor, she had a key to the small building. At nearly three in the morning, physically and emotionally exhausted, she reached her destination and flopped on the cot in the nurse's office.

Of course, I was close by her side and, as she slept, I attempted to infuse her energy field with love, for I knew she felt unloved, even rejected, by her family. As I sat on the edge of the cot, I felt a presence, and a moment later, Orillo appeared beside me. A light green cape flowed around him like leaves in a breeze. His golden hair glowed and his eyes gleamed with luminescence and compassion.

"You are concerned about her, Darci," he began as he placed a hand on my shoulder. "You must know that she is intelligent. Even though emotionally distraught, she will not put herself in real danger."

"I don't know," I sighed. "The long walk here so late at night was risky enough."

"Yet here she is, safe, with you by her side." He smiled. "All is well, Darci. The avatars are coming to Earth."

"The avatars," I repeated. "Why do they come, Orillo?"

"They arrive to usher Earth into a new time, a new golden age, a time when love and compassion are the norm and greed, hate, and war fade away."

I shook my head. "It is difficult to believe that such a time can ever manifest on this plane. I have seen such terrible things. During my apprenticeship, I witnessed horrible behavior during the last Great War. Why, only a few weeks ago, Angel's father beat her!"

"We must not dwell on the past," the prince said softly. "Instead, let us read more about the soul who is to become the elfin avatar." After taking a step back, he twirled and reached toward the ceiling of the small office. "Please, allow us to read more about Naquahris, the one who is to return."

The Great Book of Lifetimes, shimmering with luminescence, appeared above him and floated slowly down into his arms. We sat together on the edge of the cot and read the words that appeared on the pages within.

Naquahris journeyed on foot, his medicine bags strapped to his body. Considering himself a peacemaker, he carried no weapons and trusted the Creator and the Earth Mother to protect him.

After traveling south for several moons, he came upon a large encampment of Indians. Having seen one of the guards scouting the perimeter of the village, he avoided the main entrance and carefully kept to the bushes, circling around the edge of the camp until he heard sounds of girls and boys at play.

When the young twisted hair stepped from the forest, the children were the first to see him. They halted their game of tossing a moose hide ball and stared at the stranger.

"I come to tell you stories," Naquahris smiled, but the children continued to stare, their eyes wide. One small boy ran away yelling words that Naquahris could not understand. It was then he realized that the language spoken at this village was much different from his own.

Instinctively, he knelt in the dirt and offered a silent prayer as the children watched. "Dear Creator, bless my ears that I may hear what is spoken here. Bless my mouth that the words I utter may be understood. I ask this so that I may better serve You and your most beautiful Creation, Mother Earth."

Flashing a smile to the remaining children, he stood and picked up their ball, tossing it high, then catching it behind his back. He kicked the soft orb with his moccasined foot, then caught it again. By the time adults arrived, he had won the hearts of the children by showing them a new game using their ball.

Three of the tribe's women were first to arrive. The tallest glared at him and spat a demand that he sensed was a warning. Naquahris smiled and pointed to his universal hairdo. The other women nodded, but the tall one remained suspicious. "You come to tell our children stories, young twisted hair?" she shouted. "We tell them stories of our people. We do not need you for that."

Naquahris grinned, for his prayer had been heard; he understood her words clearly. "Good woman," he addressed her respectfully, "I come in peace with many stories of the plants and animals. I ask that I may be allowed to entertain those who wish to hear them."

One of the shorter women tugged at the tall one's doeskin dress and whispered in her ear.

"Come with me." The tall woman gestured to him. "I will take you to our chief."

Naquahris followed her, the other two women and the children trailing behind. As he was led through the large encampment, he noticed that it was set up differently from the familiar Cree camps. The teepees were arranged in concentric circles with one large abode in the center.

When the procession reached the big teepee, the tall woman held up her hand and everyone stopped. She then called to the occupant requesting the right to enter. Naquahris did not hear a reply, but the woman seemed to because she lifted the flap, ducked, and stepped through the entrance. The storyteller was not sure if he should follow. He knew that to enter the home of the chief of such a large tribe was an honor. When he glanced at the other women and children, he noticed that they stared at him with curiosity in their eyes. After a few moments, the tall woman appeared at the entrance and motioned for him to step through.

The interior of the abode was dark and smelled of pungent herbs. When his eyes adjusted to the dim light, he noticed bundles of dried plants hanging from poles. The old chief lay on a mat, a roll of hides behind his shoulders propping him up.

"Come." His voice nearly a whisper, he motioned for Naquahris to approach.

Without being prompted, the storyteller knelt by the old chief's side.

"Black Wolf tells me you claim to be a twisted hair."

The young man nodded. "Yes, Chief. I am Naquahris from the Northern Cree. I come to tell you and your people stories about the wonders of the Earth Mother."

"Young man," the chief's voice was stronger now, "I am Silver Eagle, chief of the Menominee. My sons and most of the other men are away on an important hunt." He shifted slightly, grimacing as if in pain. "There are no warriors here to protect the women and children."

"Chief Silver Eagle, I come in peace. What ails you? Perhaps I can help."

"I can no longer walk. My feet are crippled with pain. The longer I lie here, the weaker I become."

"May I have the honor of bestowing a healing treatment? It may relieve your pain, perhaps do more."

With a sparkle in his eyes, the old man nodded his acceptance. He glanced at the tall woman, now scowling at them. "You may go, Black Wolf."

Her mouth drawn into a tight line, she hissed and then said, "But my chief, you do not know this man."

"We will need privacy as this young man works."

Shrugging a shoulder, she promised, "I will be right outside if you need me."

Once she had stepped out, Naquahris drew back the blanket that covered the old chief from the knees down. He found the elder's feet wrapped in strips of doeskin.

Silver Eagle saw the young healer's expression and urged him on. "Yes. Take off the bindings. You must see what you are dealing with."

As Naquahris pulled away the last bandage, he saw that the poor man's feet were covered in wart-like growths so numerous that his feet appeared misshapen.

"How long have you had these?"

"The first appeared five winters ago. I have not walked for two. Our medicine people have not been able to heal me. They say it is a sign that my time as a chief nears its end."

Naquahris moved closer and spoke in low tones. "If I were to heal you and restore your feet to their normal state so that you can again walk, would you continue as chief?"

The old man's eyebrows lifted in surprise. "Do you think you can heal me?"

Naquahris smiled. "I can try."

"If you do, if I could walk again, I would see it as a sign for me to continue as leader and chief."

The young healer gazed at the bundled herbs. "I will need a few fresh ingredients for the poultice."

"My daughter will help you find whatever you need." He turned his head toward the entrance flap. "Black Wolf, please step in."

The tall, stately Indian woman was at the elder's side in two breaths. "My chief," she said softly.

"Take this young man to the medicine teepee and introduce him to my daughter. Now I need to rest," the old man said with effort. "I grow weaker by the day."

Without speaking one word, Black Wolf walked through the large encampment with Naquahris following behind. The young man was trained to observe details, and he noticed many differences between his Cree tribe and these people.

On the other side of the encampment three teepees were set apart near the edge of the forest. Black Wolf halted before the largest and spoke a greeting. A young woman emerged holding a partially plaited braid of sweetgrass. Sunlight shimmered on her long blue-black hair as she appraised the visitor.

"Your father requests that you assist this young traveler." Black Wolf's stern expression bespoke her disapproval. "I will come with you if you wish."

In both appearance and manner, the chief's daughter contrasted with the harsher older woman. Black Wolf was bony and angular while the young woman standing before Naquahris was soft, rounded, and gentle.

Her eyes glistened as she introduced herself. "I am Dream Swan."

She spoke with a hint of a smile. "How can I assist you?"

The young storyteller was drawn to her gentleness. "I am Naquahris, a twisted hair, as you can see."

She nodded.

"I come with stories for all who wish to listen, but I also travel with ancient healing knowledge. Will you help me locate the plants I need to heal your father?"

Her eyes grew wide. "Heal him? But our best medicine people have been unable to help him."

Naquahris smiled. "I wish to try. Will you assist me?"

"Of course." Dream Swan glanced back and forth between the young man and the tall, scowling woman, then said, "I will not need your protection, Black Wolf. I'll be safe enough with this man."

"But you do not know him!"

The young woman stared at the older as she gestured toward Naquahris. "Can you not see? He carries no weapons, and I can tell by his eyes that his heart is good."

Black Wolf glared at Naquahris, a look that communicated her mistrust. "As you wish," she grumbled, turning to go.

The two young people, each carrying a basket, walked into the woods, Dream Swan leading the way. Naquahris described the plants, trees, and vines he needed for the special poultice. Her people called the plants by different names, yet soon they gathered all they searched for. The chief's daughter was surprised at some of his choices but said nothing.

Once back at the camp, Naquahris began by clearing a small space between the largest medicine teepee and the forest.

"Would you bring me a lit torch?" he asked her.

Curious, she did as he requested. He wound the vines into a pile on the cleared spot, then set them on fire. They smoldered, sending a unique scent into the air. After patient tending, the vines were reduced to ashes. As they cooled, Naquahris chopped, then ground dandelion root, horseradish root, and balsam fir bark with a few balsam needles sprinkled in. Next he added fresh sage leaves to the already aromatic mixture. To Dream Swan's surprise, he spit into the mixture, not once but four times. Finally, the cooled ashes were added and the medicine was ready.

"Please come with me." Naquahris looked into her beautiful dark eyes. "Let us treat your father together, for love is a part of all healing."

They found the old chief asleep. Dream Swan kissed her father's forehead and whispered in his ear. "We have come with the poultice, Father. May we apply it?"

His eyes opening to thin slits, the old man grunted and nodded.

Using leaves to apply the paste, Naquahris sang quietly in his Cree tongue.

"I feel it," the old chief mumbled. "It tingles and makes my feet feel as if they are flying."

Dream Swan smiled.

Naquahris refused to use the old bandages. He instead wrapped the chief's feet in large comfrey leaves, tying them with sturdy grasses.

"Things are happening here." Silver Eagle nodded toward his feet.

"A fresh application each day for four days and you will walk again," promised Naquahris.

"Then please stay as a guest in our camp while you continue to treat me," offered the chief. "And tell your stories."

That night outside the chief's teepee, many of the tribe gathered to sit by the fire and hear the stranger speak. The flap of the chief's abode lay open so that he could hear what was said as he rested on his pallet.

Naquahris related the following story. "The stars in the sky told me that all on Earth is made of many tiny stars too small to see. These miniature stars are the energy of the Creator, which permeates all things. Once the stars in the sky told me this, I realized that I could also speak to the many tiny stars in all things. At that moment millions of voices entered my mind. The sound was louder than a thousand stampeding buffalo and I thought my head would explode. I pressed my hands over my ears, but the roar of all the star voices continued to fill my mind. I felt small. With yearning in my heart I prayed to the Creator for silence and stillness, and it came. Everything was so quiet I could hear dew dropping from a leaf to the ground.

"Then a question filled my heart. Why was I led to hear the voices of the many tiny stars in all things when such knowledge overwhelms me?

"At that moment a turtle walked slowly across my path. I asked the turtle why I had heard the millions of voices of the tiny stars in all things. The turtle stopped and turned toward me, training its eyes upon me. 'Naquahris,' it said, 'you have much to learn and you have taken the first step: you were humble in the face of the great knowledge. I will give you this wisdom. Your intent is the key. Just as you focused and addressed me with the question in your heart, you need only direct your attention to one thing at a time.'

"'But I do not understand,' I told the turtle.

"The wise creature took a few steps toward a plant, one I did not know. 'Focus on this plant,' it directed. 'Ask it what it has to tell you.'

"I did as the turtle suggested. Sitting cross-legged before the plant, I stared at it and asked, 'May the miniature stars, the energy of the Creator within you, speak to me. What have you to say?'

"Immediately I heard one clear voice in my mind, the voice of this plant. 'You are blessed, dear one,' it said, 'for you have learned how to converse with the Spirit-in-All-Things. I am useful to you and your kind, for my roots make syrup that can ease cough and congestion in the chest. Always remember to take only what you need for healing and leave plenty behind that we may serve another one day.'

"Amazed at what I had so clearly heard, I looked over at the turtle.

"'That is the key,' it said. 'Set your intention, focus, and ask. In the quiet of your heart and mind, you will receive the answer.'"

At that moment one of the children sitting in the front of the group spoke up. "Twisted Hair, is this how you found the cure for my grandfather, Chief Silver Eagle?"

Naquahris smiled. "That is exactly the way. I called to the plant kingdom, 'Show me who can help heal this great chief!' Then I walked through the forest and listened for the plants and trees to volunteer their healing magic."

Suddenly Chief Silver Eagle appeared at the entrance of his abode. Black Wolf and Dream Swan rushed to his side. All who had gathered for the storytelling stood in amazement.

"My chief! You are standing!" cried Black Wolf as she grabbed his arm.

"Father! You walked!" exclaimed Dream Swam, excitement in her eyes.

Smiling, the old chief waved them away. "I do not need your assistance. I can walk on my own." He took the few steps needed to reach the young twisted hair. "I bestow upon you, Naquahris of the Cree Nation, a great honor. As thanks for healing me, I give you this pipe." The crowd gasped as the chief held forward a long-stemmed pipe adorned with eagle feathers. "This gift will show all you meet in your travels that you are honored and trusted by the Menominee."

Naquahris knelt before the powerful chief and thanked him for the gift.

The words then disappeared from the pages of *The Great Book of Lifetimes*. Orillo floated to his feet. "That was an excellent story."

"A story within a story," I observed.

"Yes," agreed the elfin prince. "Now I am in even greater awe of this soul who once walked the earth as Naquahris and who will come as our avatar."

"When will that be?" I asked.

"Much depends on you, Darci, and on your charge."

We both glanced at Angel, who shifted on the cot.

"On us?" I was surprised. "Can you tell us why this is so?"

Orillo winked. "I am not at liberty to say at this moment."

"Please, Orillo," I pleaded. "Tell us our roles in the coming of this avatar."

"Right now there is only potential," he replied. "I will ask Nyna if I may tell you more." He nodded toward the single window in the nurse's office. "First light has arrived. I must go. Take good care of that young woman. She is a key to the great changes." Orillo then floated upward and dissolved into a cloud of dazzling scintilla.

I said a prayer for Angel and her family. I knew not what was ahead, but I knew now that it was monumental.

CHAPTER ELEVEN
THE PEACEMAKER

Because I study with the Master Guides, I knew that several waves of transition would bring change to Earth. The first one in Angel's lifetime occurred while she was in college.

After freshman year at an all-female school, she transferred to Boston University and lived in a dormitory on Beacon Street. She had many reasons for the move, though the primary one was music. In the mid-sixties, Boston was the center of a thriving folk music scene. In less than a month, she found her way to The Club 47 in Cambridge, home of nightly live music shows. I enjoyed watching her aura flash and sparkle with excitement as she sat stage-side at the feet of such greats as Muddy Waters, Bill Monroe, Joni Mitchell, and Mavis Staples.

The most difficult part for me was watching Angel discover sex. After all, she and I had shared deep love and passion on Earth and in spirit realms. During my last Earth lifetime in nineteenth-century England, ladies were modest, covered head to foot in clothing, and always chaperoned. Intercourse was never discussed, sometimes even between a husband and wife.

Angel, however, was propelled into the escalating sexual revolution. My heart ached as she experimented, moving from one young man to another, never really knowing love. I told myself over and over that she was experiencing the revolutionary pulse of the changing times. On the positive side, the freedom-loving young people of the sixties held high ideals for social, economic, and political change, all part of the wave of transition.

Her second year in Boston, she rented her own room in Cambridge between Central Square and Harvard Yard. One night as she slept, exhausted, after an evening at The Club 47 enjoying the Paul Butterfield Blues Band, I stood at the foot of her bed giving her a cleansing bath of white light. I was contemplating the effect big-city living was having on my charge. Angel had yet to discover how sensitive, impressionable, and psychic she was. From my vantage point, I could see that the intense vibration and overwhelming din of the city was masking her instincts. She did not always make the best choices.

An emerald glow in the corner of the room grew brighter until a figure took shape and stepped toward me. Overjoyed, I welcomed Prince Orillo.

"Darci, good to see you. There are some fine old trees on this street. They make it easier for an elemental like myself to manifest."

"I'm glad," I said with enthusiasm. "It's been too long since we had a chance to visit and talk."

"You seem concerned, old friend." Orillo placed his arm around my shoulders.

Sighing, I shook my head. "Angel is … is …"

"Grown up?" Orillo asked with a smile.

"Grown and immune to my influence. When she was a child, I could affect her, heal her, entertain her so easily. Now she is immersed in this very promiscuous society and quite distracted by it."

The elfin prince walked to the window, glanced at the shimmering shadows made by the streetlights through the trees, then turned to face me. "Keep in mind that your charge is going through exactly what she needs to."

"Why does she need to?" My frustration was showing. "Why does she need to experiment with so many boorish young men?"

"You are very attached to her," Orillo observed, "but that is good. In order for the two of you to fulfill your destiny, the bond between you must be extraordinary."

"It is."

"Yes," he nodded. "I know of your past lives together, and the training you two went through at the Spirit Guide University."

"You elves seem to know a lot."

"We know about you and Angel because you may figure into our destiny and the destiny of our avatar."

"And what might that destiny be?"

The glowing elfin being walked toward me, flinging his emerald cape open. His golden belt flashed so brightly it nearly blinded me. "Come, Darci. First things first. Your mentor Sottrol wishes us to read another excerpt from *The Great Book of Lifetimes*. It is important that we both become familiar with the background of the extraordinary soul who is to arrive as our avatar."

Orillo waved his hand and Angel, still sleeping deeply, rolled over to face the wall. The prince and I sat on the edge of her bed as the elf raised his arms to summon *The Great Book*. Appearing in a spiral of sparkling white radiance, the large tome floated down, settling across our laps. As usual, *The Great Book* opened itself. The pages seemed more luminous than I remembered.

Orillo's eyes sparkled. "Darci, I think we are going to learn something very important tonight."

We both focused on the glowing pages.

Naquahris, protected by the Earth Mother herself, continued his travels. Sometimes he was welcomed warmly by a tribe who recognized the hairdo of a traveling storyteller. Other times in other places he was regarded suspiciously, but won the people's hearts and trust with his entertaining tales and healing skills.

Several years passed. Naquahris grew into a strong, handsome, very intuitive man. As he traveled through the land that is now known as the Dakotas, he grew uneasy. The Earth Mother was warning him of unrest and hostility between tribes in the area. Soon after, he saw smoke in the distance. Heading in that direction, he came upon a small Indian encampment that had been raided by a war party. The teepees were burned and bodies strewn around on the ground. His heart wrenched with sadness; he went from body to body, checking to see if any still lived. The dead were all women, children, and elders.

"The cowards must have attacked when the men were away on a hunt!" he muttered, tears shimmering.

Movement caught his eye. A boy lying under a fallen lodge pole moaned. Rushing over, Naquahris lifted the heavy pole, then knelt at the boy's side. The lad, about ten years old, was covered in dust, a deep gash in his scalp. The healer murmured comforting words as he cradled the boy's head, cleaning the gash with water from his bison bladder canteen. As Naquahris sang a healing chant, the boy's eyes flickered open.

The twisted hair's odd appearance frightened the lad, who was already in a state of shock and panic from the vicious attack. He squirmed and tried to stand, but fell back into the healer's arms. Weak and panting, he pleaded with Naquahris. Although the healer did not understand the words, he knew the boy was begging for his life.

Naquahris radiated great compassion and kindness while praying silently, which seemed to calm the lad. The twisted hair asked Great Spirit and Mother Earth for help with communicating and healing the young Indian. Soon he was able to understand the boy's tortured words.

"Mama! Where is my mama?"

The traveler's heart ached, for he had found no one else alive. Naquahris shook his head and gazed up at the cloud-filled sky.

"She is dead? My mama is dead?" the boy exclaimed.

"She is being welcomed by Great Spirit, who is taking very good care of her." Somehow Naquahris knew how to speak these words. His highly developed inner instincts sensed that the orphaned boy's destiny intertwined with his own.

"I am Naquahris, a traveler, healer, and storyteller. I saw the smoke from the attack and came to help."

The boy seemed to relax a little. "So you are not one of the evil warriors?"

101

"No. Do you know who did this?" The healer looked around. Many dead bodies were lying in sight.

The lad shook his head, then winced. "That hurts!"

"You have a gash in your scalp. I've washed it. Now that it is dry, I'd like to sprinkle on some healing powder."

The twisted hair glanced around, locating some pieces of hide nearby that had escaped burning. Carefully sliding the boy's head onto the hide, Naquahris stood and detached a pouch from his belt. Opening it, he kept his eyes on the young one. "Stay still."

"Is it bleeding?" asked the boy, his eyes wide with concern.

"The bleeding has stopped," assured the healer, grasping a pinch from the little sack. He crushed the substance between his fingers as he spoke a prayer into the powder.

"What is that?" The lad eyed the tall Indian.

"Something to help you heal. What's your name?"

"Pacami'ita. It means 'Growing Deer.' Everyone calls me Paca."

The healer felt more than saw tears fill the boy's eyes.

Paca inhaled a shaky breath. "Most everyone who calls me that is …"

Naquahris jumped in. "I'll call you 'Paca' then, if it's all right with you."

The boy nodded.

"What about your father and the other warriors?'

Paca stared at his hands. "My father died last winter. The other men are hunting. I do not know when they are coming back."

"You need rest, Paca, but we also must be ready to leave. If the war party comes back this way, we don't want them to find us." Naquahris again surveyed the area around the smoldering encampment. "I want to carry you into those trees."

"The stream is over there." Paca pointed in the opposite direction.

"That's where everyone will look. We must be very careful. We must be invisible." The healer offered his canteen. "Have a drink. I'll go and refill the water bag once we've moved."

Paca drank, then gulped for air, then drank again. Once Naquahris had strapped on the canteen, he lifted the boy and carried him away from the camp, stopping only after entering the tree line and crouching behind thick bushes.

Just before dusk, Naquahris crept stealthily to the stream on the far side of the encampment. After filling his water skin, he heard the grasses by the stream whisper a warning, "Horsemen." As he made his way back to the boy, he felt the earth tremble beneath his moccasined feet and heard the sound of riders in the distance.

As the healer hid in the brush with the sleeping boy on the ground beside him, twenty men galloped into the camp and began yelling and screaming. Naquahris watched carefully and realized that the men were grief-stricken. They were the returning hunters. Still he waited and did not show himself, fearing he would be mistaken for the blood-thirsty warriors who had massacred the families of these men.

The crying and moaning of the men filled the darkening terrain. At length, a campfire was started and the hunting party gathered around it. The boy still slept, so Naquahris crept closer to the group in order to overhear their discussion.

"It must have been a Crow raiding party from the north," one tall hunter proclaimed.

"They were Blackfoot warriors from the west," another insisted.

The Indian in charge held up his hand. "We will track them in the morning, but some of us must stay and tend the dead."

"We need all of us together to face them," grouched a sour-faced man.

"We must be smarter than them and surprise them!" cried another as he stood and shook his fist.

"My entire family lies in the shadows, all brutally murdered," said a man whose back was toward Naquahris. "I cannot leave them as they are. I must stay and honor them."

"I will stay with you," an older hunter offered. "My wife, mother, and daughter have all died."

"We will see to all the dead," promised the first man who said he'd stay.

The heart of the twisted hair grew heavy with compassion, but he did not make himself known. Returning quietly to his hiding place, he joined the boy who continued to sleep. It was not until well after the hunters rode out of camp on the trail of the war party that Naquahris woke Paca and checked his condition.

"Some of your people have returned to camp. I'd like you to walk with me, but if you are still too weak, I will carry you."

"The hunting party returned?" Paca mumbled sleepily, his face a mask of sorrow.

"Only two remain. The others are tracking the killers. Try to stand, Paca. See if you have the strength to walk into camp on your own two feet."

The lad made a valiant effort, but he was too weak. His legs gave out as he was overcome with dizziness. Naquahris scooped him up. "Time to introduce me to your people."

When the older Indian spotted Naquahris carrying the boy, he aimed his hunting spear at the pair. When he saw Paca, he shouted gruffly, "Who are you, stranger? Why do you carry the boy?"

"I am Naquahris, the Peacemaker. I came upon the scene of this massacre of your people and found one survivor."

"He's a good man, Sharp Eye," Paca called out. "He's a healer."

Sharp Eye lowered his spear and motioned for Naquahris to approach. "Use my sleeping blanket for the boy." The hunter motioned toward the dwindling campfire. "How badly is he hurt?"

"He needs rest," replied the healer as he placed the young Indian on the blanket. "He has a head injury that I have dressed. I believe he will recover."

"Good." Sharp Eye scanned the stranger's appearance and noticed his strange hairstyle. "You are a storyteller?"

"Yes," Naquahris responded as he checked the boy's wound. "If you can help me find a clean cloth to bandage him, it will help keep the wound clean."

Sharp Eye nodded.

At that point, the other hunter strode toward them. "What is this?"

"Gray Hawk, this traveling storyteller has rescued Paca," Sharp Eye informed him. "The boy appears to be the only survivor."

"I am Naquahris," the twisted hair introduced himself. "And I will help you bury your dead."

For the rest of the day, Naquahris worked alongside the two hunters. The hard-packed earth resisted the digging tools of the three men. By sunset, they had made burial sites for eleven dead, but they needed four times as many.

That night around the campfire, Naquahris told a story to comfort the three grieving Lakota.

"Many sun cycles ago after Creation, Great Spirit gave the people a great test and a great gift. The test was death and the gift was spirit.

"In the early years, our ancestors hunted as we do. When a hunter was killed, the entire tribe grieved his death much as they do today, for they had lost an important provider.

"One autumn day, a beautiful young woman named Blossom Breeze waited for her new husband to return from the hunt. He had promised her a bear robe for the cold winter ahead. When he and the other hunters had not returned by nightfall, Blossom Breeze sent prayers to the Creator asking for the safety of the men. An owl flew silently to a tree nearby her. It hooted over and over until she heard the message that the owl was bringing.

"Sweet woman, your husband walks on the other side. He will come to you tonight to tell his story.

"Blossom Breeze did not know exactly what the message meant, but she feared for her husband. She sat awake by the fire awaiting her husband. In the hours just before the first light of day, she heard a rustling and felt a cool breeze on her cheek. From behind her came her husband's voice.

"'Dear wife, I am here.'

"She turned and smelled his scent but did not see him. 'Where are you, my love?' she cried.

"'I am beside you. There is a veil that separates us so that you cannot see me, but I am here. I killed a bear for you, the biggest I have ever seen, but it wounded me. Soon after, I found myself standing over my own body. An owl came and told me to come home to you, so I am here.'

"Blossom Breeze began to weep. 'You are dead!' she cried.

"'My body lies cold and still, but my spirit thrives. I do not feel the wounds of my past, the broken arm that healed but always ached, the twisted knee that would hurt when I walked all day. I am free of such things. And I can fly, speeding from place to place like an eagle.'

"'But can you hold me as a husband holds a wife? Can you father the children we talked about?'

"Her husband appeared before her, looking as he had when he departed with the hunting party, but there was a warm, comforting glow around him. 'Blossom Breeze, you carry my child within you, and I shall be close by to protect you and help you raise him.' He moved toward her and she felt engulfed by love.

"Next morning the hunting party returned with her husband's body and the carcass of the bear who had killed him. The tribe was stricken with grief for the loss of one of their finest hunters, and many wails and cries soared skyward. Blossom Breeze asked the chief to call the tribe together immediately. When they were gathered, most thought the new widow would make requests as to how the tribe could honor her husband. They were surprised at what she said.

"'My dear friends and relatives,' she began. 'I have not lost my husband, for he came to me last night. His spirit body glowed with magical light. He comforted me and told me I was carrying his child. He embraced me and I could feel his love surround me and comfort me. His message to all our people is that we live on after our Earth bodies fail us and die. We live on without pain or encumbrances. We live on to watch over our families and loved ones. We shall honor my husband as a great hunter and provider, and a member of our tribe.'

"From that day on, we include as a part of our ceremonies those who have passed on before us. We sing and dance with the knowledge that our ancestors are among us in spirit."

Naquahris looked around the encampment and saw the spirits of the departed. They smiled at him and radiated love to all four present. The healer noticed tears glistening on the faces of the two hunters as they stared into the fire.

Paca's eyes were wide with disbelief. "Naquahris, do you see them?"

"Yes," whispered the healer. "Their presence heals the heart, cleansing emotions of loss and grief. Your mother comes to encircle you with her love."

The glowing form of a woman appeared beside the boy and proceeded to hug him, imbuing him with her love. The four slept well that night, comforted by the healer's story and the cleansing emotions it brought.

Two days later, the slain were all buried. Rocks were placed atop each mound to discourage creatures from digging, but also to identify the loved one. In one year's time, the remaining members of the tribe would return to honor their departed.

Gray Hawk and Sharp Eye prepared to ride out at dawn the next day. Sitting by the fire that night, Paca asked what their plans were.

"We'll join the others from our hunting party," Gray Hawk growled. "We will seek and obtain revenge for the inhumane slaying of our women, children, and elders."

"I wish to come!" cried the lad. "I want to join and revenge my mother's death!"

Sharp Eye laughed. "You are too young and you are recovering from a serious head wound. You would be more of a burden than a help."

"Then what shall become of me?" Paca wailed. "I cannot lose the last of my tribe! Please, take me with you."

As the two hunters shook their heads, Naquahris spoke. "I'll tend the boy. We will follow behind you so that he can join you once he is stronger."

The next day, the hunters set off on their horses while Naquahris and Paca followed on foot. The healer was pleased to have the company of the young Indian, for he knew that Paca was gifted. The boy had seen the departed and felt his mother's gift of love.

As they journeyed, Naquahris told the boy many stories. The healer taught him about what the trees and bushes they encountered offered in the way of food and medicine.

When the moon had swelled from a crescent to a full globe, the two travelers came upon a large encampment by a river. They snuck very close in the night to see if they could identify the tribe.

"Crow!" whispered Paca. "This is the tribe my people are seeking to exact revenge, for they believe the Crow attacked our encampment."

"Do the hunters know for sure?"

Paca appeared confused. "I don't know. I heard only what Sharp Eye and Gray Hawk said."

"Do you trust me, Paca?"

The boy nodded.

"We'll make our move in the morning sunlight."

The next day Naquahris proceeded as he had done so many times before. He located the children of the camp and introduced himself and Paca. He told one of his most beloved stories about a family of wolves. Other members of the tribe gathered, and he told another story. His status as a twisted hair seemed to be acknowledged and accepted.

At the end of the day, the two travelers were invited to meet the Crow chief. Once formal greetings were exchanged, the chief asked Naquahris to tell stories to his nephew who was ill. After the twisted hair agreed, he asked the chief about the raid on women, children, and elders of Paca's tribe.

"It was not us," stated the chief. "We are gathering food for the coming winter. This clan is very big and much effort is needed to feed and care for all."

"But … but the hunters who were away from camp when the slaughter took place … they think it is your tribe who attacked and killed our people. They are coming for revenge."

The chief appeared worried. "I do not want any more of your tribe killed nor any of my own, but how can we avoid it?"

Naquahris stood tall and smiled. "I am the peacemaker. I will make sure there is no senseless battle here."

In the cool of the evening, the healer walked out from the camp, communicated with the Earth Mother, and received the information he sought: the location of the hunters. At dawn the next day, Naquahris, Paca, and one of the Crow elders walked to where the hunters were camped. A peace agreement was brokered on the spot, and the hunters were invited to feast with the Crow. Naquahris was known from that day forward as the great peacemaker.

∞

As before, the words disappeared from the pages of *The Great Book of Lifetimes*.

Closing the giant tome, Orillo smiled, his eyes glistening. "Naquahris was a peacemaker. Darci, we have learned that our elfin avatar comes to us as a peacemaker."

Remembering my apprenticeship during World War Two as well as the current war in Viet Nam, I spoke earnestly. "Good news for a world that has seen far too many wars."

CHAPTER TWELVE

SOUL MATES

Now that Angel was out on her own, she gravitated to people who shared her passion for music. My twenty-year-old charge spent time anywhere live music was offered. Starting as a waitress, she worked several nights a week at the center of the folk music scene in the Boston area, The Club 47 in Cambridge. Soon she was also helping with filing as well as designing the club's promotional flyers.

One afternoon in late spring, Angel was at the club's front desk filing new memberships. Singer Maria Muldaur, then with the Jim Kweskin Jug Band, stopped in looking for a traveling babysitter. My charge volunteered with no hesitation.

June 1967, Angel found herself for the first time in California on tour with the jug band. Although she was looking after Geoff and Maria's three-year-old daughter, Jenny, she still managed to see live music.

One afternoon, I stood protectively behind Angel in the lighting booth at the Fillmore West during a sound check. Unaware of my presence, she focused on the stage. The Doors, the main act, were playing through a test song. The volume was extremely loud, unmatched in my experience, even louder than a roaring waterfall or the guns of war. The flashing, swirling light show was another spectacle that I had not before observed on Earth. I watched exhilaration crackle through Angel's energy field as she soaked in the scene. The Jim Kweskin Jug Band did their sound check next, leaving the stage arranged for their opening set later that night.

Near midnight Angel shifted uncomfortably in a makeshift bed on the floor, the sleeping child beside her. This hilltop house in San Francisco did not offer enough beds to accommodate the entire jug band, so Angel ended up sleeping in the corner of a downstairs room with her head under a table. The rest of the household was at the Fillmore West show, so all was quiet.

My dear Angel was being exposed to so much at once, yet she thrived on the excitement. She twisted restlessly on the pallet, trying to assimilate all she had witnessed that day.

Hovering over her, I created a cloud of sparkling pink light then gently floated it down to cover and enwrap her. She relaxed and fell asleep shortly thereafter.

As I stared out the window at the lights of the big West Coast city, I felt the presence of an old friend behind me. Turning, I beheld a sphere of swirling white and gold light. Prince Orillo stepped through the luminescence, as it became part of him. I greeted him with a grin.

"It is not your charge alone who is restless," Orillo commented as he stepped beside me. "An entire generation of young people instinctively feels this first wave of transition."

"Truly I have seen and heard things today that I have never before experienced. Change is afoot."

The prince lifted his left eyebrow and smiled at me. "And this, Darci, is only the beginning."

"You definitely look as if you know things that I do not."

"Perhaps. But we must agree that your mentor Sottrol has wisdom far beyond ours."

"Have you seen Sottrol?" I missed having access to my teacher.

"I have." Orillo's smile was wide. "He sends greetings to you, Darci. He said that it is time for us to read more in *The Great Book of Lifetimes*. Shall we sit on the table or settle on the floor?"

"Let's sit on the floor near Angel."

"Your instincts are good, Darci, for the coming of the elfin avatar shall affect her, as well. One day she may write about it."

We sat close enough for me to touch my charge, then Orillo spoke a few words in his elfin language and the magical tome appeared just above our heads. This time the great book had a rosy-pink glow about it that I had not seen before. It floated slowly down to us, its pages whirring as it lowered.

As dark purple letters appeared on a light green page, I saw immediately that it was another story about Naquahris. The words informed us that the twisted hair had now lived for twenty-five cycles of the sun. During his wander west, he had developed a ceremony, which he performed upon approaching each unfamiliar encampment. Taking time, he would live in the woods near the tribe for at least one day. First he'd exchange energy with the trees and other flora, as well as with birds and animals. Chipmunks were his favorite because they noticed everything and then were more than willing to communicate. Next he would pray to Great Spirit and ask for guidance. Naquahris knew that first impressions were important for a stranger, so before entering the village, he took time to wash himself and rebraid the signature hairdo.

Outside an encampment somewhere in the rolling hills at the foot of a chain of great mountains, the twisted hair bathed himself and washed some clothing. At dusk, he wrapped himself in a warm hide and settled into sleep with the plan of entering the village the next morning. A vivid dream of radiant white deer, a doe and fawn, filled his sleep. When waking, he tingled with the memory of the magical dream animals. The healer knew that great change was coming to his life.

Preparing with diligent care, the impressive and uniquely handsome man slowly combed then braided his many tresses. When he walked into the camp, he walked with his strong shoulders squared, his spine erect, for he was walking with Great Spirit and moving to meet his destiny.

Naquahris was always happy when the first person he met in a new place was a child, in this case two. A pair of boys sat behind one of the dwellings; one was drawing with a stick in the dirt. Naquahris whistled like a bird and when the boys looked up at him, he smiled. At first their eyes grew wide with surprise, then they looked at each other and grinned. The healer sighed and relaxed. They had recognized him as a storyteller.

The boys babbled excitedly as they led him to the chief's abode. By the time they reached the large teepee, Naquahris had intuitively learned the dialect and understood what was being said. His telepathic and intuitive powers coupled with an open heart filled with compassion boosted his communication skills. For instance, when he sat with this chief, he could read the undertones of emotion as well as the words that were exchanged.

He was ushered into the dwelling by a large man, a guard. Just as Naquahris and the elder were greeting each other, they heard a woman's voice pleading with the guard. She pushed her way into the teepee and fell on her knees before the old chief. The young healer was startled, for in his eyes the woman had a white radiance about her person. He also saw tiny sparks of red light exploding in rhythm with her weeping.

The old chief looked down at the young woman, telling her to wait, but Naquahris raised his hand, saying, "Please, let's see if we can help her."

The woman's body trembled with sobs. Breathing heavily, she kept her head down and stared at the floor.

Naquahris immediately began singing softly, a song meant to calm and comfort. After a few moments, the woman's tears subsided. The healer knelt on the ground beside her. He rocked on his heels, then held one hand over her head, one over her back.

"Quiet yourself," said Naquahris. "How can we help?"

Looking up, she locked her gaze on his, a moment marked in spirit history, for two great souls met and recognized each other. Nothing was said for so long, the chief finally grumbled, "You two know each other?"

Naquahris focused on her and asked again, "How can we help?"

Her large, tear-filled eyes glanced from the healer to the elder and back. "My mother has been injured, scalded by boiling water. I tried to make her comfortable, but I don't know how to tend the burns." She drew a shuddering breath, then forced a sigh. "I'm afraid she'll die."

Naquahris looked at the chief. "Where are your medicine people?"

The old one shook his head. "Our medicine man died last winter."

The young man stood, staring in the elder's eyes. "I am a healer."

The chief looked surprised, then wary.

"I know I am a stranger to you, but you can tell by my costume and hairdo that I am not a threat. Besides my role as a storyteller, I can also heal. I was taught well by several powerful and knowledgeable medicine people."

Seeing hope in the eyes of the woman, the chief nodded. "Do what you can, Twisted Hair. Help Anamani Sunset Flower."

As Naquahris followed her across the encampment, he noticed the white sparkling light around her as it had enwrapped the deer in his dream. He observed that his own body was tingling with an electric feeling. She moved quickly and gracefully, her long dark hair fluttering against her shoulders and back.

Once he ducked into their small dwelling, he located the mother on a stack of hides lying by the center fire. Naquahris instantly saw that the injured woman had the same glowing, sparkling white light around her, with the exception of a strange mustard-colored light that clung along one side of her body.

"Mama, I have brought a healer," whispered Sunset Flower as she sat by her mother. "He is very skilled and compassionate. His name is Naquahris."

Scanning the elder woman, the healer saw that burns ran down her right arm and leg, which were left bare, the scalds red and angry in the firelight. As he, too, sat beside the woman, Naquahris could see that the boiling water had burned layers of skin away. The poor woman moaned in pain.

"This is a dangerous time with such wounds," said the healer quietly. "We must make new skin for her. Bring me a bowl of clean, cool water."

Anamani quickly brought the bowl; Naquahris extracted leaves from a pouch on his belt and placed them into the water. He gave her a quick smile of thanks and reassurance. Singing quietly, he proceeded to examine each burn while the leaves softened. Tears streamed from the young woman's eyes as she watched the healer and listened to her mother's sobs. After a few moments, the healer placed cool wet leaves carefully on the woman's wounds until all were covered.

"We will need to do more," he said, glancing up at her with concern in his eyes. "Can you ask your wisest and most talented gatherers to come to me? I will explain what I need."

Anamani hesitated to leave her mother's side.

"Your mother is in good hands," he assured her, "but we must all work quickly. Please go."

Moments later she returned with three women, one her age and two older.

Naquahris addressed them, "I need the skins of many wild onions to help heal these burns. Bring me at least twenty." He flicked his fingers indicating the amount. "Please, as quickly as you can."

The three women left, though the daughter stayed. Her mother's groans were softer now.

"I will make a tea that will help relieve the pain, calm her, and help her rest," Naquahris explained as he removed two medicine bags from around his waist. Anamani provided a gourd of water that had been warmed by its proximity to the fire. The healer sprinkled in several herbs and swirled them into the hot water, then asked her to gently lift the injured woman's head while he used a wooden ladle to administer the healing tea.

The two of them worked silently side by side, carefully changing the warmed leaves on the burns for cool ones soaked in spring water. At length, the women returned with two baskets heaped with wild onions. Naquahris asked the three to stay, showing them what to do.

"You know these gifts from the Creator." He picked up an onion and peeled off the papery outer layer. "Just inside the tough outer layer there lies a thin but resilient layer of skin." Holding the example onion near the light of the fire so that the women could see, he showed them the delicate, translucent layer. "Peel these onions down to this layer but do not remove it. When you have done so, place the onions in this container of water."

The four women began working quickly and soon there were over a dozen onions prepared as he had instructed. They watched in wonder as the healer removed the wet leaves from a burn on the injured woman's leg, carefully peeled off a wet silvery layer of onion skin, and gently used it to begin covering the open wound. Rebuilding the injured woman's skin in this way was excruciatingly slow detailed work, but Naquahris never lost his focus. On occasion he asked Anamani to give her mother more tea. Once in a while he rejected an onion because the layer he needed had been compromised.

After an hour, the three gatherers left, but Naquahris was still in the process of carefully covering each open burn with layers of onion skin. Anamani's mother was resting more comfortably now, which made it easier for the healer to continue. Once a burn had been covered with a layer of wild onion skin, he placed fresh wet leaves over it to keep the onion skin from drying out. Anamani watched him work with amazement and gratitude.

After hours of labor, each burn had been tended. "Now we wait and we pray," Naquahris told the daughter with compassion in his eyes. "Your mother's well-being is in the hands of the Creator."

Firelight played along their features as they sat on opposite sides of the wounded woman gazing at each other. One of the older women who had collected wild onions entered the lodge with two bowls of hot stew. Grateful, the two tenders accepted the nourishment.

After an hour or so, Naquahris carefully replaced the warmed leaves with cool wet ones, examining each burn as he did so. On one especially serious wound, he replaced the onion skin in part as well.

The two kept their vigil over the wounded woman throughout the night. They remained silent for much of the time except for some words of reassurance from the healer and responding words of thanks from the daughter.

Naquahris saw the resemblance between mother and daughter. Both were handsome women; both had auras of brilliant white. Anamani, despite her worried countenance, was beautiful. Her long shimmering black hair reflected the dancing firelight. Her eyes were large, warm, and brown like the sun on the Earth Mother on a summer day. When the healer's eyes settled on her lips, he felt a stirring, as any man might, but his heartbeat quickened as well. He noticed how gracefully she moved and how devoted she was to her mother. As the night wore on, he had to admit to himself that he desired her.

In all his wanderings, he had met many women, some extraordinarily beautiful. On occasion a female had wanted to bed him. He allowed himself this pleasure only after he was sure the woman understood that he was a twisted hair and would be moving on. He had never become involved emotionally, feeling it unwise to become attached.

The woman sitting across from him, being quiet, being herself, called to him as no other ever had. In the dark, predawn hours, having not slept since his dream the night before, Naquahris stared at Anamani as she soothed her mother's brow. He saw her glow with angelic white light and felt his heart swell with love for her.

The two kept their vigil throughout the night. At first light, a different woman brought them food and inquired about her injured friend. Seeing their exhaustion, she insisted on staying so that the healer and the daughter could rest. Anamani curled up on her bed nearby, but Naquahris felt it best to camp outside. He spread his caribou hide on the ground under some trees behind the lodge. Managing to sleep a few hours, he woke when the sun was high in the sky.

Upon returning, he was troubled to find that the wounded woman was delirious with fever. Despite his careful healing, infection had set in. After thanking the woman, who left to tend to her own duties, he quickly made a tea designed to lower the fever. He was attempting to administer the broth when Anamani rose and immediately realized that her mother was in trouble. She knelt by the healer's side and lifted her mother's head so he could more easily spoon the brew. The two worked tirelessly, rotating cold cloths on the mother's brow, feeding her healing teas and broths, and tending the wounds.

During the second night, Anamani insisted that the healer lie and rest inside the lodge. She unrolled a buffalo hide near the door flap away from her own bed. "I want you to stay nearby in case my mother's condition worsens," she told him.

Naquahris lay and watched Anamani tend her mother, love for her growing as each moment passed. He finally slept a little, then suggested that she rest.

"My mother is my only family," she replied with a worried look. "She must recover."

"You will do her no good if you exhaust yourself." Naquahris placed his hand on her arm and felt electricity spark as he saw a burst of rose-colored light engulf them both. He knew at that moment that his life had changed forever.

Other members of the tribe came and went over the next few days. Most brought food. Some stayed to relieve Naquahris and Anamani. The focus of everyone's attention was always the wounded woman.

On the fourth day at sunset, the fever finally broke, and the woman's eyes fluttered open for the first time since the early hours after the accident. The healer's heart thudded wildly when he saw Anamani's face blossom into a smile.

"Naquahris," she said softly, "meet my mother, White Deer. Mother, this is the man who saved your life."

White Deer moved her head slightly in acknowledgment. "Thank you," she managed in a hoarse whisper.

Although the fever had subsided, the burns required attention for many days afterward. Naquahris was secretly glad to be a guest in White Deer's lodge for a longer period of time. He made an ointment to promote healing and to keep the delicate new skin supple.

Now that the emergency had passed and White Deer was recovering, Naquahris had time to roam about the village. One sun-filled morning, he returned to see the chief.

"I hear you are a miracle worker," the old man began. "Many reports have come to me telling of your knowledgeable ways. We could use such a talented man. You are welcome to stay and join our people."

Naquahris saw the sincerity in the leader's eyes and pondered his response.

"I know you are a twisted hair and a traveler," the chief continued, "but your talents as a healer are very valuable. This is a large tribe. We need a new healer. There are several youngsters who were training with our medicine man before he died, but they do not possess your skills and experience. Please consider making our people your people."

Studying the face of the leader, he saw sincerity and smiled. "I have reached the age when a man desires a wife and children." The healer hesitated briefly. "I have one question."

"Speak it."

"Is Anamani Sunset Flower promised to any man? Is she spoken for?"

The chief sat silently, gazing at the small fire that blazed in the center of his large lodge. He turned his eyes to Naquahris, staring as if evaluating him anew. "Anamani," he spoke at last, "was promised in marriage when she became a woman seven summers ago. Women in our tribe are often matched when they are young. Because her father died on the hunt, she has been allowed to stay unmarried and live with her mother."

The healer's heart filled with a heavy, sinking feeling. "To whom is she promised?" he asked, a hitch in his voice.

"This is a large tribe," the chief replied. "We took in another clan more than ten winters ago when their encampment was raided and burned. The largest of these families has five sons. Anamani Sunset Flower is promised to that family as a wife for one of their sons."

Naquahris spoke from his heart. "I know I am a newcomer, and I have yet to learn the details of your ceremonies and your culture. I am willing to learn of your ways and practice them. I am willing to stay, to tend and heal your people, but I request the honor of having Anamani as my wife." Staring into the old chief's eyes, he said, "Since I left my home in the north, I have never stayed in one place for long. I sensed my calling was to travel, to teach with stories and to heal when called upon to do so. When I camped outside your village, the Creator sent me a dream of White Deer and her daughter. I knew my destiny had brought me here, and when I saw Anamani in your lodge that first day, I knew she was my future." He took the chief's hand with a firm grasp. "Is there any way you can arrange for Anamani to be my wife?"

The chief stared at him, then patted his hand. "I will negotiate with this family on your behalf. I can do this much for you. You will be a valuable addition to our people."

Days passed with Naquahris camped behind White Deer's lodge. Once Anamani's mother was well enough to move around on her own, the healer had insisted on giving the women their privacy. Although he and the daughter often exchanged glances of adoration, neither spoke of their feelings for each other, though the air literally crackled with the electricity between them. White Deer noticed their attraction to each other, but stayed silent on the matter as she worked to heal her wounds and regain her strength.

The weather began to turn chilly with the approaching change of seasons. Naquahris contemplated constructing his own lodge, though he felt it would be difficult for him to join this tribe if he had to watch Anamani wed another man.

While he waited for an answer from the chief, he busied himself. He gathered plants, bark, berries, and roots and dried them for winter use. By telling stories, he befriended the children and many of their mothers. He also took time to talk with the elders to learn the tribe's history and customs. The men were away most of the time on various hunting trips to stock the winter food supply, so he had yet to interact with many of them. In fact, he did not even know the family to whom Anamani was promised. The healer prayed often that he would be guided on his new path.

On the seventh day after his talk with the chief, he was summoned to the leader's lodge. The elder looked fatigued.

"Naquahris," he began, "I have spoken with the Red Shield family several times on your behalf. They have refused to give up their claim on Anamani."

As the healer's heart once again grew heavy, the old chief smiled.

"The woman herself came to me and asked to be freed from her bond to the Red Shields. I believe she cares a great deal for you."

At this news, Naquahris felt tingling electricity fill his body. "Then what is to be done?"

The old chief nodded. "We give the situation some time. I have had a sign that Great Spirit will resolve this."

Time was not the answer the healer wished to hear, but he trusted the Creator. He had lived his life putting himself in the hands of Great Spirit, and he knew that his dream about the magic deer was a true sign. Before he left the chief's abode, he secured permission to build his own lodge.

Allowing hope and faith to bolster his enthusiasm for the project, Naquahris gathered the needed materials. With the help of the flora and local animals, he chose a location near where he had camped that first night when he received the dream. Once he had begun construction, some of the older boys as well as a few of the women helped him, for the healer had become much loved among them.

The work helped temporarily take his mind off wanting Anamani until she began coming daily to assist him with his new lodge. Every time he saw her he desired her. Every day he felt more certain that their destiny was to be together. However, Naquahris was an honorable man in an unfamiliar situation, so he was kind and friendly to Anamani but did not profess his love. He could see love for him in her eyes and that was enough.

The very day that the healer's lodge was completed, a commotion was heard on the far side of the encampment. Naquahris was hanging herbs inside the lodge when two women and a man ran toward him. Their eyes were wide and filled with wild fear.

"Come, healer, come!" cried one woman.

"It's terrible!" panted the other. "You must help!"

"Of course," replied Naquahris, setting down his basket of herbs.

As he followed the women, he walked beside the man who told him, "Two of my brothers were badly injured on the hunt. The earth gave way and they tumbled down a deep ravine, one after the other. The hunting party was able to bring them back to camp, but I fear nothing can be done to save them."

Naquahris silently asked the Creator for assistance. As he hurried along with the group, he prayed that there was something he could do to help.

The two injured men still lay on the makeshift drags that were used to transport them. An older woman with gray braids wept as she cleansed the dirt from one of the men's faces.

Naquahris placed his hand on her arm. "I am glad you are here. I will need your help."

"Are you the new healer?" Tears rolling from her eyes, she pleaded, "Please save my sons."

"I will do my best," promised Naquahris.

The unconscious man had a head injury, scrapes, cuts, and a broken arm, but his breathing was steady. The other brother, however, moaned in pain. He had cuts, gouges, even thorns in his skin. His leg was twisted at an odd angle and great bruises bloomed across his ribs.

The healer moved quickly, beginning with the conscious brother. He cleaned and dressed each wound while the mother removed the thorns. When he was confident all bleeding had stopped, he set the broken leg. Straightening the leg and aligning the broken bone was painful for the man, but the hunter showed his bravery. Naquahris used two wooden splints, wrapping the leg tightly. Finally, with the help of one of the man's sisters, he wrapped his rib cage in soft doeskin, as he was sure the man had suffered several broken ribs.

The mother had cleaned the scrapes, cuts, and the head wound of the other brother, so Naquahris carefully dressed the injuries with healing ointment, then set the man's broken arm. Still the hunter did not wake, so the healer removed a pinch of powder from one of his medicine pouches and blew it into the man's nose. His eyes popped open. The mother gasped, calling her son's name.

Naquahris spent the next two days with the injured men. On the third day, once he was certain that they both would survive, he returned to his lodge, exhausted but fulfilled. With thanks to Great Spirit on his lips, he stretched out on his caribou hide to rest.

He awoke to someone calling his name. When he stepped outside his lodge, he stood face to face with a tall older man who had a commanding presence.

"Naquahris!" The man's voice was deep and powerful. "I am Makotanda Red Shield, head of the Red Shield clan. I have come to thank you for healing my two injured sons."

Naquahris nodded, staring at the man's stern countenance.

"Twice the chief has come to me asking that our family release Anamani Sunset Flower from her bond to our family. Twice I have refused this request."

The healer saw the big man's face soften slightly.

"Today, in thanks for your service to my family, I release Anamani. She is free to marry you. I speak for our entire tribe when I say we are honored to have you as a member of our village."

Naquahris married Anamani and settled with her in the Lakota encampment. The healer and twisted hair continued to win the love and respect of all. He and Sunset Flower were blessed with three healthy children, and although he did travel to neighboring tribes on occasion either as an invited healer, storyteller, or ambassador of peace, he was content to live out his days with White Deer's radiant daughter.

∞

The words on the page faded and disappeared. I looked at Orillo, who grinned back at me.

"The avatar will come as a skilled healer," said the prince. "She will be able to converse with the flora, the fauna, and with every race of people, plus she will have healing powers!"

"The more we read about this soul, the more amazed I become." I handed him the large book just as we heard noises at the front door of the house.

Orillo smiled and floated upward, the tome in his arms, then disappeared into sparkling light.

As the returning band and homeowners settled in for the remainder of the night, I stroked Angel's sleeping head. I would have so much to share with her someday.

CHAPTER THIRTEEN
FOREIGN VISIT

Even though I was with Angel all the time, she was not yet aware of my existence. Sometimes I thought perhaps she felt my presence, but there was no direct communication between us. I wanted to tell her that she was too young and inexperienced to marry. I wanted to say, "Dear Angel, I can see your energy field. I know you don't really love this man." But, alas, it was too soon for me to be a conscious part of her life, and heartbreaking though it was, I had to let her make her own mistakes.

The man she chose was a musician, of course. Gary was nearly five years older than Angel and very intelligent. Some called him a genius because he began playing his instrument, the vibraphone, when he was six years old and recorded his first LP when he was sixteen. He played in several famous jazz combos, but when Angel met him at The Club 47, he had just formed his own quartet. For their first date, Gary flew her to New Orleans to watch his jazz quartet play a concert there. I believe the phrase "swept off her feet" applies here.

Angel, a natural rebel, was at that point in her life disappointed by her parents and disillusioned with the church, so she and Gary were wed in May 1969 at a justice of the peace with no family attending. That summer she accompanied her new husband on a European tour called "The Giants of Jazz." I must admit that I was awed by the talent on that tour: Thelonious Monk, Dizzy Gillespie, the Duke Ellington Orchestra, Sarah Vaughn, the Preservation Hall Jazz Band, and more. Members of the various bands traveling with her that summer nicknamed Angel "The Child Bride." With her long blonde hair, short skirts, and braces on her teeth, she appeared far younger than her twenty-three years.

Gary, being a practical man, gave her responsibilities. Angel was in charge of waiting in line to change U.S. dollars to whatever currency was needed. She also was the one to wait patiently to alter airline reservations and tickets when necessary.

That summer tour included Romania and East Germany, at that time behind the Iron Curtain. A wall divided the city of Berlin. To cross the Berlin Wall, the musicians had to pass through an armed checkpoint. The jazz stars were generally welcomed wherever they performed, but the day their itinerary took them from East to West Berlin, their bus was stopped at the wall and boarded by several uniformed men with assault rifles. The group had to wait for hours while every piece of luggage, including all the instrument cases, were thoroughly searched.

Although Angel did not know I was there, I surrounded her with many layers of protective light. I saw other Spirit Guides doing the same for their charges. Even the stern soldiers had spirit helpers present, though they hovered in the background for the most part.

That night my charge slept beside her husband in a Berlin hotel. They were both so exhausted they did not hear the noisy city street below them. I employed a special cocooning technique I had learned from Sottrol to cleanse away her fatigue and revitalize her. Gary's Spirit Guide, Ohma, was floating by his charge's head, sending energy to him. Ohma and I had yet to work together. Now as I think back on that time, I believe we never did because the hearts of our two charges were not truly connected.

That night in the city of Berlin, Germany, Nyna appeared by the window. She arrived in such a brilliant sphere of white light that both Ohma and I gasped at the sight.

"Nyna!" I exclaimed. "It has been years! I'm so glad to see you!"

The elfin woman smiled at me. "Greetings, Darci." Then she nodded politely to Gary's Guide. "Good to see you again, Ohma."

"And I, you, Nyna," said the large Guide.

"I'm surprised to find you here in a foreign land," I told her.

She chuckled, sparkles lifting from her silver hair. "The network of elementals is global. To us, this is one place … Earth. We do not think in terms of separate countries."

"I see. To what do we owe the honor of this visit?"

Nyna glided toward me, indicating that I should sit on the edge of the large bed. I did so, as Ohma continued to send energy to Gary.

"Darci, I have come to talk about Angel. Your charge is a beautiful young woman now. We must accelerate her progress along her spirit path if she is to be ready to assist the elfin avatar."

"You have mentioned before that both Angel and I might be able to assist the soul who is to arrive as the avatar."

"One of the avatars," she corrected.

"Yes, one. There will be how many?" I queried.

"If all goes well, seven," she replied. "One for each level of Earth experience."

"Including a human avatar?"

"Yes."

"How are we to help? Can you give specifics? Perhaps that will help me guide Angel."

"The overall plan has been in place for some time now. You and Angel will fill in the details when the time is right. For now, let us talk about moving you both toward your shared destiny. If this destiny includes our beloved elfin avatar, then so shall it be."

"So our destiny does not necessarily include this special being." I wanted to be clear on this point.

"No." She placed a hand on my shoulder, and I felt electric tingles spread through me. "But you can choose her. She has already chosen you."

I was surprised. "She has?"

"One thing at a time, Darci. Let's focus on your charge. She does not consciously know it yet, but she is gifted psychically. We must begin awakening her abilities."

"How do you suggest we do this?"

"We must introduce something into her life, something that stirs her interest so that she begins to explore the possibilities."

"I can send her a dream," I offered.

"No, Darci. It must come from outside her, from her environment." She smiled, her cheeks dimpling. "With Ohma's assistance, I have already set something in place using Angel's current husband."

"Gary?" I was surprised.

"He is a brilliant man whose brain is highly developed. On occasion he has precognitive dreams. In fact, I made sure he had one about Angel before he met her."

"But … he has not mentioned this."

Nyna smiled again. "He will. And when he does, your charge must be ready for her world to expand. Darci, you must be ready to lead her to metaphysical reading material."

"Like what?" I wanted to be sure to get this right.

"Start her off with Edgar Cayce, the sleeping prophet," the elfin elder suggested. "There is quite a body of work now available about Cayce and his psychic abilities."

"Edgar Cayce." I knew the name. "He would go into a trance and diagnose people's illnesses."

"That's how he started," Nyna confirmed. "Cayce's information was so precise that he could describe a specific medicine on a certain shelf of a particular store in a town that was states away. Once people realized what he could do and how accurate he was, they began asking the bigger questions."

"The bigger questions … about life and death?"

"Indeed. All this will make fascinating reading for Angel. Cayce's story will stir her interest and hopefully begin to awaken her own abilities."

"And what exactly are those?" Not only did I want confirmation of what I already knew, I did not want to miss a thing.

"Darci, you know that you and Angel are connected through many lifetimes and many experiences. If all goes well, she will eventually be able to receive both words and images from you. Sottrol has informed you of this."

"Yes, but so far she has no idea that I watch over her. She is clueless as to my existence."

"Have patience. That will change, especially if we accelerate the expansion of her mind."

"Her world is already expanding, Nyna. First she traveled across the United States; now she is seeing Europe."

"Yes, and this is all good," Nyna acknowledged. "Now we need her to learn what is possible beyond earthly travel."

This news excited me. "How can I help?"

"When she sleeps, send brilliant white light into her mind. This activity will help stimulate the telepathic center in her brain. Telepathy is the means by which you two will communicate."

"I will do that ... and Nyna?"

"Yes?"

"Can you tell me something about how we can help your elfin avatar? I've learned much about the special gifts this soul has earned."

"All in good time, Darci." With a nod to Ohma, she smiled, twirled into a spiral of silver-white light, and vanished.

Other than my usual guidance and protection, I did not have much I could do to hurry the process for Angel. However, I did pour light into my charge's telepathic center whenever I could.

Angel did not have to wait long. When she and Gary returned from their European tour, Ohma did his part.

Gary's quartet had just finished performing at a jazz club, The Village Vanguard, in lower Manhattan. Angel and her husband sat in a late-night café waiting for the train out to their home on Long Island. With a little prodding from Ohma, Gary told Angel about his precognitive dreams, specifically the dream he'd had about her and their Cairn terrier before he had seen either one of them. I watched Angel carefully, ready to do my part.

"But how can that be?" she asked. "How can you possibly dream about things that haven't happened yet?"

"Do you think that this ..." Gary gestured toward the surrounding scene. "... is all there is?"

That question was all it took. I could see the linear thought patterns in Angel's mind multiplying in many directions. I beamed light into her mind and watched the expansion increase even further. Then, in accordance with Nyna's plan, Gary brought up Edgar Cayce as an example of someone with unexplainable psychic gifts. That very week, Angel bought a book about the famous sleeping prophet, the first of many she would read.

A few months later, Gary was in Japan on tour with his jazz quartet. The couple had decided that the trip was too expensive and too grueling for Angel to come along. She was asleep alone, her Persian cat nearby. I was performing my usual energy balancing for her when the room filled with blinding, bright light, which eventually coalesced into two luminous forms. My old friends Nyna and Orillo stood before me.

"Hello!" I grinned, knowing that a visit from both elves meant something special was afoot.

"Salutations, Darci!" Flipping his cape open, Orillo bowed.

"Greetings!" Nyna smiled. When she lifted her arms toward me, silver sparkles flew in my direction. "You have done well with Angel. She is now fascinated by metaphysics, exactly what we were hoping for."

"I'm glad you see her progressing in a positive direction. She has added a small book about Spirit Guides to her reading material. This gives me hope that she will one day come to know me again."

Orillo grinned, making a sweeping motion with his emerald cape. "You two are destined to work together. All is well."

"Darci, I just wanted to check in and let you know that you are doing a good job with Angel," said Nyna. "I have other matters to see to. However, Orillo will stay for a while."

The elfin prince took her hands and kissed her on the cheek, which increased the dancing, glittering light between them. "Thank you, Grandmother."

Nyna vanished in a tube of brilliant vertical streams of multicolored light.

A moment later after my eyes had adjusted from the brilliance, I stepped toward Orillo. "What adventure shall the two of us have tonight?"

"Evidently we have even more to learn about the soul who is to come to Earth as the elfin avatar. Sottrol explained something to me."

"How is my mentor?" I missed my former teacher.

"He is well and sends his regards." Orillo perched on the edge of the bed and gestured for me to join him. "He informed me that, like all souls, the avatar-to-be has received some training on other planes of existence. However, we are concerned mainly with the lifetimes this soul lived here on Earth."

"We spent a long time reading about Naquahris," I mused. "Did the soul of Naquahris return again to Earth?"

"We shall find out," replied the elfin prince with an excited gleam in his emerald eyes.

Holding his arms toward the ceiling, he spoke words in a language I did not understand. A deep tone sounded, followed by the appearance of a sphere of swirling gold and white marbled light. This stunning globe floated down into his arms and became *The Great Book of Lifetimes*. We smiled at each other as the pages flipped on their own, then settled. Golden pages glowed, highlighting the deep purple lettering.

The Great Book began by reminding us of all the skills, attributes, talents, and gifts that this soul had earned in former lifetimes. Listed were the courage to honor the Earth Mother, compassion for all living things, the ability to communicate with Creation in all its many forms, storytelling, teaching, and healing skills. The book also stated that only one more Earth lifetime was required to complete this soul's cycle of learning. The next Earth incarnation needed to be one of pure spiritual devotion, so this soul was born once again, this time in Tibet.

From the start, the parents of the girl child knew that she was exceptional. Had she been born a male, then the child would have been a candidate to become a lama in the great temple. Being born female forced both the parents and the child to be more creative, to think and act outside the structure set by Tibetan society. *The Great Book* explained that the elfin avatar will be required to break into new territory, to do things that have never been done before. Therefore, the added challenge of being female was included in this lifetime.

To our surprise, the words then disappeared from the page.

"The story has barely begun," I uttered in dismay. "Why did this happen?"

Staring at the blank pages, Orillo shook his head. "I do not know, but I intend to find out."

At that moment, the telephone rang, waking Angel. Gary was calling from Japan to update the flight information for his return. Orillo floated to the upper corner of the room.

Following him, I wondered aloud, "Do you think the book sensed that this phone call was coming?"

The elfin prince hugged the great tome to his chest and protectively pulled the luminescent emerald cape over the tome. "I have a feeling there is more to this," he responded. "I will be back in touch soon. This story holds information that is important to both of us, Darci." He nodded his good-bye and vanished, leaving a cloud of white and emerald scintilla.

Time for humans is measured and linear. This is not so for those of us in spirit form. However, while watching over Angel, I noticed that I was far more aware of linear time because she lived within its structure. In the spirit world, time is almost irrelevant. I say "almost" because we who operate in spiritual dimensions must sometimes interact with structured time. Although it probably seemed like an instant for Orillo, for me living with Angel in linear time, many months passed before I saw the elfin prince again.

Gary's group was playing a concert in Newport News, Virginia. Sea breezes blew mist off the ocean, surrounding the hotel where the band was staying for the night. Angel was in crisis, swamped by negative emotions. Not wanting to wake and upset her sleeping husband, she dressed and made her way outside to the manicured hotel lawn. Finding a quiet bench in the shadows away from the entrance, she sat alone. The spot probably had a stunning ocean view on a clear day, but in the murky, misty night, all that Angel knew was that a foghorn moaned nearby. Once there, she wept. This was another instance when I wished she knew I was there to comfort her. I could see by her aura that she felt heartbroken and alone. She wanted more for herself and her life than this loveless marriage; she wanted to express her own creativity on stage, not just watch her famous husband. Living in his shadow was unacceptable, and she felt trapped. The urge to run away was strong, but she had no place to go. As she cried and sobbed for over an hour, I helped by streaming cleansing white light through her like healing rain. Between the two of us, we washed away enough frustration and heartache to allow her to return to the hotel room and sleep.

Once Angel's emotional crisis had truly subsided, I stood by her bedside pulling waves of golden light over her. Gary's Spirit Guide, Ohma, was reenergizing his charge. The large Guide gave me a concerned glance as he sent streams of bright orange light up through the arches of Gary's feet.

In the hour before first light with the fog horn still sounding, I noticed a glow on the balcony of the hotel room. As I moved toward the sliding glass doors, Orillo appeared, this time shrouded in a hooded purple cloak, though a flash of his gleaming golden belt gave away his identity.

I joined him immediately. "So good to see you, old friend."

"Darci, you've had a rough go of it with your charge tonight."

"Yes, but she is quiet now."

Orillo studied the small woman asleep on the king-sized bed. "I came to visit earlier in the evening, but you were busy with Angel."

"I was."

The elfin prince put his hand on my shoulder, filling me with exhilaration. "Darci, I have news. The Master Guides and mentors who are preparing the way for the arrival of the avatars want us to meet with the Spirit Guide who watched over the soul we are researching, the soul who is to become the elfin avatar."

"The Spirit Guide for her lifetime in Tibet?"

"Yes. Evidently we are to do more than simply read about this incarnation. That is why the words on the pages of *The Great Book of Lifetimes* disappeared. The next time we meet, I shall bring this Guide, who has become a Master Guide now and is quite busy."

"I look forward to our next visit," I said with a sigh.

"Dawn approaches, Darci. I must go. Take good care of that charge of yours, for she may play a pivotal role not only for the elfin avatar, but also for the well-being of the planet." With a knowing expression, Orillo wrapped himself in his purple cloak and became part of the foggy night.

In the days that followed, I pondered why Orillo and I had been given only the beginning of the next story. The last Earth lifetime for any soul is important. I recalled initial experiences after passing from my last Earth incarnation when I was told that I had earned the right to begin Spirit Guide training. The soul we were reading about was returning to Earth as an avatar, a leader who could influence and change life on this material plane. Surely the earth lifetime in Tibet was highly significant for this soul. While contemplating this, I realized that the only new facts Orillo and I had been given pertained to this soul needing a highly spiritual lifetime and being born a female with incredible talents in a society that allowed only men to become holy priests. I wondered how this gifted soul would handle such an obstacle.

CHAPTER FOURTEEN
THE GIFTED CHILD

Angel was in transition. She had met Gary while still in college and had married him only days after her graduation. Now she was divorced and truly on her own with no husband or parents to support her. Through a connection with one of his vibraphone students, Gary helped Angel find a job designing knitwear for a mill in Connecticut. She had been creating her own knit garments for several years and had even designed her own line for a manual knitting machine. She was well qualified for the job.

During this time of change, Angel spent time with her family, who had moved into a new house. The fields and farmlands around her childhood home were in the process of being developed into circular, color-coded neighborhoods. Her parents sold their old house and moved into a new one in Yellow-Yellow Circle. Many people new to the area migrated to the neighborhood, and soon both Angel and her sister were dating young men whose families had purchased homes in Yellow-Yellow Circle.

I knew that Angel was disillusioned with marriage. She next chose a man who was quite opposite her former husband. Rob was undemanding and relaxed. I could see that he was an attentive lover who took the time to please and awaken her senses.

The two couples rented a small house in a crowded neighborhood of homes overlooking a lake. Her sister and the two young men were attending the University of Connecticut while Angel worked at the mill. This was a transitory situation, as all three of her roommates were finishing college and near graduation.

Rob's Guide, Sophia, was a gentle spirit who had spent her most recent lifetime on Earth as a nun. Instead of clothing herself in robes as many of us do, she preferred to wear a nun's habit.

One early spring evening while Sophia and I were tending to our sleeping charges, a bright violet light manifested outside the bedroom window. A moment later, Prince Orillo appeared beside me, as the brilliant purple light continued to pulse outside.

"Darci, finally I have returned," he spoke almost breathlessly. "With me is the Master Guide I told you about. Shall we go down to the lake for a few moments? We may not have this opportunity again anytime soon."

Glancing at Angel, I saw that she slept soundly.

"I will watch over her for you," Sophia offered.

"Thank you. Please let me know if she needs me."

The spirit nun nodded, and I followed Orillo outside where a resplendent being waited. The female Master Guide was tall, vibrating with vertical streams of luminescent violet light.

"Darci Stillwater." Her voice had a magical ring to it. "I have heard about you and your charge. I am Thujora."

"Greetings, Thujora." I bowed to her.

My eyes were still adjusting to her brilliance when she and Orillo began floating toward the lake. I trailed behind them, finally catching up when they stopped at the end of a wooden dock.

"When visiting Earth, I prefer to be near water," she explained.

Orillo and I moved closer as the beautiful Master Guide spoke.

"The soul who is destined to come to Earth as the elfin avatar was my charge during her last lifetime on Earth. Before becoming her Spirit Guide, I studied her past lifetimes, as you have." She turned her gaze from the calm surface of the water to me. I saw the reflection of the lake in her pale blue eyes. "Darci, this is your first time as a Spirit Guide. When Angel has completed this Earth incarnation, you will team up with a scribe and enter her lifetime into *The Great Book*."

I nodded, remembering that Sottrol had mentioned this to me.

"However," she continued, "because the elfin avatar's soul journey is so important to the survival and evolution of the earth plane, I am preparing a special text for you and Orillo." She smiled at the elfin prince, then at me. "I want you to visualize, understand, and relive every nuance of my time as Spirit Guide to this exceptional soul."

As she reached beneath her voluminous violet robe, a light breeze brought dancing ripples across the lake. Drawing forth a small book, she clasped it to her chest.

"As a Master Guide, I am busy with many things. I sit on the committee that is in charge of commissioning the Seven Avatars. We all want the seven to be successful on Earth. As you know, Earth is undergoing tremendous energetic changes. It is a do-or-die time for the planet, so we Guides are assisting in every way we can. I feel that my personal notes on this Tibetan lifetime are not only helpful, but they are also necessary for you to prepare for the elfin avatar's arrival."

I wanted to reach for the book, but knew it was not yet time. She would pass it to us when she was ready.

Thujora studied the waters for a few moments, then turned back to us. "I have not completed this book, but there is enough written here for you to begin reading. I encourage you to contemplate what you read in these pages. Once you have finished reading this, I will return with another excerpt. Orillo will pester me until I do." She smiled fondly at the elfin prince.

As she handed Orillo the book, a strong breeze brought crested waves to the lake, and she whirled into the wind. I heard her voice bid us good-bye, but I did not recognize the language.

Orillo read my thoughts. "Thujora said in Tibetan that she will see us again."

The book glowed purple in his hands, so I nodded to two lawn chairs on the grass at the end of the dock. "Shall we?"

Orillo grinned, his excitement apparent on his face. We drew the chairs closer and sat side by side, anxious to see what the magnificent Master Guide had prepared for us.

The pages glowed white with lavender letters. The first page said simply "The Gifted Child." Orillo turned the page and the story began. It was written in the words of the Master Guide herself.

The story that I tell is one of mystery and magic. My name is Thujora and my assignment was as Spirit Guide to Jing Lei Khan, a beautiful girl born in the mountains of Tibet. Her parents had already lost two children to hunger and disease, so she was much loved and well cared for.

To make sure his new daughter and wife were fed, Jing Lei's father traveled to the nearest village he could reach on foot and labored in the market there. He would return each night with his satchel stuffed with vegetables.

When Jing Lei was two and walking in the dark hovel, her parents noticed that she seemed to illuminate every corner. As Jing Lei's guide, I was partially responsible for this phenomenon, for I increased the energetic vibration in and around the girl. This was my way of awakening her parents to their child's destiny.

Her mother and father proceeded as I had hoped they would. They journeyed to the village with the child and brought her to the temple there.

The night before this pilgrimage, I worked with her mother's Spirit Guide to deliver a dream. We prepared the images energetically and slid them into her mind in a sphere of brilliant magenta light. The dream simply showed Jing Lei dressed as a boy. Upon awakening, she convinced her husband that the dream was a sign and that they must do this to protect their daughter. So her mother dressed her in pants and a little jacket, items that had been made for her brother who died. When Jing Lei was presented to the priest in the temple, he mistook her for a boy.

"I have seen bright light around my child," Jing Lei's father told the priest as he placed her in the lama's arms.

As Jing Lei sat in the lap of the priest, I sent spheres of brilliant white light into her until she shone like a polished jewel. The monk observed this, then nodded and told the parents to bring the child back when she was seven and ready to live at the temple.

In the five years that followed, Jing Lei's parents observed her doing extraordinary things. When she was four, they found that she had risen before them and made a kind of bread they had never seen before.

How could this occur? The truth is that Jing Lei could see and communicate with me. Most babies can see their Spirit Guides but lose this ability when they begin interacting more with their Earth environment. I knew that Jing Lei and I could continue our conscious contact if we both wished to. In the early morning hours before the miracle bread was made, I sent my young charge a dream of a beautiful bejeweled loaf. When she awoke from the dream, I was sitting on her bed.

"Can we make such a loaf?" she asked me as her eyes glittered with excitement.

"Let us try," I replied with a smile.

I told her to gather all the ingredients she could find and lay them on the table. The jar of ground rice was not easy for her to reach, but she was a good climber.

When I had walked the Earth in a human body, I had the responsibility of feeding the clan. I used this knowledge to help the little one combine the ingredients to make the dough. She then decorated the moon-shaped mound with seeds and small pieces of vegetables that were left over from the evening meal. The coals in the hearth were glowing hot, perfect for baking. The aroma of the magical bread woke her parents, who marveled at their tiny daughter's accomplishment.

Jing Lei would often talk to me out loud, sometimes when others were present. Her parents and relatives knew she had an imaginary friend, though they did not realize it was her guardian angel, nor were they aware that they all had Spirit Guides helping them.

Jing Lei's favorite game was drawing in the dirt. Choosing different sticks to make wide or thin marks, though her fingers were her favorite tool, she spent hours making elaborate drawings that filled the yard. We then sat together in the doorway watching the wind change them or the rain wash them away.

Two months before she turned seven, her mother began making special clothing. The little girl was fascinated by the process and watched every step with interest. Using their limited resources, they traded for the finest cloth her father could find in the village marketplace. Jing Lei had never felt anything so soft and could not believe the material was for her.

One morning as she watched her mother sewing, she asked, "Why do you not make yourself a new robe? Or one for Father? You both work so hard and take such good care of me."

"We want you to have the finest clothes so the monks will know how special you are."

Jing Lei's face became sad as she twisted her hands nervously. "I don't want to go live in the temple, Mother. I love it here with you and Father."

"We talked about this." Her mother touched the girl's face tenderly. "You have gifts beyond our comprehension, gifts that need to be fostered by the holy monks."

Jing Lei pouted a little, so I distracted her by whirling around in the doorway and sprinkling sparkles of light toward her. Her eyes brightened; she giggled and soon forgot her approaching move.

However, the day came when she celebrated her seventh solar return. For her birthday she received a traveling satchel and a haircut. When the family walked into the monastery the very next day, Jing Lei looked like a seven-year-old boy.

The girl's future and her ability to stay with the monks depended on me; I knew I had to work fast. She had been instructed not to cry, so only a few fat tears rolled from her eyes as she watched her parents walk down the steps of the temple. Two young monks led her to a cubicle, a tiny room with a pad for sleeping and a table with a candle. Daylight came through a slit high in the wall. She could hear the birds singing in the courtyard as she lay down to wait. Moments later an elder monk, one of the lamas who taught the boys, came to her cell and introduced himself.

"Good day, Master Lei," began the lama. "Your holy instruction begins tomorrow. I am Xin Fau, your caretaker. Your welfare has been assigned to me."

This is the moment I had been waiting for. I immediately floated toward the two Guides who accompanied this elder.

"Greetings. I am Thujora."

"Welcome to the monastery," replied the male. He was tall and shone with a bright blue light which radiated from his entire spirit body. "I am Bodu and this is my assistant Celestina."

The female guide, his perfect complement in pink, bowed to me. "The white light around your charge is strong," she observed. "I see why he was brought here."

I did not pause. "I need your help, since you and Xin Fau will be caring for my charge."

The two Guides looked at each other, then back at me, then at the child.

"Something is wrong with your charge?" questioned Bodu.

"No, not at all. In fact, this little one is talented beyond comprehension. It is very important that the child be instructed by the lamas, for only then will this talented being fulfill the destiny we designed."

"I do not understand the problem," said Celestina as she floated closer to Jing Lei, who now saw us and smiled at the beautiful pink Guide.

"The child can see me!" exclaimed Celestina.

"Yes! I would introduce you, but Jing Lei is now listening to the elder monk."

"Such talent must be fostered by the holy lamas," Bodu agreed. "I do not see why you need our help."

This was it. I had to tell them now. "Because she is a girl."

The two guides gasped and retreated to an upper corner of the tiny room.

I hovered next to Jing Lei, showering pink and white light upon her. The little one was nervous and missed her parents.

Xin Fau completed his orientation speech with an invitation for Lei to join the other students for rice and soup. "When you hear the small temple bell ring, it is a call to sustenance. When you hear the large bell, it is a call to prayer."

Jing Lei nodded as she watched the elder's Guides approach me.

"We will help you if we can," said Bodu.

Celestina nodded as they floated behind the monk down the hallway.

That night after Jing Lei fell asleep, I joined the two Guides in the room of the elder. Bodu shook his head.

"Xin Fau will learn that Lei is a girl tomorrow when he brings her to the baths. This could be an embarrassing moment for all. We must try to prevent this, but I do not know how."

I had a plan. "We must help him see how special she is. He must make an exception for her somehow."

"There have been no women in this part of the monastery since it was built hundreds of years ago!" Bodu exclaimed.

Celestina was less sure. "Bodu, how do you know? I, for one, would like this talented child to have the opportunities she deserves."

"Then let us give the lama a dream, a vivid dream that he will never forget," I suggested.

So the three of us set about designing a long, colorful, complex dream that showed Jing Lei's potential as well as her gender. We spun the images into a great glittering ball of light and slowly slid it into the mind of the sleeping elder. We watched his eyes roll under their lids as he experienced it. Suddenly he sat up, awake, trembling and perspiring. He began to pray and continued until the first glimmer of light arrived in the east.

We Guides watched as the monk donned his robes and vestments, then walked directly to Jing Lei's cell. I flew ahead to be with my charge when she woke to find the priest by her bed.

She rubbed her eyes. "I thought I was still at home with Mother and Father," she said softly. Then she saw me. "At least you are still here."

"To whom are you speaking?" asked the elder curtly.

"My angel, Thuji. Your angels are right behind you."

"I have angels with me?"

"You cannot see them? I thought priests could see angels and that was why I was brought here. Mother said I need to be instructed by the holy men."

The elder was silent for a moment, then asked in a whisper, "Young Lei, please answer truthfully. Are you a son or a daughter to your parents?"

"Father told me I was not to say. That's why they dressed me in my brother's clothes."

"Ah, I see." The priest smiled. "I guess I might have done the same if I had a daughter like you."

At that moment, I beamed brilliant white light into my charge so that she vibrated with high holy energy. My fellow Guides were impressed.

"The child can handle such an intense vibration?" asked Bodu.

"This and more," I replied as I circled around behind Jing Lei to steady her.

Xin Fau saw the glow emanating from the child as they sat together in the dark cell.

"The question is … what do I do with you? Lei, do you know that girls are not allowed in the monastery?"

"I am dressed as a boy."

"That does not make you one, dear child."

"But my parents said …"

"Your parents wish you to be instructed by the lamas, but we have no programs for girls."

"Why?"

"Now that I've met you, I wonder that myself."

Jing Lei hung her head in disappointment. "If you send me home, my parents will be sad. They worked so hard to get me here. My mother made these beautiful clothes. Can't I stay?"

As the priest sat thinking, Celestina, Bodu, and I moved in a circle around the two humans, swaying and dancing until the room was alive with joyous vibrations. We knew the child could see our cosmic dance, and the elder could feel it. The energy fields around both of them filled with luminescent bubbles of pink and gold.

The lama finally spoke. "Extraordinary child, you shall have your schooling. I shall see to it myself. However, you cannot live with the other boys. My niece has a home in the village. Let's visit her today. Perhaps she has a place where you can stay. Remain here. I will return with food, and then we shall venture out into the sunshine."

$$\infty$$

The white pages in the small book began to glow brighter and brighter until light obscured the words. Orillo closed the book, then held it out before him toward the lake, releasing it. On its own, it rose and turned end over end until it vanished in the cool spring night. I followed the book's departure with my eyes, sighing deeply when it disappeared.

The prince glanced at me. "Thujora will return the book once she has inscribed more of this tale."

"I was hoping to read this story through to the end," I told him.

"I know, Darci," Orillo sympathized. "We were given what we need to know for the time being. Besides, you have your hands and your heart full with Angel."

"You're right. I'd better get back to her."

We floated together up the hill to the small house. Orillo said good-bye outside, and I returned to Angel's bedside.

CHAPTER FIFTEEN
THE COSMIC JEWEL

After sharing a house with her sister and their two boyfriends, Angel lived alone. She moved to an upstairs apartment rented out by the family who inhabited the floors below. Despite her loneliness, I was glad there was no man around to distract her. I wanted her to focus on her spiritual studies.

As for her job designing knitwear, the garments she created for the company were distributed internationally. Even though she was making the owners millions of dollars with her artistry, she did not earn even two hundred dollars a week. She recognized this fact and it disheartened her.

On the positive side, along with constantly reading metaphysical material, she had begun doing yoga at home on her lunch breaks. The practice aligned her spine and brightened her energy field. My daily routine of sending light into her mind was having effects as well, and I hoped that soon she would be able to hear me speak to her telepathically. I decided to try an experiment.

After doing yoga, she would recline and relax for a few minutes before returning to the mill. I had decided that this was the time to impart a very simple message, but first I wanted her to feel my presence. Bathing her in brilliant golden light, I ran ripples of pink love energy from her feet to the top of her head. I did this over and over. Enjoying the sensation, she stretched and sighed. Encouraged by her reaction, I increased the intensity until she whispered, "Who's there? Who loves me this way? Is this how Krishna loved the thousand gopis?"

In Hinduism, there is a story of Krishna, beloved of all who knew him. Each gopi or doe-eyed peasant girl who saw this divine youth hoped that he would dance with her and love her. Each asked him to dance and to each he gave his promise. When the time came, a miracle seemed to occur. Each gopi truly believed that Krishna danced with her and loved her. Angel wondered if she was being loved by Krishna or by some other god. She was not far wrong. I am not a god, but I was loving her with my energy just as Krishna had loved the thousand gopis, though I focused on her and only her.

Her aura glowed rosy pink with my love. Sending a beam of bright white light into the telepathic center in her brain, I relayed the message, "I love you. Please start a metaphysical library."

She reclined in a blissful state for a few minutes, then rose and penned a few words about the experience in her journal. I was thrilled. She had felt my presence and my love and had received the message. She wrote, "I was told to begin a metaphysical library." Elated, I beamed a fresh burst of love to her.

The very night after this milestone, Orillo visited. I was sitting on Angel's bed, loving her more with every breath, when I heard the prince's voice, "Your charge is doing beautifully, thanks to you."

I glanced around, but did not immediately see my elfin friend. A shower of white and emerald sparks drifted down from above, so I looked up. Orillo hovered near the ceiling holding a small purple book.

"Good news, Darci! Thujora has gifted us with more of Jing Lei's story."

Enthused, not only because I was glad to see him but also because he usually brought unusual experiences, I invited him to sit beside me.

"Thujora and I met not long ago by the ocean," he told me. "She gave the book back to us. Now we can continue to learn about the soul who is to become the elfin avatar."

I recalled our last meeting. "We read that Jing Lei was just seven years old and spiritually talented, and because of those talents she was befriended by a Tibetan monk."

"Yes, Darci." An excited gleam flashed in his emerald eyes as he opened the book. "Little Jing Lei could see and hear Spirit Guides."

The pages danced with white light. A moment later, we were able to discern the words as Thujora's account continued.

Colorful prayer flags snapped in the breeze as the priest and the little girl made their way down the steps of the temple. Bright sunlight contrasted dramatically with the dark, somber atmosphere inside the monastery making Jing Lei squint as she followed close behind the lama toward his relative's home.

Xin Fau's niece lived in a small, clean, stone hovel at the edge of the village. A lively mountain stream ran behind the abode and, from the front stoop, the view over the valley below was magnificent. Jing Lei waited patiently outside while the priest entered and spoke with his niece and her husband. Soon he reappeared at the door and motioned for her to join them.

"Come in, little one. Meet Shen Lu and her husband, Meelam."

Because I, Thujora, was her protector, I hovered behind the girl as she entered the room. We found ourselves in a simple, well-kept home filled with Spirit Guides.

"I am Jing Lei." My charge bowed. "My, you have so many angels living with you!"

Shen Lu smiled and patted her pregnant belly. "They are watching over this baby who will make an entrance into this world very soon."

Xin Fau bent over and looked Jing Lei in the eye. "You may stay here as long as you are well behaved and helpful."

Meelam motioned toward his wife. "I cannot be here all the time to help her. You can see she does not move so easily. If you can make her tea … bring her things … then your presence will be a welcome one."

The elder explained that the little girl would be allowed to come into the temple at certain times for instruction, then he taught her a simple prayer to sing. As Jing Lei sang it back to him, Shen Lu joined in.

The old monk smiled. "It is a good prayer for the baby. Sing it often."

The priest and Meelam left and with them Bodu, Celestina, and another Guide. There were still at least a dozen Spirit Guides filling the hovel. My charge sat quietly as I introduced myself to the one nearest me. She appeared to be ancient and wise and wore a luminous red jewel on her forehead.

"I am Thujora," I began as I dipped my emerald robes in a half-curtsey.

"You and your charge are welcome," spoke the Guide in a low, booming voice. "You may call me Mother Ruby. I am here to facilitate this birth. There are many on the spirit side who watch with interest."

"Why is that, Mother Ruby?"

"Not all is as it should be, so many spirit helpers stand by."

The girl watched, listened, then asked the expectant mother, "Do you feel well?"

Shen Lu raised her eyebrows and sighed. "I feel pregnant. I don't know if I feel well or not as I have never carried a child before."

Jing Lei narrowed her eyes and looked at the mother-to-be. Sometimes the girl could see light around people. She remembered a year ago seeing rays of gold streaming from a pregnant woman in the marketplace. I understood what Jing Lei was trying to do, so I beamed a ray of white light into her forehead. As soon as I did this, the girl's eyes grew wide with wonder. She saw what I saw, what all the Spirit Guides saw: rippling maroon and black emanations radiating from the young pregnant woman's midsection.

"What is it?" asked Shen Lu with a tremor in her voice.

"I don't know," the girl answered truthfully.

"Mother Ruby, what is the trouble here?" I queried, for if we were to help, we needed to know more.

"Look into the aura," came the resonate voice. "Look beyond the dark ripples."

I did as the wise woman guide instructed, though I had to reposition myself. Once I was floating directly over Shen Lu, I saw two spirals of purple light going in opposite directions. There were two babies!

Mother Ruby read my thoughts. "Yes, there are two, and they are positioned badly."

"How do you mean?" I responded. It had been many years since I walked the earth and birthed a child.

"The babies are heads up, feet down. She cannot birth them feet first. She will die trying."

"Is there a midwife here in the village who can help her?"

"Only other women who have given birth. None who can do what needs to be done. That is why I am glad that you and the girl are here. It was no accident that you came now to this home. We need your assistance."

"What can we do?"

"May I have your permission to address your charge?"

I knew Jing Lei had been listening to our conversation intently, so I nodded and Mother Ruby lost no time.

"Jing Lei, my dear, can you hear me?"

"Yes," she said aloud.

Shen Lu had a mystified look. "To whom are you talking?"

"To one of your angels, the one with the red jewel on her forehead."

"My uncle told us you are strangely gifted, but I had no idea. What does the angel want?"

"She is about to tell me, then I will tell you."

Mother Ruby glided close to the child and looked her in the eyes. "You mustn't frighten Shen Lu. She must remain calm. Tell her to relax."

"The angel says to relax."

Shen Lu took a deep breath and shifted her bulk.

Mother Ruby led the girl closer to the expectant mother. "Listen carefully. You can try to do this on your own or we can wait until Meelam returns and have him attempt this."

"Do what?" said Jing Lei again out loud.

"Do what?" Shen Lu echoed.

"Dear girl," said Mother Ruby patiently, "you can think your questions to me. You do not have to speak them aloud."

"That's magical," thought the girl. "What shall I tell Shen Lu?"

"Say that the angels are going to guide you in a special ritual."

The girl repeated this to Shen Lu, then sent another thought to Mother Ruby. "I am only seven years old. Are you sure I can do this?"

"You must try. If we wait until Meelam returns, we may be risking her life and the life of her babies. Do not fear, little one. We are all here to guide you. We cannot affect physical change on Earth, but we can offer assistance to you as you do so."

Jing Lei began to speak out loud, then remembered to send a thought instead. "I'm afraid, but I'll try."

Mother Ruby nodded. "Good. There's a pot of warm water sitting on the hearth. Take a clean cloth from the stack on the table and soak it in the warm water. Tell Shen Lu you want to place the warm cloth on her belly."

The girl related the first step of the so-called ritual to the expectant mother, then went to carry it out. She let the steaming cloth cool for a moment so it would not redden Shen Lu's skin.

"Why do I do this?" Jing Lei sent the thought to the wise woman Guide.

"We must relax all the muscles in her midsection. When the cloth begins to cool, warm it and reapply. Continue until I say to stop. Please, little one. You could save three lives."

For the next hour Jing Lei warmed Shen Lu's belly with cloths. Finally, Mother Ruby interrupted and asked the girl to brew some relaxing tea, specifying the herbs to be used.

"I want the woman to be so relaxed she falls asleep," said the wise woman Guide.

By the time the sun had climbed overhead, Shen Lu was dozing in her chair.

"Suggest she lie on the pallet ... and please, Jing Lei, help her move."

"The angel says to lie down," spoke the girl. "Let me help you."

Shen Lu's legs were shaky and she nearly fell, but the little girl steadied the mother-to-be as she relocated. As soon as the woman lay down, she fell asleep.

"This is good," said Mother Ruby when the girl looked at her for advice. "Let her rest. What happens next is very important."

As Jing Lei and I sat next to Shen Lu, we observed two intensely brilliant spheres of light circling the sleeping woman. My charge was delighted as we watched these two luminous balls dance closer and closer to the expectant mother. I had seen this cosmic dance before, but it was a new phenomenon for Jing Lei. The spheres of light finally came so close to the slumbering female that they were rolling around on her pregnant belly. Suddenly one disappeared, then the other.

"Oh!" Jing Lei made a sound of surprise, then smiled and uttered, "Ohhhhhh," as Shen Lu's belly began radiating streams of bright golden light, for she had seen this before.

The girl turned to me. "What just happened, Thuji?"

"The beautiful souls of those two babies just entered their new homes."

"Thanks to you." Mother Ruby nodded at the child. "Because these babies were sure to be stillborn, no souls would enter. Now you are here, all has changed."

"The babies remain in the wrong position," I pointed out.

"With Jing Lei's help, we are about to change that. More warm cloths, my dear. I will tell you when to stop."

After several more applications of warmth to Shen Lu's midsection, Mother Ruby zoomed in front of the little girl so that they were eye-to-eye.

"My child, you are a cosmic jewel. The fact that you can see and hear all Spirit Guides makes you invaluable. We will work together to save these babies and their young mother. Are you ready?"

Jing Lei nodded, then looked at me with uncertainty in her eyes.

"Just do as Mother Ruby says," I encouraged her.

The wise woman guide surveyed the room. "It will take all of us, every Spirit Guide here, to make this happen, but you, little one, *you* are our hands. We can assist energetically, but that is all. You are the one who can physically change the situation. Do you understand?"

The girl nodded again.

Mother Ruby rose and seemed to increase in size and luminosity. "All Spirit Guides, gather and listen. The two souls who have just entered the womb of this woman know they must shift the positions of the bodies they have entered. We can work with them to accomplish this. Jing Lei will be the channel for our energy. Please form a spiral. I shall be right behind the girl, then Thujora, then you and you …"

The wise woman Guide pointed to one spirit after another until there manifested a line of illuminated beings that spiraled around the room and up toward the ceiling of the hovel.

"Now let us each place our hands on the shoulders of the Guide in front, like this …" Mother Ruby instructed as she laid her hands on Jing Lei's shoulders.

I followed suit, placing my hands on the wise woman Guide's shoulders. Glancing around, I was amazed at the resplendent train we had created. Jing Lei's eyes were as wide as I've ever seen them, for she perceived the chain of at least a dozen Guides, all attached to her.

Mother Ruby inspected the alignment, asked two of the Guides to shift their positions slightly, then nodded indicating all was ready.

"Jing Lei," the wise woman Guide spoke softly, "tell Shen Lu you are going to place your hands on her belly."

The girl did as she was asked, then sent the thought, "Where do I place them?"

"You are a talented, insightful girl. You can tell where the babies are inside Shen Lu. Take your right hand and locate the head of the twin on the right. You will know when you have found it."

The girl gently placed her small trembling hands on the woman's belly.

"Relax," I told my charge. "You can do this."

I watched the little girl move her hands slowly up the mound until suddenly she smiled.

"He's right here!" she exclaimed aloud.

The expectant mother shifted a little but did not waken.

"Best if you talk to us with your mind, child. Now keep your right hand there and move your left to find the head of the other baby."

It took Jing Lei only a moment to locate the twin. She was so small, and Shen Lu's belly so big, she looked as if she were hugging the mother-to-be.

"Dear one," Mother Ruby whispered in her ear, "we Guides are going to send you energy. Listen closely to my instructions. Do not remove your hands from the heads of those babies no matter what you are experiencing. When I tell you, use your hands to show the twins how to move."

Jing Lei looked over her shoulder; her eyes revealed fright. "Move?"

"Yes, my dear. The babies must change position. Indeed, they must invert themselves. Their little heads need to move down and their feet up. Just follow my directions and keep your hands on their heads."

The girl gave a slight nod.

Mother Ruby then spoke words in a language Jing Lei did not understand. However, I knew what she said, for she was using the multidimensional language of the Spirit Guides. As she uttered the syllables and tones, first sparks, then luminous clouds, then glowing shapes and symbols manifested in the air. It was a prayer and a blessing.

Jing Lei did not notice this phenomenon because she was focused on keeping her hand positions just right.

Mother Ruby spoke two more words, and the room became alive with dancing energy. The shapes and symbols the Guide had created surrounded the expectant mother and rotated slowly around her as the chain of Spirit Guides, including myself, sent energy to little Jing Lei. Watching my charge become illuminated so brightly that I could no longer see her features, I discerned only her little hands, which were vibrating as we sent pulses of energy through them into Shen Lu's belly.

"We all now tell those babies it is time for them to move. We all see them shifting," declared Mother Ruby in an authoritative voice. We followed her instructions, though not in unison.

"More energy!" the wise woman Guide commanded. We complied.

Jing Lei was now shaking, though she kept her hands in place.

"Now!" Mother Ruby shouted. Then more softly she spoke to the girl. "It's up to you to guide these babies as they rotate. Start with your left hand, child. Do you still feel the baby's head?"

"Yes." Jing Lei's voice sounded tiny, distant.

"Imagine you are moving a melon down from a shelf. Does that make this less scary? Come now, bring your left hand down followed closely by your right. Slowly. Keep a steady motion."

As I watched and listened, I prayed for my charge, for the mother-to-be, and for the twins. I visualized the babies turning in the womb and prayed again.

Shen Lu fluttered her eyelids and moaned.

"Tell her to breathe deeply," instructed Mother Rose.

The girl did so.

The deep breathing was the final ingredient, for I saw that Jing Lei's hands had moved down. The babies had inverted themselves.

Mother Ruby raised her arms toward us. "Now, dear Guides, let us make a circle around these two females, the mother and the girl."

Abandoning the spiraling chain formation, we floated into a circle. When I did so, I noticed that the patterns of light within Shen Lu's womb had changed dramatically. The two purple spirals I had seen before were now brilliant ovals of white light pulsing with life.

"Thank you for your help." Mother Ruby bowed to us. "We will keep a vigil until these babies are born, though we have done what we can for now." She turned to the girl. "Jing Lei, special thanks to you. We could not have shifted these babies without your help."

"Will Shen Lu be all right?" The little girl's voice trembled as she asked.

Mother Ruby stroked her hair. "She and the babies have a better chance now. Get some rest, little one."

Jing Lei climbed into a chair and curled up. She was exhausted but still tingling from all the energy she had conducted. I sat by her side and showered her with soothing blue-green light to help calm and restore her.

The sun had disappeared behind the slope of the western mountains when Meelam returned. He had brought extra food for their new house guest. As Jing Lei helped him unpack his satchel, he showed her where to store various items. They were talking about preparing the evening meal when Shen Lu wailed so loudly it made them both jump. They ran to her side to find her garment soaked and a frightened look on her face.

"It's time!" she gasped.

Meelam grasped his wife's hand and kissed her forehead. "I'll fetch your helpers and be right back!"

Shen Lu's eyes were squeezed tightly as she let out another wail. "Go!" she screamed through clenched teeth.

Jing Lei took her hand as Meelam dashed out the door. The girl spoke words of encouragement. "Remember, you have many angels here to help you and your babies."

"Babies? What are you saying, child?"

"There are two babies. Didn't you know?"

"Two?" Shen Lu choked on the word.

"You are blessed," the girl said calmly. "Much has already been done to help you and your sons."

"Twin boys?" Shen Lu couldn't believe what she was hearing. "But how do you know?"

Jing Lei didn't have a chance to answer, as another wave of pain rippled through the birth mother. She squeezed the girl's hand so hard it hurt.

Mother Ruby moved to the girl's side and suggested that she take a fresh cloth and wet it with cool water for Shen Lu's brow. Jing Lei was glad to be able to do something for the mother-to-be. The girl had never seen anyone's face change and contort so much. She wished she could take away Shen Lu's pain.

I heard her thought and reminded her, "You have already removed the pain of certain death for this woman and her children."

Meelam and two women rushed through the door to Shen Lu's side. They lay blankets and a large clean cloth on the floor, then helped the expectant mother to the birthing location. As they were positioning pillows under her head and arms, Shen Lu experienced another contraction.

"This baby comes soon," said one of the women.

"Babies!" cried Shen Lu.

"What?" exclaimed Meelam and the two women.

"Babies," repeated Jing Lei. "There are two."

"More blankets! More clean cloths!" shouted one of the women. She then looked at the other woman and whispered, "I've never helped to birth twins." The second woman shook her head.

It was a long and stressful night for everyone. Jing Lei stayed by Meelam most of the time and did her best to comfort him. At one point she told him there were even more angels in their little home. Indeed, there were, for the Spirit Guides of the babies and the two village women were present along with two resplendent angels who arrived to bless the birth.

The father-to-be felt very helpless and was so restless he could not stay in one place. It was difficult for him to listen to the cries of his wife. Jing Lei had never heard such sounds coming from anyone. Since neither the husband nor the girl were directly involved in the birth, they stood sometimes in the doorway, sometimes against the wall of the little house. They could hear the two village women whispering to each other, but could not understand what was said. However, I could hear that the two were supporting and encouraging each other and Shen Lu. It was a new experience for everyone.

Shen Lu's cries became louder and more frequent and the women's whispering more intense. Meelam paced and prayed.

Jing Lei and I watched the light and energy around the birthing mother shift. Early on, radiant ripples streamed from her belly. Now she was entirely circled by multicolored bands of buzzing, sparkling light. I was glad my charge could see the many levels of this miracle of birth.

Then came a gasp from the women helping Shen Lu, followed by urgent whispering. Meelam paced faster and wrung his hands. Suddenly a whooshing sound filled the room as Jing Lei and I witnessed a bright flash of light. The first baby was born.

We were all relieved. Meelam was ecstatic as he held his first-born son, but concern quickly overspread his face as he saw his poor wife lying there exhausted but still in labor. He prayed again that she would survive the ordeal.

As the first rays of sun peeked through the eastern mountain range, the second baby was born. He was smaller than the first, but healthy. Shen Lu lay completely spent, but had just enough strength to hold her twin sons for a few moments.

When Xin Fau arrived to check on his niece and new student, he found the peaceful scene lit by the strong morning sun. There was much joy as the elder embraced Shen Lu and welcomed his new relatives.

Mother Ruby glided over to my charge and me. "Time for me to go," she said, smiling for the first time since I had met her. She looked at Jing Lei. "My dear little one, remember this day. You are the one who made this event joyful rather than tragic. Just look at the energy in this room!"

The wise woman Guide allowed us a moment to take in the splendor. Great pink and gold bubbles of light filled the room. They danced, bounced, and spun as the new family beamed with happiness.

"Thank you, my cosmic jewel," Mother Ruby continued. "You are able to see much of the magic and mystery of the universe. Use your gifts well and many will benefit." She bowed to us, looked at the new mother once more, then floated up and out of sight.

My charge was tired and finally ready to sleep after the longest, most exciting day of her young life. She curled up in a big chair and slept as I held her in my spirit arms. She had done well.

The book closed itself on Orillo's lap.

"That was truly amazing," I commented. "What a truly gifted soul!"

Orillo grinned. "We elves are so honored that she comes to Earth again to become one of us."

"If Angel knew about this soul, I know she would want to assist her. I certainly wish to help in any way I can."

"Excellent, Darci." Orillo smiled. "Continue to work with your charge. I must return this book to Thujora, but I will visit again. I leave you with a message from your dear mentor Sottrol. He said to tell you that big changes are afoot for Angel."

Before I could ask for details, he seemed to dissolve into a whirling spiral of tiny orbs of emerald light, which rose up toward the ceiling and vanished.

CHAPTER SIXTEEN
KARMA CALLS

After the breakup of her marriage, the one thing Angel missed the most in her life was music. While sitting for hours in her office at the mill designing knitwear, she listened to the radio constantly. With her confidence bolstered by experiences with her famous husband and his band, she walked into her favorite FM radio station in Hartford and made friends with the deejays. One of the announcers was a long-haired, spiritually minded woman who introduced my charge to the wisdom of the I Ching and astrology. In a life-changing event, she drew Angel's astrological birth chart for her.

When my charge first saw the pattern, I was standing right behind her. Her aura expanded and brightened many-fold. Subconsciously she connected to the chart for two reasons: she had been a skilled astrologer in a former life, and she had been shown the chart prior to her birth in preparation for this incarnation. The drawing resonated so deeply that even consciously she knew she had seen the chart somewhere before. Thus a new phase began for Angel in which her focus changed to radio and astrology.

Within two years, she was hosting a radio show at the University of Connecticut's radio station. She lived in a cottage, which she shared with a college student, by that same lake near campus. I was glad her residence was near water again, for it had a soothing, calming effect on her.

The metaphysical library that I had encouraged her to start was growing. Angel's passion for astrology prompted the purchase of many books on that subject. She learned how to calculate and draw up natal charts and began constructing them for people just as she had lifetimes ago in ancient Egypt.

One summer night after my charge had fallen asleep, Orillo and Nyna visited me. As always, I was pleased to see them. Nyna's presence made my heart surge with love.

The elfin elder placed her hand on Angel's head and smiled. "She is coming into her own, Darci. She has reconnected with knowledge from her former life as an astrologer. I can see by her energy field that you have been doing your part, too."

"I followed your suggestion, Nyna," I confirmed. "I beam white light into her mind on a daily basis."

"It shows," the prince agreed. Dressed in trousers and a tunic made of iridescent golden fabric, he stepped toward me. "Nyna wants to sit with Angel for a while to evaluate her progress in more detail. Why don't we walk over to the lake? It's a beautiful night."

Glimmering stars reflected in the mirror surface of the lake as Orillo and I sat side by side on a wooden dock. The air was warm and still and carried the fragrance of sweet blossoms.

"I think it's very interesting that Angel has begun broadcasting on the radio," he told me. "Our elfin avatar will be known as the Great Communicator."

"She will?" This was news to me. "Why, Orillo?"

"Because she will be able to communicate between worlds, just like Jing Lei. Your charge has the potential to do this as well. That's one reason you and Angel have been chosen to help us usher this extraordinary being to the earth plane."

I shook my head. "Every day I wish Angel could hear me, see me, know me. After one instance, she seems to have closed down. Each day I hope she might hear me, but aside from that one time … nothing."

Orillo placed a comforting hand on my shoulder, and I felt buoyed. "First of all, rejoice at the fact that she did hear you, and second … be patient, my Spirit Guide friend. Your charge needs time for her telepathic receptivity to develop and mature."

"I know you're right." I sighed. "Do you have any idea when she might be ready?"

"Even if it's a decade or more, it is worth it, Darci. She is still young, not yet thirty. There's plenty of time." He gazed out at the surface of the lake as if looking for something.

"What is it, Orillo?"

"Sottrol informed me that Thujora requested a meeting with us tonight."

"I remember that Thujora prefers to be by water when she visits the earth," I mused. "I guess patience is the watchword for both of us tonight."

We sat enjoying the peaceful scene. Once in a while a sound from the quiet neighborhood would reach us. At long last, the water before us began to glow with a purple hue, and Thujora appeared in a cloud of lavender vapors. Moving toward us, she joined us on the dock, and we greeted her warmly.

"Gentlemen," she began, "thank you for waiting. As a Master Guide, I seem to be constantly busy." She glanced from me to the prince. Her oval face held an especially serene expression as she reached under her violet robes. "Here is my narration of more of Jing Lei's life in Tibet. The more you know about this exceptional soul, the better you shall be prepared when she incarnates again on Earth."

She handed the book to Orillo while looking at me. "Darci, please know that Angel can be key in this soul's return. Take good care of your charge."

I wanted to say, "I will," but the Master Guide immediately twirled herself into a spiral of white and purple light, which shot skyward and was gone. Orillo and I followed her departure with our eyes, then looked at each other.

"Shall we read?" he asked, gesturing with the little lavender book.

I nodded my assent and the book opened, gracefully flipping its pages.

After Jing Lei assisted with the birth of the twins, she was a hero in the village. She continued to live with the lama's niece and her husband for ten years, helping raise the twin boys, doing housework, cooking, and amusing the family with stories. Her weekly meetings with the priest for lessons and wisdom were her favorite activity. Jing Lei slowly grew into a beautiful young woman.

As her Spirit Guide, my preferred times to speak with my charge were evenings when she returned to her small room or mornings when she woke. On one particular day, however, I felt the need to interrupt a visit with her aging parents. They had traveled to see her for her seventeenth birthday. The three of them were sitting in the sunshine outside the small house where Jing Lei lived with the lama's niece and family. They enjoyed a view of the brook and the valley below as the sun warmed them. I was standing behind my charge exchanging news with the Guides who watched over her parents when I noticed something strange. Her father's aura had a gray spot about the size of his hand that pulsed with his heartbeat. It drifted from his chest area to his abdomen to his knees, then meandered around to his lower back. When this animated gray spot finally hovered above the man's head, I asked his Spirit Guide, Najar, about it.

"Ah, you see it, too," he replied. "I have tried to cleanse it from his energy field for some weeks now with no success. It does not seem to affect his work, though he may tire more easily."

Moving over to Jing Lei's father, I floated before him, keeping my eyes on the moving patch of gray.

The young woman noticed what I was doing and asked me telepathically, "Thujora, is something wrong?"

"I am trying to discern that," I told her. "Can you see your father's energy field?"

"I see a slight glow around most people," she replied. "I do not see auras as clearly as I see Spirit Guides." She squinted at her father, then again asked with her mind, "What do you see?"

I began to tell her, but at that moment, her mother gave her a birthday gift of a lovely, colorful jacket that she had made for her daughter, so Jing Lei was distracted and did not hear my reply. When her parents departed, I watched her father carefully. He seemed to drag his feet a bit, but other than that only the gray spot seemed different.

That night I spoke with my charge as she pulled the covers up preparing to sleep. "My dear one," I began, "I think you should visit your parents very soon. I saw something in your father's aura that concerns me, and I would like to study this more closely. Perhaps we can offer him a healing."

"I trust you, Thujora," she told me. "I shall visit my childhood home right after my lesson with the lama."

Her parents' home was high on a mountainside a half-day's walk from the village. Jing Lei set off at dawn and arrived when the sun was overhead. Her surprised parents welcomed her. As they shared a simple noontime meal, I examined her father with the help of Najar. Although it was difficult to be certain, it seemed that this gray spot was attached to his spine by a strand of dark thread that was not always visible to us. The patch would move this way and that, up, down, back, and forward, but remain anchored in the man's body.

When I pointed this out, Najar remarked, "I think I see that now. So this is why I have not been able to cleanse the gray spot out of his energy field." The Guide looked at me. "What does this mean?"

"Impending illness," I speculated. "We must do a healing ceremony to detach this looming ailment before it entrenches itself further and affects him adversely. I believe it is already slowing him down."

"But, Thujora, I have always been able to heal my charge quite easily. Why is this ailment so difficult to remove?"

"It must be karmic," I answered grimly. "It is the sticky spiderweb of karma that holds the illness in his aura."

"Ah, I see," declared Najar. "That makes sense. But if it is this man's karma that has attracted the problem, then we cannot remove it. He must be the one to counteract its effect."

"Yes, it is meant as a lesson to him. We cannot remove this and nullify the karma, but we can help him deal with it." I gazed at Najar with his dark skin and white robe. "You helped your charge prepare for this lifetime. Do you know what actions from a past incarnation may have brought this challenge?"

While Najar was contemplating this, I focused on Jing Lei. She was sitting next to her father, talking quietly while her mother cleaned up after their meal.

"My dear daughter," he was saying, "you cannot live in your current situation forever. The twins are old enough to watch out for themselves. It's time you moved on."

"But, Father, the family has asked me to stay. I must receive instruction from the lama or from my Spirit Guide before I change my life."

"It's your life, Jing Lei. You must choose how to use your gifts."

The young woman shifted uncomfortably. "I will move when the time is right, Father. Please don't force me to do otherwise."

Najar motioned to me. I glided back to his side.

"I believe I have the answer, Thujora." He did not look happy about it.

"It must be a major life challenge," I reasoned. "We Spirit Guides cannot remove such karma, but only help our charges resolve it."

The gray patch pulsed in the center of the man's back as if taunting us to try to remove it.

Najar began his explanation. "In one of his former lifetimes, he was the commander of a great army. He made life and death decisions every day."

"What decision has brought him this ailment?" I asked.

"The army was on the move. Illness overtook some of the soldiers. He commanded the rest of the men to march on, leaving the ailing soldiers behind. His sense of duty overcame his compassion, and the men left behind struggled and died. He must now face a similar situation to balance his karma."

"But how?" I wondered. "He has a wife and daughter to care for him."

"Then this karmic illness will overtake him when he is alone," Najar reasoned. "So if this is the case, how can we help him?"

"In whatever situation he finds himself, he must choose compassion over duty," I offered. "He must let go of control and replace it with understanding."

Najar looked at me. "And it is my task to see that he does this."

"Yes, though I do think that Jing Lei and I are meant to help somehow. Otherwise, I would not have seen the gray spot."

"I am glad to have your assistance," admitted the swarthy guide. "Jing Lei's father is my first charge, and although I have been well trained, I have yet to practice all I've learned."

"The most difficult part of being a Spirit Guide is to allow your charge to enter situations that may be harmful, but are meant as karmic teaching aids," I told him gently. "I'm sure that's what will happen here. Stay close to him, but allow him to meet his challenge."

"That does sound difficult indeed," Najar agreed. "Thank you, Thujora."

On the way back to the village the next day, Jing Lei asked me about her parents. I was honest with her.

"Dear one, I have seen an animated gray spot in your father's energy field. This is not just an approaching illness slowing him down," I told her. "Your father is slated to face one of his major life challenges."

"He's getting older, Thujora. He cannot do what he used to. Perhaps his slowing is due simply to aging, something all humans face."

"In your father's case, it is more. Take heart. We may yet be able to help him." Moments like this made me very grateful that Jing Lei could see and converse with me.

Several weeks passed. One cool, gray day, a man arrived with a message for Jing Lei. Her mother wrote that her father had gone missing. My charge wanted to go to her mother immediately, but her parents lived too far away; it was too late in the day for such a journey. Instead, she went to see her teacher, the elder priest, Xin Fau.

"What shall I do?" she asked the lama. "I fear my mother will go looking for him, but she is no longer young. She may become lost, too!"

The wise elder sat quietly for a few minutes. Jing Lei knew to be patient and wait. Finally, he looked at the young woman and spoke.

"Send a message to your mother. Tell her to stay near home. Tell her to call her husband to her with her mind and heart. Say that you do not wish to lose both your beloved parents. She will understand."

"Can we organize a search party? We must do something!" she pleaded.

"Yes, we can do that," said the lama, "though I do not think we will need to."

Jing Lei's eyes widened. "What do you mean?"

"Go. Write the message. There is a trader headed in that direction soon. I will ask him to personally deliver the letter to your mother. Be sure to tell your mother that we will send searchers to look for your father, so that she will stay home. Once the message is on its way, we will talk further."

After Jing Lei had given her letter to the merchant traveler, she came to meet me at our special place. Because my charge lived with a family, she did not have a great deal of privacy, so long ago we had chosen a meeting spot, a place of power. To reach the site, she walked upstream to a warm flat rock. Even though a beautiful, open view of the valley spread out before her on the ledge, she was protected from the winds by large rocks around her. Jing Lei would go to this spot when she was troubled, as she was on this day.

"Thujora," she called. "Thuji."

I came near. "Yes, my dear one. I am here."

"Your presence comforts me," she said aloud, then sent the following thought, "This is what you warned me about. My father's karma has manifested."

"Yes."

"You said we could help him. How can we help? I do not know where he is."

"You do not need to know. We can help him from this very spot right now. Then make plans to travel to your mother first thing in the morning."

"But what can we do from here?" She looked so worried.

"First, we will send a prayer for his well-being. Together we shall pray that he receives the help and guidance he needs, and that he accepts that help so that he can learn, change, and heal. We both know his Spirit Guide Najar. We both know that Najar will do all he can to help."

"Can we not do more?" my charge pleaded. "I love my father so. He has done so much for me."

"We can send him a vision," I told her.

"A dream?"

"He may experience it as a dream or a waking vision. It depends on his state of awareness. I will show you how."

This was another of many moments when I was so thankful that my charge could see and hear me. "Your connection to your father is strong, so we will use that. Here. Let us sit across from each other."

Wind whistled around the rocks and down the mountainside, but the sheltered ledge was calm and peaceful.

"Does your father understand karma?" I asked her.

"I'm not sure. We've never discussed it. I have studied karma with the lama, so I know that karma winds itself through many lifetimes. Humans immersed in their present incarnation do not often see karma's big picture."

"And therefore dismiss its existence," I added.

"But Father isn't like that," she insisted. "He will understand the vision. I know he will."

"Very well. Ready?"

She nodded.

"Place your hands out like this." I showed her. "As if you are lightly holding a great sphere."

She did so, and I moved closer so that I could position my hands to hold the imaginary orb with her.

"Now see the sphere as a ball of white light," I instructed. "We are using our hearts, our minds, our energy to create this."

Jing Lei nodded, and instantly the sphere of white light appeared in our hands.

"Now we will place the vision for your father inside this globe."

My charge took a deep breath before asking, "What shall we show him?"

"Let us show him the origins of the karma he must face."

She was quiet for a few minutes, then spoke softly. "I see my father as the commander of a great army ... but he is leading his men away from an encampment. I see the men he left behind. They are injured and ailing. My father seems very focused on arriving somewhere in time to do battle." I saw her shudder. "He does not look back to the men he leaves behind to suffer a slow death."

"Place this vision into the sphere of light," I told her. "The images you saw were real. Your father must see them, too. A part of him must remember."

She breathed a heartbreaking sigh. "But I want to send him something positive, too ... something that will help him."

"The memory of his past life as a commander will help him understand why he faces what he does in the present."

"What does he face, Thujora?"

"He is alone and ill, much like those men he abandoned in that long-ago lifetime."

Tears glistened in her eyes, and her voice quavered. "Will he die, too?"

"Not if he faces his karma and learns from it," I assured her. "Over a dozen men died because of his decision to abandon them. He must discover how that feels. He must ask for forgiveness. This is the process of balancing his karma. Now place your vision into the sphere."

"But cannot we do something else? Something to help him? My heart breaks when I think of him alone and suffering."

"Jing Lei, my dear, this is something he must experience and now is the time. That's why neither Najar nor I could remove the gray spot from your father's energy field." I could see her reluctance to send the karmic information, so I suggested, "Why don't we include another picture, a comforting one that will inspire him to fight and live. Send him love, Jing Lei. Send him your image radiating love."

She nodded, then sat for a while focusing on the radiant sphere of energy we had created. I saw the lighted globe flush pink and knew that she had added her love.

"Now, let us lift the globe and send it," I told her.

We raised the sphere, now filled with images and energy.

"Great One, Creator," I spoke slowly, reverently, "take this orb to Jing Lei's father and to his Spirit Guide Najar. May it assist them both."

We watched the sphere of light rise, then become caught in the crosswinds and sail across the valley.

"It does not seem to be traveling in the direction of my parents' home," she said with concern.

"Be assured, it will reach your father and his Guide. Now we must prepare to leave at dawn to go to your mother."

"Yes," she agreed. "And I want to talk to the priest about the search party. Hopefully they have gone out looking by now."

When Jing Lei arrived at her parents' home the next day, she found her distraught mother being comforted by a female neighbor. The woman excused herself as mother and daughter reunited. I spoke with Florina, the Spirit Guide watching over Jing Lei's mother, who was sending waves of comforting love to her distressed charge.

Florina gave me a knowing glance. "When karma calls, no one escapes. Najar and I were expecting something like this."

"As was I," I told her.

"At least you can converse with Jing Lei," she pointed out. "You are so fortunate to have that conscious link."

"Yes. We did earn it, but it comes with great responsibility," I sighed, remembering Jing Lei's face when she had the vision of what her father had done in a past life. "We worked together to send something to help the man recognize his karma and make amends. Najar will help, too."

"That's what we do," said Florina, moving to rub her charge's back, as Jing Lei and her mother embraced and wept.

Meelam, father of the twin boys, and two other men were searching for my charge's father, but by nightfall, no word had come from anyone. With her mother sitting worried and awake by the small fire, Jing Lei collapsed into a troubled and exhausted sleep.

Curious to discover what was happening, I asked Florina to watch over my charge while I went off to find Najar. Spirit Guides can communicate with one another telepathically, especially when they are involved in one family as we were. I located Najar and Jing Lei's father in a deep ravine several miles away. As I suspected, the man was injured and ill. He had taken a bad fall, rolling down the mountainside and ending up in a stream. He had managed to pull himself out of the water, but his leg was broken, so he could not climb. Wracked with pain, he was shivering with cold and hunger.

Upon arriving, I told Najar, "There is a search party out looking. Jing Lei and I sent energetic help to aid him in resolving his karma."

"Thank you for that," responded Najar with a concerned expression. "He is at the point of hallucination, not far from death."

"But he still has a chance," I offered. "He must realize that he is reliving what he did to those soldiers he abandoned. He must realize his own mistake."

Najar shook his head. "Yes, he must do so soon, before he dies of exposure."

At that moment, I heard Jing Lei's voice in my head, but I was not the only one who heard it. Najar did, too, and from the look on his face, so did the injured man.

"Compassion and love," said Jing Lei. "Karma is dissolved in compassion and love."

"Jing Lei!" cried her father weakly. "Jing Lei! Help me!"

The brilliant sphere of energy that Jing Lei and I had created then appeared above the man's head. It lowered and engulfed him. Najar and I watched the man experience the past-life scenario we had sent to him. He wept for those abandoned men, for now he knew exactly how they felt.

Again, my charge's gentle voice entered our minds. "Love, compassion, and forgiveness, Father. Apologize to those you have wronged and forgive yourself."

"I'm so sorry," he cried aloud. "My desire to be successful in battle overrode my compassion for human suffering. I was so wrong. I'm sorry."

Even though Jing Lei slept miles away, her spirit was with us there in the rocky ravine. It was then I truly realized how gifted and powerful she was.

"Jing Lei, my dear daughter," wept her father. "I will be a better man. I will not force my ideas and desires on you. I want to see you again. I want to see my beloved wife. Jing Lei! Help me! I am so sorry!"

Najar and I looked at each other. The man had faced his karma, recognized his mistakes, offered a heartfelt apology, and asked to be forgiven.

"He is ready to be saved to go on and live life," said Najar. "But how?"

"I can wake Jing Lei and we can lead the search party here," I suggested.

"There isn't time, I'm afraid," said Najar ruefully. "He will die before morning light."

Just then we heard shouts on the path high above us.

"There!" yelled one man. "He's down there!"

Next came the thud of feet and the sound of loose gravel and pebbles skittering by.

"Here!" cried the injured man, but his voice was small and weak.

Somehow, the rescuers heard. Somehow, they located the injured and ailing man. Najar and I were surprised.

As one of the men wrapped a warm blanket around my charge's father and another examined his broken leg, he asked, "How did you know where I was? How did you find me?"

"Your daughter," answered Meelam. "We saw her on the mountain path in front of us carrying a lantern with a strange glow. She led us down the hillside, too." He glanced around. "Where is she? I thought she'd be right here by your side."

Najar and I looked at each other. It seemed that my talented charge could also project her astral body so powerfully that the searchers could see it. We had heard her but not seen her, yet all three men swore they saw the young woman leading them with a strange light.

My admiration for the gifted soul who was Jing Lei expanded many-fold. I feel truly blessed to have had her as my charge.

$$\infty$$

Those were the last words written in the lavender book. A breeze arrived from down the lake, herding ripples before it on the surface of the water.

Orillo closed the book and smiled. "Darci, as I learn more about this soul, I must admit that my anticipation of her arrival grows."

"I am excited to meet her," I told him. "Do you know when that will be?"

Fixing me with a steady gaze from his emerald eyes, he replied, "When you and Angel are ready." He paused, and then uttered the following words before he disappeared. "We want you to be her parents."

CHAPTER SEVENTEEN
THE KARMIC INJURY

Orillo had departed before I could ask him anything about his surprising statement. How could a Spirit Guide and a human woman parent the elfin avatar? It seemed an impossibility. My mind wrestled with Orillo's words until I thought I might implode. Finally, I called for my mentor, Sottrol. He is the wisest, most experienced teacher I know. Surely he could explain Orillo's statement. To my surprise, both Nyna and Sottrol appeared just inside the door of Angel's bedroom. Their luminosity shone so brightly that the room was awash in celestial light.

"Greetings, Darci," began my mentor, the crystals in his beard glimmering.

"Sottrol, Nyna … thank you for coming."

"We never want to leave a fine Spirit Guide like you confused for long," assured the elfin elder. "For a while now, Orillo has wanted to tell you that you and Angel might parent the elfin avatar. We finally gave him permission to pass on this information. I want to make sure you know, Darci, that this path is your choice, yours and Angel's."

"I understand that this realm, the earth plane, offers free will," I told them. "I was not sure it extended to me."

Sottrol put his arm round me, and I immediately felt a strange combination of comfort and exhilaration. "Darci, you have free will as far as how you choose to work with your charge, as long as you follow the basic Spirit Guide Creed."

I got right to the point. "I've been considering the scenario that Orillo presented, and I don't see how it's possible."

Both luminous elders smiled.

Nyna stepped to my side as well. "Dear Darci, surely you know that the possibilities in the universe are many. Earth life is but a physical manifestation of Spirit, and when you work with Spirit, the potential is great."

"I guess I understand," I replied, not certain I did. Trying another approach, I went on, "Orillo is so excited about the arrival of the elfin avatar. Why is he not the avatar's father?"

Sottrol smiled. "You are just beginning to learn about the realm of the elementals. They do not arrive on Earth through conception, pregnancy, and birth as humans do. When they choose to enter the earth plane, they do so for a very long time, for hundreds, even thousands of Earth years. Spirit Guides and elves alike foster their arrival. The arrival of each new elfin being on this plane is celebrated, for these comings are few and far between."

Nyna continued, "The elves arrive as infants and are nurtured and taught much as human children are, but they grow and learn more quickly."

"So Spirit Guides foster elfin births? Why did I not hear of this before now?" I asked.

Sottrol chuckled. "You had enough to do watching over your charge. We wanted to be certain that you could handle that much. Besides, not all Spirit Guides become involved with the world of the elementals."

I shook my head. "I still don't understand how Angel figures in to all this."

"You and Angel have parented many children in your past lifetimes together," said Nyna.

"I know this," I responded. "But we were both humans then."

Sottrol patted my shoulder, and I felt tiny zings of energy pulse through me. "Both you and she can call on those past experiences in parenting."

Nyna jumped in. "Though the elves will raise her."

"What about Angel's involvement?"

Nyna smiled. "That's the exciting part. Listen carefully, Darci. The avatars come to Earth to break new ground, to penetrate through barriers that before were insurmountable."

"Keep it simple, Nyna," suggested Sottrol. "The lad has quite a bit to process already."

"But you must know this much, Darci, for you to understand," the elfin elder continued. "The elfin avatar's purpose … one of them … is to involve humans in the world of the elementals. The Earth has suffered greatly in the past century. All must change. Humans must embrace a new reverence for the planet. The elfin avatar will help this occur because she will be able to cross the barrier. She will be able to appear to humans."

Sottrol could see that I was overwhelmed by this information. "Surely you've learned what an extraordinary soul is coming to fulfill this destiny," he said. "In the past life that you and Orillo recently read about courtesy of Thujora, this soul could see and communicate with Spirit Guides and could also astral project and appear to humans. She will use these experiences and more when she arrives on Earth as the elfin avatar."

"I still don't see how this involves Angel."

Sottrol's smile grew wider. "The elfin avatar is the breakthrough link between elementals and humans. She needs not only a Spirit Guide to foster her arrival, she needs also a human to do so."

"She needs a human mother," simplified Nyna.

"And a Spirit Guide father," added Sottrol. "Darci, I'm sorry, but we must go. I hope we answered your questions. Remember, more is possible than you might think."

They encircled me with their spirit arms, and I felt buoyed beyond belief. Stepping back, they disappeared into a sphere of blindingly bright white light, which floated up and dissolved, leaving tiny sparkles on the ceiling of the room.

Standing by Angel's bedside, I gazed lovingly at the sleeping woman, amazed and overwhelmed at the possibilities that stretched before us.

As I went about my daily activities as Angel's Spirit Guide, I constantly wondered how we would get from where we were currently to a place where she and I could communicate, fall in love, marry, and parent the elfin avatar. The journey seemed unachievable, yet Sottrol and Nyna said that it was possible.

The first step was activating telepathic communication between my charge and myself. We had the one breakthrough when she thought I might be Krishna, but nothing since. She continued to read metaphysical material and to practice astrology, but she was too busy for the quiet needed for telepathic communication between us.

Within two years, Angel moved from college radio to a commercial radio job at that same station in Hartford. She was given the coveted afternoon drive air shift. Now she was right in the middle of the music world and she loved it, taking to radio like an eagle to the sky on a clear, breezy day.

Between her job and her social life, she was on the go constantly. To her credit, she did learn to meditate, and this practice helped keep her centered, but I needed her to be somewhere far more quiet and serene in order for regular telepathic contact between us to be possible. This took a few years to accomplish. I knew her well, knew what drove her decisions, so I used both radio and men to change her life. Making sure she had heard about an enticing radio job in Maine, I was very pleased when she took the position and moved there. Sadly, my charge soon discovered that radio is one of the least stable professions. Angel held four different radio jobs in the span of three years, jobs that took her from Lewiston, to Portland, to Boston, then back to Maine.

The men in her life changed as quickly. In fact, I made sure she met one fellow, a British lad, on a voiceover job at the University of Maine in Augusta. They began seeing each other and eventually she moved north to the foothills of Maine's Appalachian Mountains. Luckily there was an AM-FM radio station in the county seat that employed her.

"Now we're getting somewhere," I thought. I was not entirely correct.

Still she did not slow down, and I can't say that I blame her. She was in her mid-thirties and thriving. Her radio show received the highest rating in the surveyed market. I thought that perhaps the heartbreak she suffered when the British man cheated on her would slow her down, but she had an appetite

175

for relationships that stemmed from low self-esteem. She felt she needed a partnership with a man to feel good about herself and her life. Little did she know that I waited patiently to be her partner.

With her mother's help, she bought an old house on five acres of land. I led her to the place through friends. The land had a large blackberry patch, apple trees, space for a garden, and blessed quiet. The pre–Civil War cape had no plumbing except a hand pump in the kitchen. It did have one outlet for electricity so she could listen to music. It was a joyful day for me when she moved her collection of vinyl records into the place.

Angel was almost thirty-seven in June of 1983 when she signed the papers to purchase the house and land. Finally, she had fulfilled one of her goals, owning her own home. I was delighted because it was located on a peaceful dead-end road on the edge of the great Maine wilderness.

Even living in such a remote area did not slow her down that much. She became a founding member of an all-female a cappella comedy group; she taught astrology and began an astrological practice; she continued to work on the radio, attend concerts, and enjoy a flourishing social life.

One example is the connection she made with a soon-to-be-famous rock band. Intrigued by their first release, Angel made it a point to see and hear a young band from Athens, Georgia, open for the English Beat. She knew instantly that the southern boys had a powerful sound that would take them far. Tape recorder in hand, she ventured backstage to find REM alone in their dressing room, where they recorded a station ID for her.

She befriended the lead singer, and they spent time together off and on for the next few years. My charge was fascinated because she and Michael are astrological opposites. He was born on January fourth; she was born on July fourth. Not only are their natal suns opposite each other, their natal moons are as well, and she proceeded to study this phenomenon.

One warm May evening when Angel was visiting Michael in Athens, I sat by her bedside cleansing away stress residue from travel. She was in a guest room at the front of the house. I had just helped her slip into a deep sleep when Michael woke her. He asked her to remove a tick from his scalp, which he figured had latched on while he was rolling around in the grass with his two dogs. Sleepy-eyed, she successfully removed the parasite despite his long, curly hair. He then let her return to sleep. Their friendship was deep, but not sexual. After seeing his astrological birth chart, she decided that a solid friendship with him was more important than occasional sex.

That night around 4 a.m. once Michael had finally retired, Nyna visited me. I was very surprised to see her, as Angel and I were so far from home.

The elfin elder smiled. "I am an elevated elf. My domain is the entire Earth plane. I can locate you and Angel anywhere you go."

"I am very pleased to see you, Nyna, though you usually visit with a purpose."

"Yes, Darci. Sottrol and I have been discussing you and Angel. First, we commend you for leading her to a quieter, more rural residence."

"But it does no good if she continually travels, going to concerts, visiting friends," I lamented. "I often wonder if she will ever stay still long enough to hear me talk to her. I have beamed light into the telepathic center in her mind ever since you made that suggestion, Nyna. I honestly thought that Angel and I would be communicating by now."

"Patience, Darci, patience," said Nyna, patting my shoulder, sending comets of energy zinging through me. "I am here to have a serious talk with you. It is time to make sure that Angel hears you. Since she has not chosen a cloistered existence, it is up to you to make sure she finds that quiet place where she can begin to listen."

"I've thought about this a lot," I told her. "I'm not sure how to do it."

Nyna sighed. As she grasped my hands with hers, I saw much compassion in her eyes and felt gentleness and kindness flow through me.

"My dear Darci, sometimes our charges must go through experiences in order to learn things, to face their karma. You know this."

I nodded, for indeed I had already seen this with Angel and others.

"In this case," she went on, "I fear the only thing to do is to bring a karmic injury into her busy life."

"Injury!" I exclaimed. "I would not hurt my charge for the world!"

"But, Darci, you want her to face her karma. You want her to move toward fulfilling her potential destiny. Sometimes a step on this path is suffering an injury."

"What kind of injury?"

"Let's look back to her incarnation three lifetimes ago when, in a fit of anger, she kicked and mortally wounded her eldest son."

My heart leapt. That was a very difficult incarnation. I was her partner in that lifetime. We struggled. We had eight children, and it was difficult for Angel, then a tall thin man named Gabriel, to make a living, though he tried. The most devastating part of that entire situation came after the child died. Gabriel never forgave himself, locking himself away. Because his right leg had been the agent of his son's demise, he blamed it and flailed it constantly. The broken man refused help from anyone, from me, his wife, from the priest, from the other children, from family, friends, and neighbors. Slowly he wasted away, censuring himself and his leg until the essence of his soul had shrunk to a tiny sphere.

Angel's spirit then had to go through much rehabilitation. Even though she had come a long way from the despair and self-loathing of that long-ago lifetime, she still carried some of its karma. I knew that the injury Nyna spoke of would involve my charge's karmic right leg. When she was born this time around, she was yanked out with a ghastly tool known as forceps. Because of its use, she became caught on her mother's pelvic bone. The attending doctor rotated her in the birth canal, and in the process, her right leg was twisted in and remained that way. This made it difficult for her in many ways. For instance, in elementary school, the main activity at recess was kick ball. My poor charge with her twisted leg and turned-in foot could kick only foul balls, and received much teasing and taunting from the other students.

So I knew that this leg would be the focus of her adversity, but I didn't know how I was supposed to facilitate an injury. I looked at Nyna, who was watching me, reading my thoughts.

"Darci, you will not have to do much," she told me. "There need be only one situation in which she puts herself, and that will be easily manifested with a little encouragement from you."

"You must give me some guidance, some hints at least," I said a bit desperately. "I really cannot force myself to do anything to harm her. It's not in my being to do so. I love her too much. Why, it's even written in the Spirit Guide Creed that we must never harm our charges. Nyna, I don't understand what you're saying."

Nyna's emerald eyes glistened, as her expression remained serious. "There will be a situation where she will be involved in doing something quite physical and at the same time she will be stirred to anger. That will be all it takes. After all, it was anger and her physical reaction to it which produced the karma in the first place three lifetimes ago."

Sighing, I tried again. "I still don't understand what I'm supposed to do. I don't know if I've ever felt this confused since becoming a Spirit Guide. Bringing an injury to my charge goes against my grain, against everything I was taught in Spirit Guide training, against my great love for Angel. Even though she does not yet know it, we are partners. Hurting her hurts me!"

"I do have a suggestion," responded Nyna, again with much compassion in her eyes. "Angel can do some repetitive activity that will prepare her for the injury, then in that instant when anger swells within her, you will know to prompt her to do something physical that will manifest the damage. I know it's not easy, Darci." Pausing, she stared at my sleeping charge. "Here is my idea. She has been yearning to play music, much as her first husband does, much as her rock star friend does. She has many songs within her. Helping her create them is something you can enjoy, too. Guide her to a simple instrument that she can use to compose songs."

"She likes guitar," I said.

"Very good. Something along those lines, something she can use to allow the music within her to pour forth into the world. Once she begins this process, she'll love it. You know she will. She'll sit for hours practicing. And if she sits with her karmic leg tucked under her while she plays, this repetitive position will put her in exactly the right state for this injury to occur."

"I just do not want to see her in pain," I reiterated even more strongly than before.

"Darci, if you want her to hear you, if you want her to know you, if you want her to love you, then help this injury come to pass. Think of this: it will be your joyful duty to help heal her. Through your attention and healing, she will come to know and love you. This will all turn out for her greater good, though it may not seem so at first."

Sighing, I shook my head. "I certainly can encourage her to write songs. I know she wants to. I certainly can bring her inspiration for songs. She is receptive to music of all kinds."

"There, you see?" said the elfin elder. "You can find your way through this. I know it's not easy. We are available to help you should you come upon stumbling blocks. For right now, see that she becomes immersed in writing, playing, and singing her own music. And then be on the watch for that moment when you can prompt her to physical action when she is angry. The injury will take care of itself." Nyna smiled, though there was sadness in her eyes. "Bless you, Darci, and please know in your heart that this is Angel's true path, karma that she must face, and in the long run, you are truly helping her. Sottrol, Orillo, and I will not be far."

With those words, she moved toward the window, gazed out into the warm Georgia night, and became a funnel of glittering radiance, which moved upward, vanishing through the ceiling.

Angel was an artist, creating all the time. Not long after her journey to Georgia, she purchased a baritone ukulele, an instrument that is tuned like the top four strings of a guitar. Since she had some experience playing guitar, the baritone ukulele was easy for her and exactly the right instrument for her to use to write songs. She played for hours, learning different chords and hand positions. She would choose a key, learn the chords in that key, then write a song in that key, including lyrics. Music poured out of her, song after song. I was amazed at the quality, the words, the emotion she wove into each piece. My charge had an eye for beauty and a reverence for nature that she was able to put into her songs. I was happy because she was happy. She was creating and loved nothing better. Sitting on the edge of her futon with her right leg tucked under her, day after day she played and wrote, strumming, singing, composing songs.

On a beautiful spring day in May 1989, Angel brought home trays of vegetable plants she had purchased. Dressed in her rag-tag gardening clothes, she went about placing the little plants into the freshly dug soil in her garden.

I must preface this next section with the following observation about Angel and the men with whom she became involved. There was intense restlessness inside of my charge, and I knew why. She was searching for me. I was her destined partner, but she did not find me in any of her lovers. When Angel was planting her garden that May, she was in transition between one man and another. She had been living with an eccentric artist, who was an odd sort of fellow, though he did care about her quite a bit. Her new infatuation was a student involved at the college radio station where she volunteered.

Then it came, the moment that Nyna had mentioned. The artist, who was sitting in the kitchen of the old cape, was extremely angry. He had just realized that Angel was moving on to a new relationship, and his anger filled the small room. Angel was washing the garden dirt off of her hands in the sink using the pump, and I could see that she was becoming very upset. My charge has always been extremely sensitive to the emotions of the people around her, and she immediately picked up on this man's rage. The anger overtook her and they argued. The entire kitchen was permeated with red, jagged light, and the situation was very uncomfortable for me, as it was for my charge. When I saw the fiery red vibrations and the bristling energy of anger, I knew that the karmic moment had arrived.

The physical activity that she was called to perform was watering the newly planted vegetable seedlings. She couldn't stand to be in the house anymore, so she stomped outside, slid the wooden cover off of the well, and began using a bucket to haul up water. She was standing awkwardly at the edge of the old stone well, her body twisted as she pulled up one heavy bucketful of water after another. I saw it happen. I saw the ligaments between her karmic leg and her hip shred to bits. She felt it go. I could see it in her face as her pelvis tilted and rotated, and the pain began.

It all happened rather spontaneously, much as Nyna said it would. I really did not do much more than lead her to the baritone ukulele. Glad that the elfin elder had prepped me, I was ready. I was there for her when the injury occurred. The damage was extensive, but initially she thought it was another muscle ache. Driving to her college friend's apartment, she took a long hot bath, which exacerbated her condition, causing the swelling around the tear to increase. In fact, nothing she did seemed to help. This was her first major injury in this incarnation, so she did not know to get immediate assistance. Of course, I did what I could, working with her energy field while she slept, but initially my healing attempts gave her little relief.

My heart broke for her. It was time for me to have a serious talk with Sottrol.

CHAPTER EIGHTEEN
FIRST CONTACT

On July 4, 1989, Angel's forty-third birthday, approximately seven weeks after the injury, I continued to stay close to my charge. For the last decade, she had been involved in an eccentric, unusual, rather anarchistic celebration of the country's independence, and this year was no exception. A group of friends, artists, musicians, and thespians wrote and produced an annual play, which they performed in a gravel pit. Hundreds of people attended every year. This particular year the theme was a spoof on the terrible oil spill that had occurred in Alaska that spring. My charge had written a song for the play to be sung by a group of women who were portraying the oil spill clean-up crew, "The Waltz of the Revolutionary Char Women." I could see that she was very excited about debuting the song. I had to hand it to her. Despite the ever-present pain, she performed well. She did not allow the injury to quell her creativity.

That night as Angel slept restlessly, I sat by her side, gazing out the window at the fireflies blinking in the field. Once again, I called for my mentor, Sottrol, and this time he came.

"Greetings, Darci," he began. "I apologize for not visiting sooner. I know you have been requesting my help these last few weeks." Sighing, he smiled a little. "Ah, but unfortunately, being a Master Guide means that I have many things to attend to."

"I'm glad to see you as always. You must know why I have been requesting your presence. Angel is in constant pain, and my healings do not seem to be helping. Watching her suffer is very hard for me."

"My dear Darci, I do not have to tell you that Angel is hurting because of her karma, which originated three lifetimes ago. She has a very serious imbalance in her soul, and that is why her injury is so severe and why she endures a great deal of pain."

"This doesn't seem right," I told him. "I cannot bear to watch her suffer as she does. I want to help her, but what can I do?"

"Do what you've been doing," he replied. "I know it doesn't seem like enough, but continue to balance her energy, heal her, love her. Stay as close as you can. Talk to her, Darci. Talk into her ear. Send loving thoughts into her brain along with the light that you daily send there. Keep it up. It will not be long before she does hear you. This is a breakthrough time for her and for you." Pausing, he stared into my eyes. "Being a Spirit Guide takes a great deal of patience, Darci. A conscious connection between you and Angel will come to pass. Focus on her, love her, care for her, talk to her, tell her who you are, and one day soon she will hear you."

"I understand your words, but they do not comfort me," I admitted.

"Look at it this way, Darci. You accomplished what was necessary for conscious contact to take place. She now lives in a quiet remote area. She has slowed down. She again lives alone, removing the distractions a roommate brings. Now that her birthday has passed, she will return to a more solitary existence."

"Sottrol, I have a question. A while back, Nyna came to visit me to tell me about the upcoming karmic injury to my charge. I was very surprised that she was the messenger. I thought it would be you bearing such news. You have been my mentor since I began training to be a Spirit Guide. I thought Nyna was mainly concerned with the elves and the arrival of the elfin avatar."

Sottrol smiled and moved closer, moonlight reflecting from the crystals in his beard. "Ah, you see, we are all working to make the arrival of the avatars possible, and the fact is that Angel has to clear her karma before she can be ready to foster this soul. It is in Nyna's interest and in the interest of all the elves that your charge faces and processes her karma." He studied my expression, then went on. "It may still be a while, Darci, for once Angel hears you, she'll have to learn how to communicate with you on a regular basis, which is precisely what we want to occur. Her body will have to adjust to new, unfamiliar energy. She will not be accustomed to constantly interacting with your high vibration in a conscious way."

"I know I can help her with any adjustments," I offered.

"You also must be aware of the project the Master Guides have chosen for the two of you. We discussed this before Angel was born. It has a high priority and must be completed first before you move on to help the elves."

"Oh." I was surprised. "So this undertaking with the elves, fostering the avatar, may be years away."

Sottrol nodded. "Yes. And in fact once you and Angel telepathically transcribe the important text for the Master Guides, information that is vital for human beings at this great turning point on Earth, then you may wish to have her write your story. This is a highly significant time for humanity. Finally, humans learn that there is far more happening on Earth than what their five senses provide to them. In particular, it is essential for humans to learn about their Spirit Guides, and having Angel write your story will be of great assistance to humanity." He gazed at me again, one eyebrow raised, evaluating my receptivity. "Once that second book is completed, then it will be time for your participation in the arrival of the elfin avatar."

Now that I had Sottrol with me, I wanted to ask the questions that had been circling around in my head. "Can you be more specific about the potential between Angel and me? What is our destiny?"

"Oh, Darci!" The radiant elder chuckled. "You know that you and Angel are meant to be partnered through the veil between worlds. The bonds you form between the earth plane and the Spirit Guide Plane are monumental. Your partnership will help many."

"I guess I don't understand exactly what's possible." I wanted details.

"Everything." His smile was wide. "Yes, you can partner her. Yes, once she knows you and grows to love you and understand your relationship, there is potential for marriage, and potential for you to parent the elfin avatar. Ah, but we get ahead of ourselves, Darci. Right now, focus on Angel, for she needs your healing love. Then, things will unfold just as they're meant to. It is your diligence, patience, perseverance, and kind attention to your charge that will make all this possible. Once she has conscious communication with you, she also will join us in helping all of this come about." He clapped his hand on my shoulder, causing a burst of electricity to pulse through me. "It's really wondrous, Darci. Please look past her current situation and her pain. Having Angel face her karma is a cleansing process. Soon you will be able to tell her why she suffered this injury. You will be able to remind her of the past lifetime in which the karma occurred. Once she understands, she can reach deep inside herself to forgive the man that she was in that long-ago lifetime, the man who kicked his son in anger and caused his death. Forgiveness will cleanse the karma that she carries from that incarnation. Once this has happened, Angel will be open and ready for so much more. Your Angel can help the earth plane immensely with you as her guardian and husband."

That word, "husband," shook me to my extremities, for I hadn't realized until that moment how much I wanted to be that for her, how much I wanted to love her as a partner and a wife. At that moment, it seemed both impossible and possible. On that day, her forty-third birthday, she had yet to hear me and know me, though I knew she felt my presence. Yet there was Sottrol, in his purple robes with his amazing luminosity, the wisest being I had ever known, telling me it was possible for me to be Angel's husband. The elder had never deceived me. He had always told me the absolute truth.

"It's up to you, Darci," he spoke quietly. "You can help her through this. The coming weeks may be challenging as she seeks answers and healing. It is appropriate for her to find a doctor, for she will need physical as well as spiritual assistance, for she has experienced a serious injury. As she receives physical help, you can provide help from the spiritual side. You can assist in bringing her to a point where she processes the pain, the karma, and rises out of this. I will offer your lovely charge a birthday present. Let us heal her together. Stand at her head, and I will stand at her feet. Let us send energy through her, cleansing the pain and preparing her for your arrival in her life. It's the next step of many on a glorious path that will help humanity, the elementals, and the earth."

So my mentor and I worked together to heal her. I saw that the cleansing and soothing we did, helped her to sleep more deeply, and I was glad.

The next few months, however, were tough for me and especially for Angel. My heart cried out for her, for she was in so much pain all the time. The discomfort caused her to isolate herself socially. That summer, she visited a local chiropractor, but when he examined her, he realized that the situation was serious, that she had waited too long after the injury. He instructed her to go home and apply hot towels to her lower back every day for a week, then come back to see him. She did as he asked, but an hour after this doctor tried to push her tilted pelvis back into alignment, her entire back went into spasm. I felt so helpless and my heart ached as she lay in utter pain on the floor of the college radio station, tears streaming down her face.

At that moment, I vowed to increase my efforts to help her. There simply had to be a way to turn this situation around.

However, initially nothing improved. I came close and surrounded her with my energy, loving her twice as much as I had before. I prayed for her; I prayed with her. Entwining my spirit arms around her, I stayed as close as breath, so close in fact that she began to consciously feel me.

One of her favorite stories was Jane Austen's *Pride and Prejudice*. She picked up the book to reread it while she was going through this period of pain, as the story distracted and comforted her. Being very creative, she began writing her own sequel to Austen's novel. In fact, she had notebook and pen with her when attending another doctor's appointment, a physician recommended by an acquaintance. She was hopeful that this doctor would be able to help her. Since it was a beautiful summer day, she sat outside his office writing away.

The doctor examined her and was rude, saying he couldn't help her in any way. The constant pain had broken down any self-restraint, and she began to weep as she left his office. She was crying so hard that when she backed her car out of his driveway, she accidentally dropped the car into a deep ditch and needed to go back inside to phone for a tow truck. Her eyes were red and swollen from tears and her hip and back throbbed with pain. I was at my wit's end and called for Sottrol's assistance again, but I had to wait patiently.

Finally, Sottrol visited me one evening as I sat near Angel, who was asleep on her pallet. It was the end of summer, and I was watching moonlight play on the leaves of the maple trees outside the old house.

"I know you are concerned about her," said my teacher as he put his arm around me.

"Sottrol! Greetings! Have you come to assist me? Angel is in need of so much help. She has not only injured her back, she has also lost her job and much of her confidence."

"Ah, you see, this is good," winked Sottrol.

"How can this be good?" I exclaimed. "She suffers so, and as much as I try, I cannot seem to help her."

"See the bigger picture, Darci," said my teacher softly. "In order for the conscious connection to be made between the two of you, Angel has to let go of much Earth business and slow way down."

I brightened immediately. "It's time! Sottrol, you're telling me it's time!"

Sottrol chuckled. "A little anxious are we, Darci? Yes, it's time, though you must proceed gently. Think of coaxing a seed to sprout, then nurturing the tender young plant as it pushes its way up into the world."

"All right. I understand," I said, perhaps too curtly, "but what's next?"

"For the next few weeks, do the following exercise. As Angel sleeps, activate the vertical energy flow through her body."

"Isn't that easier with two Guides?"

"Very good, Darci. Yes, that's correct. For that very reason, I'm sending you an assistant. She will arrive shortly, bringing instructions with her for the next steps."

"Who is she? Where is she?"

"Patience. Caroline will join you soon. There is something you can do on your own. Project an image into her mind."

"An image? Of what?"

"Of you, Darci. Choose carefully. This is how she will picture you for the remainder of her lifetime."

"I didn't learn this in class, Sottrol."

"Each and every relationship between a Spirit Guide and a human is unique. You know that. Many Guides focus on creating auditory connections with their charges because much precise information can be imparted in this way. For you and Angel, both the auditory and visual links can be easily established."

"So I must choose an image to project."

"Yes. Select one she will identify with and embrace. Now flood that little one with love. She has a great journey ahead of her."

My heart swelled with anticipation and love for Angel. I looked at her sleeping, curled up, oblivious to the conference that was taking place by her bedside. When I turned back, my teacher had vanished, though he left a hint of sweetgrass in the air.

Pondering what Sottrol had told me, I wondered what Angel would respond to … what would draw her to me? I reviewed the many lifetimes Angel and I had shared. Recalling our time together in Egypt, I speculated that perhaps projecting an image of myself as Hett, tall, dark, and devoted, might stir her, for she was now an astrologer as Tuura had been. When I lived as the Roman statesman Alger Matticus, I had been handsome and statuesque. Perhaps such a likeness would intrigue her. Then I saw myself as the Mayan corn farmer, Zontyl, muscular and brown. Maybe this picture would entice her, for she grew corn in her garden. But no. I stopped myself. "She will not consciously recognize these images. Her subconscious self may know them, but what will speak to her conscious mind?"

Gazing around her room, I found the answer. By her bedside lay the book *Pride and Prejudice*. In my last lifetime, I had been acquainted with Miss Austen. Her father was the pastor of the church that my family attended.

I chuckled when I recalled the day my aunt bustled into our sitting room for a visit. Evidently I was the object of the latest gossip. Word was out that young Miss Austen had written a novel in which one of the main characters was patterned after me. How cosmically appropriate that Angel had begun rereading this story and even writing her own version.

Since passing into spirit, I had continued to use the likeness of myself from my last incarnation; most souls do. It became clear to me that Angel would easily identify with a spirit friend from that era. It was an image she could see, accept, and embrace. This is how I eventually became known to her as Darci. She chose the variation on Austen's character Mr. Darcy. My spirit name is actually much longer and more complicated.

The next night as I again sat by Angel's bedside, I saw two female Spirit Guides floating across the field from the east. One was slender, wispy, vaporous, and looked very much like the Master Guide Esther. The other guide radiated just as much luminosity, but was plump, rosy, and dressed like a peasant woman.

"Greetings, Darci Stillwater," said the slender Guide wrapped in pastel veils. "You know me. I am one of the Esthers."

"Yes, hello. You were Life Guide to Angel's grandmother. I remember you."

"Darci, may I introduce Caroline? She is an expert in health and healing." The plump female Guide curtsied and smiled widely.

"Caroline, I'm very glad you're here," I said earnestly. "Angel is suffering tremendously."

"We can help her, Mr. Stillwater," Caroline replied.

"Please, call me Darci, and let's begin right away. Dear Angel needs relief."

Caroline directed me to kneel at Angel's feet while she sat at her head. Esther hovered over us, observing. Caroline worked quickly, first establishing a stream of white and green light between her hands on Angel's head and my hands cupped around her feet. Once the flow of energy was strong, Caroline nodded to Esther, who floated to the head of the bed. The plump, rosy Guide then moved to Angel's midsection and placed one hand above the injured area, the other below. I was surprised to see electricity crackle between Caroline's hands. She continued to pierce the injury with lightning bolts for quite a while. I watched the redness in Angel's aura dissolve into a light peach color.

Caroline looked at me and smiled. "She'll sleep through the night and awake rested. However, the injury is serious. She'll need more healings, and she must find real help on the physical plane as well."

The two female Guides then led me to a corner of Angel's room. Esther's green eyes glowed as she spoke. "Do you see how this injury is a gift to both of you?"

"A gift? You mean so she can process her karma? You must know that I dislike watching poor Angel suffer so."

Caroline chuckled. "Have you not been waiting for a chance to connect with your dear Angel?"

I nodded, as realization flooded through me. It was time for Angel and me to connect consciously through the veil between worlds. I was so elated that I danced a little jig. The two female Guides laughed, but quickly became serious again.

"Darci, please calm yourself. You must prepare her," Esther informed me. "Let me show you." She moved gracefully back to the pallet. I watched as the slender Guide created a sphere of golden energy between her hands, then slowly lowered the brilliant orb into Angel's head.

"Do this daily," said Caroline, as we watched the glow of sparkling golden light. "This gives extra energy to that part of her brain that receives telepathic communication."

"So she'll finally hear me talking to her!" I blurted excitedly. "I have been waiting so long for this. When … ?"

"Just keep at it." Caroline put an arm around me. "How soon Angel responds depends entirely on her."

Promising to return, the two female Guides took their leave. I sat the rest of the night at Angel's head whispering, "I'm here. I love you."

The big breakthrough, the moment I had been anticipating for over forty years, came shortly thereafter. It was September and the morning was bright. Mist lay in the glen, and dew outlined the fallen leaves. I drew very close to my beloved Angel. My heart ached with compassion as I saw her force herself to wash the dishes, a simple task for most, but very difficult for her. She primed the old hand pump in the kitchen and laboriously forced the handle down again and again until water spilled into the sink and the kettle. She then lifted the heavy kettle and moved it to the woodstove to heat.

An idea came to me. Perhaps music would cheer her. Projecting the image of a tall, dark-haired, English gentleman, I encircled her with my spirit arms and spoke softly in her ear.

"Might we listen to some classical music today?" I suggested. "You rarely listen to classical."

She stopped. She had heard me. My heart began pounding wildly. I knew I must continue speaking. "I'd like to hear some Mozart." I beamed the words into her telepathic center. "Though I believe you have but one Beethoven record."

"Classical?" I heard her say aloud. She walked into the back room where there was a wall of vinyl records. I guided her hand to the one Beethoven album. When she slid it from the rack, her eyes widened in awe, and I heard her gasp. "You really are here!"

She indulged my request, playing the entire record, scratches and all. As we listened, I again sent her the image of myself from my former lifetime, a gentleman of noble birth, handsome and refined, standing tall and proud in an elegant long coat. Her eyes glossed with tears. She not only saw me, she felt our deep connection, nearly swooning as I filled her aura with love. We were together again. This was the sweetest moment I had ever known.

CHAPTER NINETEEN
THE EXTRAORDINARY SOUL

Angel was elated, walking on air despite her continued discomfort, for now she had met me. I was exhilarated as well. The breakthrough had occurred. My charge began writing about me in a small journal.

Shortly after our first conscious contact, she visited her mother who at the time was managing a motel in Connecticut. From her mother's apartment, Angel traveled to Providence for a rock concert. She was particularly excited because another of her music friends, Natalie, and her band Ten Thousand Maniacs was opening for REM. There was a glorious moment when she and Natalie were in the lobby of the old hall. They grasped hands and spun each other around very fast, much like whirling dervishes.

I could see the difference in my charge: she was lighter, not so burdened. The contact between us had done amazing things for her energy field. As the two women spun faster and faster, they laughed, and I was happy. I knew that Angel had a long road of recovery ahead of her, but at least her spirits were high. During the concert, she danced, though often leaned against a column for support to give her back a rest. As the music filled her, she thought of me. Soon I would tell her about the book we would write for the Master Guides, but not yet. Right now we were just getting to know each other.

Late that night after the concert Angel was back at the motel, exhausted and asleep. As I was doing my usual round of energy work on her, Nyna arrived on the balcony in a blazon of white and emerald light. She floated through the glass sliding doors and embraced me.

"Congratulations, Darci. This breakthrough is the beginning of a wonderful relationship between you and your charge, one that will make a great deal of difference not only for humans but for the elves as well."

"Thank you, Nyna. Even though I want to tell Angel everything right away, I must restrain myself. I must proceed slowly, carefully, so that she continues to trust and believe me."

"No worries, Darci. You have plenty to talk to her about right now. Know that I am very interested in the progress that you make. The Seven Avatars are being prepared, though they will not arrive on Earth until the next wave of energy has lifted the consciousness of all."

"What wave is this?" I asked her. It seemed as though there was always more for me to learn.

"Physically, humans will see the wave as a band of photons surrounding the earth in her orbit. We from the spirit side call it a new ray of energy that has arrived to help the earth with the upcoming changes. It is meant to increase the vibration of the planet and all upon her so that all are open to much new information, including the arrivals of the avatars, though these events are still a number of years in the future."

"This new ray of energy, Nyna ... tell me more about it."

"It is a gift from the Creator," she replied with sparkle in her eyes. "The Earth is coming into a time of great transition, and instead of letting humans flail about, not knowing what is happening, the Creator is providing this helper ray to prepare them and provide information, guidance, and direction. This new ray brings a great opportunity not only to humans, but also to the elementals. You and Angel will write about it in this first project for the Master Guides." She stared into my eyes for a moment, then continued. "I come with a message specifically for you, Darci. The Master Guides wish to meet with you before you tell your charge about the project. They want you to read through the text and make sure the material is organized properly for humanity to receive. It is important that the information is easy for humans to read and understand. The Master Guides have done a fine job preparing it, but they want you to look it over. After all, your name will be on this book, as well as Angel's. If you wish, I'll stay with your charge while you meet with Sottrol, Arcillis, and the other Master Guides involved in getting this material ready. It is almost time for the text to be transcribed." She then smiled wider than I had ever seen. "Darci, I cannot tell you what an exciting time this is upon planet Earth. Probably in the entire history of this plane of learning, there has never been a time like this! And you and Angel are at the forefront … with others, of course. For now, just focus on her and the work that you do together so that it may manifest."

"So … I am to go and meet with the Master Guides now?" I was surprised.

She nodded. "Yes. And while I'm here with Angel, I shall bring a loving, healing touch to her, for I see how restless she is, how she is not comfortable in her own body. Even though you have now had conscious contact with her, she still has a ways to go as far as her personal healing is concerned. There is much to do, Darci, so go. Meet with the Master Guides."

Although I never liked to be far from my charge, I knew that this meeting must be important, so I agreed to go. As soon as I stepped outside the motel, Sottrol was there, ready to guide me to the conclave. Because I was with a skilled and experienced elder, our journey to the Spirit Guide Plane was nearly instantaneous.

Sottrol held onto my arm to steady me, as I needed a moment or two to adjust to the high vibrations and the blinding radiance of the meeting place, so very different from what I was used to on Earth. My first lesson as a Spirit Guide trainee had been spirit breathing, so I used that long-ago lesson to center myself and adapt to my new highly luminescent surroundings.

The others who were present waited patiently until I could see them clearly. Seven Master Guides, three females and four males, stood in a semicircle in front of a horseshoe-shaped bench. There was a separate seat for me in the opening. Once the introductions were made, the Master Guides sat, and I took that as my cue to sit down also. Three of the members of the Elevated Council, whom I had met before, were in attendance. Sottrol was to my left, the Master Guide Arcillis was to my right, and the Master Guide Esther across from me. All seven were exceedingly radiant, with their eyes being their most prominent feature, and they all had their amazing eyes on me.

The tallest Master Guide passed a tome to Sottrol, who presented it to me. "This is the text that we wish you to telepathically send, page by page, to Angel," my mentor told me. "It contains extremely important information for humanity at this juncture in the earth's evolution. We've taken the trouble to organize it, and we wish you to look it over. When you're sure that Angel is ready, begin transcribing daily a page or so at a time. The project will take the better part of a year to complete doing it this way, but this information is eternal."

Arcillis stood. "I'm the head of this project. It is I who wish to tell Angel about it, for this text is so important that it could make the difference between humanity's survival or extinction during the upcoming transition on Earth."

I'll admit that I was quite shocked when I heard this. "We will do everything we can to make sure this is exactly as you wish it to be," I told the seven.

"Good." Arcillis nodded.

Sottrol said, "This is an excellent exercise to strengthen the telepathic ties between yourself and your charge, so this benefits the two of you, as it benefits all of humanity, as it benefits us." He motioned toward the others in the group. "So this is very, very important."

I held the book close to me. It vibrated with an intensity that is difficult to describe.

"Begin soon," directed Arcillis. "It's best if your charge is transcribing this material by the time the new year begins."

"We think that she is ready," added Sottrol.

I nodded. "She is. She's ready and so am I. Thank you for this opportunity."

They all stood, and I automatically followed their lead. As I bowed to the others, Sottrol took my arm and led me from the room. We passed under an arched doorway. Everything was bright as we moved through hallways glowing with rich golden light. After several turns, I asked Sottrol exactly where we were.

"We're in a special wing of the Spirit Guide University used for conferences and meetings," he replied.

"Ah, back to the Spirit Guide University," I exclaimed. It was here that I had received most of my training to become a Spirit Guide, but it had been almost forty-four Earth years since I had been here.

Sottrol guided me to an intricate door that appeared to be made of wood, though I could never be sure of anything on the Spirit Guide Plane. The entire arched door was covered with intricate carvings of plants and animals. Sottrol pulled the handle on the giant door, which opened with ease. Everything seemed easy for my esteemed mentor. We walked into a garden. I gasped because I had never seen anything like it when I was here training to become a Spirit Guide. It appeared to be a garden from Earth except that the foliage glowed and the blossoms sparkled. There was a path of multicolored marbled stone, which we followed for a while until we came to a tall hedge that formed a small alcove. In the semicircle grew white roses, their smell so sweet that I felt light-headed. In the center was a bench made of that same multicolored marble.

"Let's sit here," Sottrol suggested. "There's one more important meeting I want you to take before you return to your charge."

"What meeting?" I asked, sitting beside him. I was impatient to return to Angel, though I knew she was in good hands.

He patted my hand, then surprised me by saying, "I'll be right back." My mentor stood and simply disappeared. He was so good at that.

I enjoyed sitting among the fragrant white roses, though all I could think of was Angel and how much she needed me. But I did not have to wait long.

Through the opening to the alcove stepped Sottrol and the most beautiful child I had ever seen. She looked to be about seven or eight years old. In a white dress with lace overlay, her hand in Sottrol's, she walked slowly toward me. Her rosy cheeks and deep golden hair curled in ringlets set off her astonishing emerald eyes. Around her was a halo of radiant white, and in her free hand, a single white rose.

They approached me, and she held the rose out for me to take.

She said simply, "Hi, Papa."

I was taken aback. "Hel-lo," I said haltingly.

The child and I stared at each other.

Sottrol spoke. "I want you to meet the soul that you have been hearing and reading about. You've known her in other lifetimes. This is your daughter to be, Emer-Aye."

She smiled at me, and I felt my own essence light up as if a giant fireworks display was going off within me. "Hello, Emer-Aye," I managed to say. "I've heard so much about you."

"Nyna told me that you have been reading about other Earth lifetimes I have lived. My most important lifetime is yet to come, and I really do want you and Angel to be my parents."

"I thought meeting her might motivate you," said Sottrol, with a twinkle in his eye. "She is beautiful, is she not?"

"Very," I smiled. "Emer-Aye, why do you appear to me as a girl? Are you not a fully matured, evolved soul? Or if you are preparing to enter the earth plane, would you not appear as a babe?"

She giggled, and I swear the roses bobbed in response.

My mentor answered this question. "You and Angel will write many books. The one that you hold on your lap is but the first. The second will be your story, Darci, the tale of how you became a Spirit Guide. And the third will be Emer-Aye's story. It's very important that humans learn about her. She will be a presence on the earth plane for hundreds, even thousands of years. Her purpose is to help humans understand the world of elementals. She will have the unique talent of being able to appear to humans."

"I see," I said, still puzzled, for he had not answered my question.

"Wait, Papa. He has not finished," she giggled. "You see I will be seven going on eight years old when you and Mama write my book. I thought that this would be the best way to present myself to you, because as you two are writing about me, this is how I shall look." She laughed again.

Sottrol moved to my side and lifted the tome off my lap. "Hug your daughter, Darci."

She ran into my arms. The energy of our embrace was so strong that we actually levitated. I recalled all the lifetimes that I had learned about. This magnificent soul had been Jasmina, conceived in a sacred temple ceremony;

Rahid, the boy who understood elephants; Leijasa, who heard the trees speak; Naquahris, great healer and wise storyteller; and Jing Lei, who had the ability to see and hear Spirit Guides. And now she was going to be my child once again, though many times more evolved. Then I thought, *but I, too, have evolved, for I am a Spirit Guide now.*

She laughed, then kissed my cheek. "Give a big hug to Mama. I think she probably needs it right about now."

"Yes," said Sottrol, as he lifted Emer-Aye out of my arms. "I think it's time for you to return to Angel, Darci. Now you have your motivation."

I could not take my eyes off the radiant little girl with her elfin ears and her bubbly, effervescent energy that I had experienced around Nyna and Orillo. The sparkling shimmering light around her was second only to her amazing emerald eyes.

"I don't want to let you go yet," I told her. "I've just met you again. Your essence is so beautifully green. You are just … so lovely."

"Thank you." She did a little curtsey.

"She carries an emerald essence because she represents the earth's flora," Sottral informed me. "She has, as do all the elves, ties to the flora, and her brilliant green energy means the flourishing of the plant life on Earth. You should know that, Darci. Thank the elves, for they are the ones who keep the plants and trees healthy and thriving. They are the ones who heal the flora, who spread the seed and see that it is fertile. The elves are extremely important on the earth plane, yet most humans don't know about them. Emer-Aye will change this."

"I can't wait to meet Mama," she said.

At that moment, a female elf appeared in the opening of the hedgerow. She looked much like Nyna, though younger.

"Serina, you may take her now," Sottrol told the elfin woman. "Darci and I must be getting back to the earth plane."

Serina quietly took the little one's hand and began leading her away, though Emer-Aye kept her eyes on me. The elfin girl gave a little wave before she disappeared.

Sottrol placed the book back in my hands, motioned for me to stand, then hooked his arm in mine. Several flashes of light later, we were standing outside the Connecticut motel again. This time I had a tome in my arms and much love for sweet Emer-Aye in my heart.

When we entered the motel room, Nyna was sending pulses of white and green light down through Angel's head. The light was circling around my charge's hips where the injury was located.

The elfin elder saw us and smiled. She could easily see the difference in me. "You've met her," she said. "You've met the elfin avatar."

I nodded, speechless, motioning toward her with the book.

"This has been an eventful night for you, Mr. Stillwater. Sottrol and I will leave you to assimilate all you have experienced."

"Angel had a big night, too," Sottrol observed. "She visited her famous rock-and-roll friends."

"And I met the extraordinary soul who is to be our daughter," I managed to say. "Sottrol, Nyna ... I really want this to come about. I want to do everything I can ... not only to help Angel, but to make these things you speak of possible ... the books you say we will write, and the birth of our daughter. It's astounding to me ... awe-inspiring."

Sottrol put his arm around me and hugged me, which seemed to center me and settle me down. "All in good time, Darci." He nodded toward the book in my arms. "Now you have your first project, something for you and Angel to focus on. This is good. This is as it should be."

Nyna said, "Hold in your heart the image of the elfin avatar, for she will become a part of your life before you know it."

"One step at a time, Darci," Sottrol told me.

"Yes." I lifted the book, stroking its glowing white cover. "I understand that this project is significant."

Sottrol moved in front of me and looked me in the eyes. "Make sure that Angel hears every word correctly. Practice telepathy with her in other ways before you begin sending her the text. I know how diligent you are, Darci.

You were one of my finest students. I know you will do an excellent job with this. Angel will want to do a good job, too, once you and Arcillis explain the project to her. Together you and your charge will be an unbeatable team, working between worlds to help the Earth and other realms as well."

After uttering those words, Sottrol escorted Nyna out through the glass doors onto the balcony. The elfin elder waved as my mentor nodded, then they transformed into glowing spirals of light. Sottrol's funnel of light was brilliant white and blue; Nyna's was bright white and emerald. The spirals revolved for a few spectacular moments, then lifted up and out of sight, leaving a slight glow on the balcony.

Amazed at what had transpired that evening for both of us, I sat on the corner of Angel's bed, holding the tome. This was certainly a night to remember. Yet as I gazed at the sleeping woman, I realized how much lay ahead. I hoped that she would understand all of it. I had faith that she would agree to partner me in all the endeavors. At this point, we had just made first contact, so I had to nourish our telepathic communications, then focus on writing this first book. In my heart, I held the hope that in the not-too-distant future, we would be husband and wife, united through the veil between worlds, and we would become the parents of the beautiful child I had met. My inspiration high, I knew it was my job to educate Angel in everything I had learned and to make sure that she, too, was highly motivated. "Not an easy task," I sighed, "but very worthwhile."

Lying next to her, I placed my spirit arms around her and simply loved her. I loved her until the entire room was filled to overflowing with brilliant pink light. Her energy field began to shimmer with the intensity of it, and somehow I knew that everything would work out.

Three months later, the week before Christmas, Angel visited her mother again. She brought with her fresh-cut boughs of fir, strings of lights, candles, crystals, and decorations for the guest room where she set up a magical environment. In this quiet space she meditated every day and received healings from Esther, Caroline, and me. By the time Christmas arrived, my dear Angel shone bright as a beacon. On Christmas morning she went to wish her mother Merry Christmas and to have breakfast. The television was on with news of a great revolt in Romania where the people had killed the king and his family. It was horrible news for such a holy day, and Angel took it very hard. She returned to her room to cry. I could see grief for the plight of humankind pouring out of her.

"Darci, when will this end?" she sobbed. "When will humans stop killing and torturing each other?"

I comforted her and watched as the tears cleansed her energy field even further. Once she had cried herself out, she meditated. I was pleased. I could see that her aura was sparkling and she was vibrating at a very high rate. The daily meditations had truly made a difference.

As I was holding my dear one, Esther floated through the window with the message that Arcillis would be arriving soon and wished to speak directly to Angel. Master Guides do not often make their way to Earth, though Arcillis had told me that he wanted to tell Angel of the first book himself, so I knew this was a significant event. The vibratory rate of a Master Guide is very high, and most humans, even those who connect consciously with their own Spirit Guides, would not easily communicate with a Master. However, I knew Angel was ready. Just to be sure, I filled her aura with gold and white light.

The weather had been incredibly cold for December, but this Christmas Day the temperature moderated enough for Angel to bundle up and go out for a walk. Arcillis arrived, ready to introduce her to the next phase of our mission. He began talking to her the minute she stepped into the cold, crisp air. Angel knew immediately that it was not me speaking. She could discern the slight ringing sound that accompanies communications from Master Guides. I stayed very near and listened in on the conversation.

"Greetings. We see your sorrow for the earth. All will change," began Arcillis.

Angel heard. "I can't wait," she said aloud as she walked down the driveway.

"How would you like to be a leader in the new time?"

She stopped in her tracks. "What exactly does that entail?" she asked skeptically.

"First, we'd like you to telepathically transcribe some information and make it available to humanity," Arcillis answered.

"What is this information?"

"Humans are ready to know more about why they are here and how to improve their lives. All the material has been carefully prepared by the Master Guides. We would like you to rise each morning and work with your Spirit Guide, Darci. He will give you the data sentence by sentence."

She agreed to try this, and at that moment our mission together began in earnest. I was joyous. At last we would be working together as a team on a daily basis. At last we would be moving forward, pursuing our purpose on Earth.

On December 28, 1989, we began writing what was to become *The Dawn Book*. I taught Angel a condensed version of the grounding and clearing meditation that she could use each morning to get herself in the proper state to receive the information. It worked beautifully. She was a natural at this kind of work. At first light I would awaken her. We would then sit together in the corner of her bedroom. I would speak and she would write in a notebook. Later each day, she would read that morning's entry. Often it would surprise or astound her. I was proud of my Angel because she was consistent and devoted to the work.

During the year that we were writing this book together, Angel and I became even closer. As data flowed from me to her, our channel of communication strengthened and widened. Without telling her, I made a resolution to court her. She was alone, no man in her life. If she gave me a chance, I could show her that I was the one she had been searching for all those years and that I could love her as well if not better than any Earth man.

CHAPTER TWENTY
CRUCIAL UNION

Opening Angel's heart and mind to the possibility of taking a mate through the veil between worlds was not an easy task. There were many hurdles. The first challenge taught me a great deal.

Angel was still adjusting to her newfound telepathic abilities. Because our connection was so strong, the dialogue between us flowed easily for the first few weeks. One gray autumn afternoon as we walked the country road by Angel's home, she asked me quite pointedly, "Who are you? I know you are my Spirit Guide, but who are you really?"

I suppose I could have answered in a number of ways; however, my heart spoke for me. "Your husband," I said.

As soon as she heard those words, a curtain of static flew up between us and communication was cut off. She mistrusted what she heard, thinking that it was her imagination. All had been going so well, but now a seemingly impenetrable wall stood between us.

That evening sitting on the woodpile near the house, I was very discouraged. I had tried several times to reconnect with Angel, but the static surrounding her made any communication between us impossible. I sighed deeply, then perked up as the aroma of sage floated by.

"Ho, Darci," said a familiar voice. "One little setback and you are downcast. That's not like you."

"Sottrol, I am so glad to see you." I hugged my mentor with gusto.

The elder settled on the log next to me. "You cannot blame her, Darci. She's lonely. She lives out here on her own, away from society. She thinks solitude inspired her imagination."

"She thinks she invented me to ease her loneliness," I added.

"Dear Angel has longed for your connection since her birth. It's difficult for her to accept that it exists, and that it is here, now."

"Sottrol, she knows me. Her soul knows me. Surely she'll come to accept that I exist … that I am real."

"Tell her that, and send her love. Love is the one thing that will penetrate that shield of static she has unwittingly erected. Love, Darci, that's your tool. Now use it."

With those words the wizard rose, took two steps toward the house, and disappeared to the sound of tinkling bells.

I wasted no time. Angel was just retiring for the night, so I sat by her bedside and pumped love into that wall of static. I aimed for her heart, though I couldn't see much through the crackling and popping. At that moment I wished I'd had a class in penetrating static.

My persistence paid off, though it took nearly ten days to clear Angel's energy field enough for us to begin communicating again. She wanted to reconnect. In fact, she sat down with her ukulele and wrote a song, which contained many of the questions she held in her heart about relating to me. I treasure it to this very day, a beautiful song called "Quarter Turn."

From that first static-filled situation, I learned to be cautious and gentle when approaching the subject of marriage with Angel. Patience was my watchword. I did not bring up the subject again for over six months.

When warm weather returned in the late spring of 1990, Angel walked to her favorite giant ash tree located in the middle of a remote field, sat beneath it, and gazed out at the mountains. I waited until she had settled down, then sent down a stream of white light into her mind followed by rays of radiant pink with the message "I love you." I watched her relax as she received the love bath.

"I love you, too, Darci," she spoke aloud.

I moved so close to her that my spirit body was pressed against her human one. "Please do me the honor of becoming my wife," I whispered to her while radiating as much love as I could.

This request surprised her, and I thought perhaps static would negate communications between us again, but at this point her heart and mind were more open.

"How can you be my husband, Darci?" I heard her project telepathically. "Can you carry firewood? Can you haul water? Can you fix the brakes on my car? Can you make love to me?"

"I love you so much," I began my answer, "and I can help you with many things. Yes, yes, yes ... I can love you better than any Earth husband."

"Darci, I need time. Your proposal is too much for me right now. Let's just focus on completing the book. We can talk about this again after it's done."

I was not disappointed at all for I had perseverance and thought her request a sensible one. She would warm up to the idea of becoming my wife because I would continue to love her so dearly she would not be able to say no. Doing as she asked, I did not bring up the subject of marriage for many, many months.

It took us nearly one full year to write *The Dawn Book* together. By December 1990, she had completed the text and four illustrations. After the holidays, she began typing the handwritten pages on an electric typewriter. War in the Persian Gulf was occurring at that time, and this upset her greatly. Typing the book brought her comfort.

In her search for help for her lower back and hip, Angel first went to see some healers privately, then began attending their monthly meetings. At each gathering, there would usually be a presentation of some kind, then healings, then refreshments. Angel and I offered information from *The Dawn Book* at one of these meetings, and there was much interest.

Later that spring, a friend came to Angel with money for her to self-publish a limited edition of *The Dawn Book*. She designed a simple cover. A deep rose color at the bottom, which faded to white at the top, it looked like the glow in the eastern sky at first light on a clear morning. In July 1991, one hundred thirty soft cover books were ready, and the project, at least in my eyes, was complete. I was pleased and excited too, because the time had come to once again ask her to marry me.

I had to find a way to show her that I could be a real husband to her. Surely I could touch her as deeply as I had before. Knowing that if I came to her in a dream, it would not be real enough for her, I decided to reach out while she was awake and fully conscious. Besides, utilizing our conscious connection was a part of our mission. I came up with a two-part plan.

I saw the opportunity to implement part one on a beautiful summer day. Angel was in her neighbor's field sitting under the giant ash. The mountains in the distance were misty blue in the hazy summer air. I moved close so that my energy field nearly engulfed hers and sent rays of powerful white light to her entire spine and head, opening all her chakras. Next I beamed brilliant pink light to her lower three chakras and pumped love energy into her; she was surprised at her arousal.

"Darci, is that you?"

"Yes, dear one. I love you."

"What are you doing?"

"I am showing you that I can love you as a husband loves a wife."

"I wondered when you would bring up marriage again."

"The book is finished, and I would like you to consider my proposal."

"Darci, I'm on Earth. I have to deal with reality. Would marrying you mean I couldn't take an Earth husband?"

"You can still marry a human if you so choose."

"I'll have to think more about this, Darci."

I expected such a response and was glad she was at least considering my offer. I had long ago processed jealousy out of my energy pattern, as all Spirit Guides do. If she chose a human partner, I would still love her, whether or not she married me. I would love the man as well, and work with his Guide to keep the two of them on their spirit paths.

Part two of my plan was brilliant, if I do say so myself. Angel was scheduled to lead another healing group meeting. She planned to take the group through a meditation and visualization that would help the members consciously connect with their Spirit Guides. During the days leading up to this meeting, I focused on sending her pure love all day and all night. Never was she out of the stream of radiant pink energy that I was projecting to and around her. The morning of the meeting, she sat at dawn with Caroline, Esther, and myself to prepare. The two female Guides knew of my plan and encouraged me to implement it. We told Angel that after she led the group into meditation, Spirit Guides would bring gifts to their charges. At the end of the meditation, each member would describe the gift that he or she had received.

Angel followed the outline we Guides had designed, including the specific visualizations she was to use. When all were deep in meditation communing with their Guides, I knelt before her with a bouquet of luminous spirit flowers and formally proposed marriage once again.

I poured my feelings out to her. "Dear one, we have been partnered many times; we are bonded through time. I love you so very much, and I would be honored if you would become my wife." I followed this with an intense surge of love energy that caused her to vibrate and tingle.

Her heart chakra opened like a beautiful rose, and she telepathically sent a one-word reply that would change our lives. "Yes."

I was overwhelmed with joy. Such exuberance filled me that I wished to tell my mentors and teachers the good news, but had to be patient. Angel was leading a class, and I was there to support her.

Once all the other members of the group had related their experiences in meditation with their Guides, it was Angel's turn. When she told the group that I had proposed, and she had agreed to marry me, her Spirit Guide, they were astounded at first, then supportive. Congratulations came from every corner, and Angel invited them all to our wedding. I had done it! We were engaged!

It was some time before we set the wedding date. As an astrologer, my mate wanted to select it carefully. With a little guidance from me, she chose November 1. For centuries, humans have held that the veil between worlds is at its thinnest and most transparent on October 31 and November 1. The first of November is a sacred day because it begins the Celtic New Year, an excellent day to begin our married life together.

All Saints Day dawned cloudy and rainy, but this did not dampen our joy. In fact, the downpour was helpful in making the connection between worlds. Rain cleansed the atmosphere, making it easier for Angel to work with higher vibrations.

The one main room in Angel's little rustic home was clean and filled with white chrysanthemums. The small group of friends brought food, including a wedding cake. Candles were placed around the room and an altar on the table. The elder from the spiritualist healing group stood and gave a blessing.

On the spirit side, there was much activity. Literally hundreds of Guides gathered to witness our marriage. All the Guides I knew from my studies at the university and all my teachers were there, plus many of the Guides we had met through doing readings for humans. The crowd was tremendous. Arcillis, Sottrol, and Nyna stood with me as Angel and I exchanged vows.

An incredible plume of light, a fountain of radiance, rose from that humble little farmhouse. The energy connecting the Spirit Guide Plane with Earth was flowing freely back and forth between my partner and me. As the rain poured down, the light got stronger until a beam of brilliant white engulfed Angel on Earth and me on the spirit side. Our marriage not only made this extraordinary bond possible, it also made this blessed connection permanent. As long as Angel walked the earth in a human body, this shaft of white light would connect us. This was our gift from the Creator.

For the next several years, Angel continued to practice astrology, work on commercial radio, and volunteer on noncommercial radio. During this time, she and I helped people by doing readings. Her telepathic ability to see and hear me meant that she could see and hear other people's Spirit Guides as well. Before every session, she would prepare very conscientiously in dawn meditation, grounding and clearing herself in order to trust what she was seeing and hearing from the visiting Spirit Guides. Learning early on not to depend on her own finite energy, she asked that energy from the Creator flow through her and power each session. Because Angel was new at this, she asked people to donate whatever they felt the reading was worth to them.

My charge was basically a humble person, uncomfortable in the role of being the link between people and their Spirit Guides. Although Angel was happy to help people, she grew to feel that she could help them more by teaching them how to see and hear their Guides for themselves. With encouragement from me, she moved from doing readings to teaching small groups, always ending each session by doing readings for those present. When conducting seminars, she sometimes explained her motivation by using the adage: Give a man a fish, and he eats for a day. Teach a man to fish, and he eats for a lifetime.

The time was right for such classes. Connecting through the veil to spirit helpers was becoming easier. The vibrations of the planet and all upon her were increasing due to the new ray of energy. The telepathic centers in people's brains, long dormant in most, were finally being activated. Human beings were ready for the information and teachings that Angel and the Spirit Guides offered.

∞

In July of 1993, Angel joined the cast of the musical *Annie Get Your Gun* at the local historic summer theater. There she met Graham, another cast member and her future Earth husband. On their first date, he bought a copy of *The Dawn Book* from her, so Graham knew about me and my relationship to Angel from the start. It did not deter him. They married in 1996, a joyful event.

The year of their wedding was significant for another reason. The government of the United States passed the Telecommunications Act of 1996, which eventually changed her life and the lives of many. This act allowed corporations to buy up several local radio stations in the same market, something that was not possible before. The face of radio changed as the profession became a shadow of its former self. No longer were many stations locally owned and operated. They were managed and programmed by corporations based in Texas or California by people who had never set foot in the Northeast. In Angel's mind, this change destroyed the very purpose of radio, originally meant to serve local communities with public service announcements, advertising, and requests. One after another, the local stations became computerized or broadcast satellite feeds and cut staff members. Somehow, my charge managed to keep a commercial radio job until the autumn of 1999.

I knew she was heartbroken because radio was in her blood. She continued to volunteer at the Colby College station, keeping her finger on the pulse of new music. However, she no longer had a job or income, and I could see that her self-esteem suffered from this loss.

Losing the job freed up her time for a new project. Wanting to help her heal, I told her that it was time for her to write my story. Though I had mentioned it before, I had not given her any details until this moment.

"Please, dear one, write the story of how I became a Spirit Guide," I requested.

She and I spent the first year of the new millennium doing just that. This was a year when we became even closer because I told her about a number of the lifetimes we had shared. I also detailed all the training I had received to become a Spirit Guide, which was an eye-opener for her.

Graham and Angel had built a cozy, cedar, passive solar house on the same land as the old place, an efficient dwelling with the bedrooms downstairs and the living space upstairs. June brought the blackberry blossoms, so the air was sweet with their fragrance. My charge and I were writing about our incarnation in Egypt, a lifetime when Angel was a healer, a teacher, and an astrologer to the pharaoh. That night as her husband's Spirit Guide, Lilyanna, was attempting to move stress out of his body through his feet, I was sitting on the edge of my charge's bed with my spirit hand on her tender stomach settling her emotions. Gazing out of the window, a glimmering glow in the garden caught my eye. The glow became a globe of swirling white light, and I knew we had a visitor. Nyna appeared and moved toward us.

Standing, I greeted her through the open window. "Nyna, hello! I have not seen you for many years!"

"Darci, so good to see you. As you well know, I have been preparing Emer-Aye for her arrival on the earth plane."

"Will this happen soon? The vibrations of the planet have increased significantly."

"Yes. The time is near." She smiled and her aura brightened further. "In fact, the children being born now are coming in already programmed with the energy of the new time. Emer-Aye is no exception."

Moving outside the window, I opened my arms. Nyna floated over and embraced me, filling me with an electric tingling sensation.

"Darci, you have done wonderfully well," she told me, stepping back. "*The Dawn Book* is magnificent. The work you do with Angel is excellent and very much appreciated by those of us in spirit."

"Thank you." I bowed slightly, then stared into her vibrant green eyes. "The arrival of the Seven Avatars is quite soon. I can feel it."

"Correct. You are very perceptive." She held my gaze. "I am here because it is time for you to talk to Angel about parenting the elfin avatar."

"I have not yet mentioned it to her," I confessed.

"This is the perfect time," she told me. "You and Angel are working together daily, writing the new book. Your telepathic link is stronger than ever. Tell her now. She will hear you clearly when you explain." She saw my hesitation and continued, "Look, Darci. She trusted you enough to marry you through the veil. She will trust you again when you suggest that you and she parent this amazing elfin child."

"But, Nyna, tell me exactly what will happen to Angel. I know her. I must explain everything in detail before she will agree to anything. Will she become pregnant as an Earth woman normally becomes pregnant? What do I say to her?"

"Of course it will not be as Earth children are born, Darci. However, this is what's important here. Emer-Aye needs to have the experience of being inside an Earth woman's body. Her soul will actually enter Angel's womb for several weeks before the birth, as is usual in a human pregnancy." Nyna could see I was processing this information, but she continued. "Once Angel agrees to parent the elfin avatar, tell her that the pregnancy is for eight instead of nine months. In a human birth, the mother grows a fetus, then the soul enters the fetus in the days or weeks before birth. In Angel's case, the fetus is a sphere of energy. Tell her that we will prepare her body to receive the high energy that comes with this advanced soul. We will make sure that her body is ready. As the months go by, her vibration will increase until she is ready. This will be her pregnancy."

After a pause, I asked, "What about the birth?"

"Emer-Aye is to be born at the end of October 2001. The actual birth will be painless and joyful. Angel will experience sensations, but they will be exhilarating."

"This is a great deal of information to tell my charge," I pointed out. "A lot even for Angel."

"My dear Darci, you make love to her. You bring your energy inside of her. She will understand this." The elder moved closer. "Angel is a natural mother with nurturing instincts. In her past lifetimes, she has had many children. Indeed, the two of you have parented dozens together. Remember when I visited you the evening of Angel's first birthday? It was then I told you of the Sabian Symbols."

My mind flashed to the very moment. Sottrol had helped me find the reading for the symbol that pertained to Angel.

"This is what the Sabian Symbol is about, Darci." She placed her hand on my arm. "Look, there have been several great souls who have in the past returned to Earth to help humanity. Jesus, Mohammed, Buddha, and others were extraordinary teachers, and so will the Seven Avatars be. These are all highly evolved souls who will arrive on Earth in different ways to help with the upcoming transition. This is a joyful time, Darci, for even though the Earth is facing great chaos, disruption, and change, not only is the new ray of energy in place, but these seven great teachers are due to arrive also."

"Will they all come as babies?"

"It is true that most of them will still be children when the transition occurs, but they will be old enough to help, and then they will take leadership roles in the new time, each in her own way. Emer-Aye, as you know, will focus on the flora. The vegetation has the potential to save humanity in this time of change. Understanding propagation of plants, their properties, and uses for food and for healing will be Emer-Aye's forte. She'll teach new ways to approach the flora. But you know all that, Darci. What is important now is to tell your charge."

Overwhelmed by all I'd heard, I stood speechless.

"The Sabian Symbol for the day of Angel's birth is the symbol for degree one hundred two of the Great Wheel. The image is three Tibetan monks sitting at the feet of a mother who is nursing a baby. The newborn in her arms glows with the incandescent brilliance of an advanced soul."

"I remember," I managed to say.

"This is your destiny, and hers. You both have been primed for this. And it will feel right to her. Trust her instincts and her intellect. You just have to have the courage to tell her."

"Yes … courage," I murmured. "I wish I could spare Angel all of this and carry the child myself. I wish it could be me."

"Darci, it must be an Earth woman, a human, and Angel is the best candidate. Emer-Aye needs to be inside of a human body to understand all the workings of a human being and to connect with humanity the way she needs to. Yes, she has walked the earth as a human in former lifetimes, as you well know, but this experience simply must begin for her inside the physical body of a woman." Nyna stared straight into my eyes. "I suggest that you radiate much love to your charge as you explain all this. She will feel it. Well, Darci … will you ask her to partner you in this extremely important endeavor?"

"How much time do I have?"

"The conception is to be next February, and she will need to prepare even for that. Convince her soon. You can do this." She drifted backward toward the garden. "As soon as Angel agrees, I will return with more information. Blessings to you, dear Spirit Guide."

Her radiance grew brighter until it obscured her features, then her form, and became a sphere of rotating bands of white and emerald light. The orb rose higher and higher until I could no longer distinguish it from the many stars overhead.

CHAPTER TWENTY-ONE
LIGHTING THE FLAME

Two days before Angel's birthday, the field outside of her bedroom window was filled with fireflies. Their blinking blended with the starry sky, sparkles emanating from both heaven and Earth. Angel was alone, as I had asked her to spare me some time. Graham had gone on to rehearsal for the Fourth of July play, so the house was quiet. I wasted no time, loving her with as much energy as I could project, asking her if I could deposit some of my love luminescence within her. I mentioned the possibility of children. She was stunned and unsure if she heard me correctly.

The next day my charge sat writing in her journal as she did most mornings. Often she would close the day's entry by allowing me to say a few words.

"Darci," she wrote, "last night I thought you said we could have children. How is that possible? Can you explain?"

"Good morning," I replied telepathically. "Of course, Love. You heard me correctly, as you usually do. Our union is blessed and unique to heaven and Earth, so we have the opportunity to take it to new places. We unite what is above with what is below. Your physical body is beyond having human children, but is just right for having a spirit child. A number of things would be similar to a human pregnancy, yet taken to a new level. Step by step we shall go if you are willing. You are a wonderful, trusting partner. I love you so deeply. We can change the norm."

After writing down my words, she said, "I don't understand how this can happen. I'm a human woman and you are my Spirit Guide."

"There are many possibilities for us," I told her. "First, please know that nothing negative is associated with our union. It is blessed and constantly held in light. As you have learned by writing my story, which is really our story, we have parented many children throughout a number of lifetimes. Think about this. If our union is truly about uniting two worlds, then children are a possibility."

Sighing, she wrote what I said, word for word. After a few moments, she replied, "This is way too strange, Darci. I'm uncomfortable with the idea of having a child with you. I can't do everything you ask, you know."

"I know. It is very good that we can communicate like this because any misunderstanding can be corrected. First, let me say that my love for you is so deep and so strong that I find it difficult to adequately express the torrent of feelings I have for you. I continually look for new ways. One possibility is very familiar to us both, the process of fertilization, pregnancy, and birth. What may appeal to you, my independent and innovative wife, is the pioneering concept that one in spirit and one in human form can share such an activity. The result would not be a human child. Only the Creator has that power. However, with the Creator's blessing, we can have a spirit child together. We would be creating a vessel for an energetic being, not a physical, carbon-based one as in a human pregnancy. Let me conclude by saying that my intention is to encourage our exchange of love, deepen our connection, and be of assistance to the Earth Mother."

Ten days later, Angel's cat Luna gave birth to five kittens. While my charge was meditating, listening to the sound of the mother cat's purr, I sent her the image of fertile silt washing from the hills and mountains into a river valley. Along with this picture, I radiated nourishing love light to her. As usual, she knew what I was doing.

In her journal, she wrote, "Darci is helping create a fertile, nourishing environment in my womb, something I have not had in my current lifetime. This opportunity waited until I was unmistakably in menopause. Long ago I decided not to load another human baby onto this planet, which needs no more people. Now Darci tells me that I can participate in a spirit pregnancy and birth if I wish to. I trust him. He has never led me astray. If this can truly happen, then life is strange, exciting, and beyond anything I'd imagined. I ask for protection and guidance as I make this decision."

That night as moonlight illuminated the features of my sleeping charge, a globe of glimmering gold and green energy appeared in the field outside the window. The form of Prince Orillo emerged from the ebullience.

Moving toward him, I grinned. "Orillo! It has been far too long! I'm glad to see you."

"And I, you, Darci," he replied, flipping his shimmering emerald cape behind his shoulders. "I'm officially moving to the neighborhood now that our avatar will be born here."

"B-but that is not yet certain," I stammered. "Angel has not yet agreed to allow the pregnancy. She is mystified by my request. Part of her feels that it is an imagined fantasy to make up for the fact that she has not birthed any human children in this lifetime."

Orillo laughed outright. "Darci, surely you remember. In a former lifetime you and Angel were responsible for repopulating an entire region of China after a great flood. She has done her duty as far as birthing human babies. You both have."

"Yes," I sighed. "Sixteen children. I remember."

"You, my friend, are a great persuader," the elfin prince encouraged, "plus Angel loves and trusts you. Why have you not succeeded in enlisting her assistance?"

"She hasn't said no."

Moving closer, Orillo stared at me with his amazing green eyes. "Darci, let me help. Let me talk to her. I'll explain how important this project is to the elves and to the earth."

I smiled. "You're right. Your input may be the missing piece Angel needs. I'll encourage her to walk by the river tomorrow. Meet us there."

Angel loved to amble along the riverside path that had originally been built as a railroad bed. It was level, so walking there was easier on her injured hip. The next day, the Kennebec River reflected its banks and the sky like a polished mirror. Dusk was approaching and many birds serenaded Angel as she walked from the dam to the bend in the river.

"My dear Angel, I have some friends for you to meet," I began. "I'd like to introduce elfin royalty, Prince Orillo."

Sensing the prince and his entourage, she ventured, "Hello, Prince."

"Greetings, beautiful one," said the prince. "On behalf of all the elves, I am here to encourage you to partner with Darci to parent a spirit child, our elfin avatar. The elves need a couple who works through the veil as you do to accomplish this."

Hearing Orillo clearly, my charge asked, "We would have an elfin baby?" She swallowed. "An avatar?"

"Yes," responded the prince, drawing very close to Angel. "The elfin avatar comes to help the Earth Mother in the new time. You and Darci can be of great assistance to her and all the elementals."

She stopped walking to gaze out at the river. "A girl? Our spirit baby would be a girl?" Glancing down at the sandy path, she added, "I do not feel qualified. I know nothing about raising an elf."

Orillo spoke softly into her ear. "Do not be concerned. You and Darci are highly qualified. We would not have asked if you were not. You will have interaction with the babe, but we elves will raise her. Your role is to sponsor her arrival by being her human mother. The soul who comes needs to experience being within a human mother, for her purpose is to improve communications between humans and elementals. Will you do this for us? For the Earth Mother?"

Angel sighed deeply. "How can I say no? I have dedicated myself to serve the Earth, and if this is a way I can do that, then yes. Yes, I will."

The next morning when she made an entry in her journal, she asked me to elaborate on this project.

"Good morning, my brave Angel," I began. "You are truly a spirit warrior for the earth plane now. I'll gladly discuss anything you wish. The elf project is one I'd dearly like to undertake. We are already favorites with the elfin community, and this would endear us to them even more.

"As far as the process is concerned, take your cues from human pregnancy. As I mentioned before, we will be working with energy forms as opposed to carbon-based forms. That's the basic difference. You will not gain weight; only increase the love energy within you. Elfin babies are small, so this will not tax you physically, though you will have to adjust to the change in energy. Such a pregnancy will, in fact, enhance your health and well-being because of the amount of love that will be showered on you and our child. You are older, more open, more accepting, more trusting, and now no longer able to bear human children. You are in exactly the right place in your life to undertake this spirit pregnancy."

∞

Near the end of July on a misty summer's night, Nyna visited. Her radiance seemed even brighter than usual as she floated across the field.

"Congratulations, Darci. Angel has agreed to help us. The most important step has been achieved, thanks to you."

"And Orillo," I added.

Her countenance then turned serious. "I have come to prepare you for what is next, for it may not be to your liking."

I was stunned. "I thought insemination was next, and that's something I will enjoy immensely."

The elfin elder placed her hand on my arm, and I felt soothing compassion flow through me.

"I know how much you love Angel," she began, "and that is as it should be, but you must detach for a moment."

"I don't know if I can," I admitted.

She forged ahead. "The pregnancy and birth will go much smoother for Emer-Aye if Angel burns off more of her karma. Remember, Darci, your charge incurred much karma around anger and injury of a first-born child."

I sighed. "What does this mean for Angel?"

219

"Darci, please. In the long run this will be best for her and for Emer-Aye." Nyna stared into my eyes. "Even though the injury to the hip and lower back still bothers her, she will deal with another problem, one that brings sharper, more immediate pain."

I knew immediately. "Her right shoulder. She injured it last March skiing down an icy hill. But at this point it has only marginally bothered her."

"She will develop what is called 'frozen shoulder,' a crippling condition, and will be forced to focus on healing this."

"Oh, Nyna, you know how I dislike seeing Angel in pain. Is this absolutely necessary?"

"Think of it this way. You will work even more closely with her to heal this, and it can be healed."

After Nyna left, I returned to Angel's side and examined her. She was sleeping on her side, curled in almost a fetal position. I saw how her instinct to lie on the uninjured left side played havoc with the injured shoulder. I remembered back to the spill she took on that icy hill. She had broken her fall with her elbow. The force of the impact had driven her upper arm bone through a tendon in her shoulder, making a hole. Her current position in sleep was twisting her ribs and collarbone even further out of alignment. She would need help soon.

Despite her discomfort, she continued to telepathically transcribe my story, which was quickly becoming an epic book. By mid-August, the shoulder injury was usurping her attention.

On August 24, she wrote the following entry in her journal. "My shoulder bothers me and my neck hurts again today. I have to go into the problem areas of my body and change the cells to white light, working through the karma associated with the pain."

At least she understood that the pain was karmic, and I loved her even more for it. I tried to help by telling her details about our upcoming endeavor with the elves.

On the last day of August, I telepathically sent her this message, which she wrote in her journal. "We are about to undertake a project that is a way to unite two worlds, three actually. When you, a human, and I, a Spirit Guide, mate in love, our offspring will be one of the elfin folk. She will be part human, of course, and this will allow her to appear more easily to humans than most elves can. She will have more understanding and compassion for humanity because you will be her mother. She will be an elf queen, reigning for hundreds of years, a great asset to the earth."

By September, she could not move her right arm behind her back, and neck aches were a daily trial. From my vantage point, I could see a bright red in her aura around the injured shoulder. I confirmed her suspicion that the pain was karmic.

"Dear one," I told her as she wrote, "yes, I sense your discomfort, and I see it in your energy field. Please remember that the human body is the crystallization of the spirit and spirit's purpose. One of your challenges is to bravely face what your body holds. In this case, your lack of employment has manifested in this shoulder pain. Your right side, your material side, is deeply wounded and has been since your lifetime as Gabriel. It is not an easy thing to heal, but we can do it. We must heal you on all levels, emotionally, mentally, physically, and spiritually, for the healing to be complete. Today say to yourself, 'The universe supports me and I am worthy of that support.' Repeat while breathing white and gold light into your entire body. I will help by focusing some of that on your injured areas. Together we can heal this."

Two days later as she was meditating on her slant board, I showered her with a vibrant and intense bath of love light. The fact that she was bravely facing both the pain and her karma evoked much love from me.

She wrote about the experience. "One thing I love about Darci is he doesn't mind my aging. I'm just getting good, as far as he's concerned, because now I am consciously aware of him, and I'm becoming aware of what we can share. The book we're writing is covering that now. I was meditating on my slant board, just letting go. Suddenly I was overwhelmed with Darci's love energy. It flowed over me and through me and literally took my breath away. In fact, sometimes Darci has to remind me to breathe. Deep breath makes the experience more intense. Where are the adjectives when I need them?"

Despite the increasing pain in her frozen shoulder, she continued to write and teach classes in astrology and Spirit Guides. This amazed me because between the pain and the hot flashes, she did not sleep much. When October arrived, she took two days off from writing because her arm pained her severely. She thought penning longhand aggravated the problem, and while it may have had some effect, I knew her sleeping position was also to blame. I tried to tell her, but she was becoming increasingly hard to reach because of the growing pain.

On October 9, Angel walked out to meet her husband driving home from work. Her mind was closed to me as it circled around asking the same question over and over. "Why live if I'm in pain all the time?" When she slid into the car and tried to close the heavy door, she screamed in pain. I lost sight of her because of the angry red flame that filled her energy field. As her worried husband drove her home, she cried, holding her arm, which was now weak and almost useless. Shortly thereafter, her physician scheduled a test, an MRI, to see exactly what was wrong.

The next weeks were extremely difficult for Angel as she went from healer to healer. These were not easy days for me either, as I truly hated seeing her suffer. As much healing as I gave her during the few hours she managed to doze, I knew she needed physical help, too. She prayed constantly that she be led to the best healing path, and I tried to help her any way that I could. For instance, when she went to see the orthopedic surgeon who would operate on her frozen shoulder, I made sure that she met another of this doctor's patients. This man had already had a similar operation and had returned because he felt it had worsened his situation. Also, while in the surgeon's office, my charge saw the MRI film and the hole in her superspinatus tendon. I sent the thought, "If it's a hole, then we can heal it."

Unfortunately, I could not keep her from every medical mistake. One doctor ignored the possibility of an actual tear in her shoulder. He tried to force the shoulder to move. My poor Angel went into a type of shock. Her body froze. Her legs wouldn't move. She told Graham that she felt as though bees were filling her body from feet to head. She collapsed, but Graham caught her. Sobbing in pain on the ride home, she cried for herself as Gabriel, the father who struck and killed his son out of anger; for herself as Shalia, the girl from Bombay born with no leg; for herself as little Tony, the orphan boy. I watched her karma dissipate.

As our ninth wedding anniversary approached, I distracted her by describing elfin life. "The elves are another Earthbound form for souls to take," I told her. "They do not reincarnate over and over as humans do. They come to Earth but once in elfin form and stay hundreds of years to learn what they need to and do what they need to. Elves have many races, as humans do. They vary according to where on the planet they dwell. Although some do live underground, most choose life on the surface because they are especially tied to the flora. They experience much delight interacting with the trees, bushes, flowers, grasses, etc. Know that a new time is coming for the elves, just as it is for humans.

"Nature spirits such as the elves exist on Earth on another vibrational level, so they cannot be easily seen by humans. When a human does see an elf, it is because that person has expanded his or her vibrational field to include the elf. The nature of their societies is complex, and there have been skirmishes, but they do not die as humans do. They do, however, leave the earth plane by force under certain circumstances.

"Elves have chosen their ether bodies because long ago they were estranged from humans. Now is a time of healing the ties between elves and humans. Humans can learn much from elves because of their ingenuity on this planet. No, they do not make toys or shoes, but they do work with the flora.

"The elves love you. You did your time as an elf many thousands of years ago when human civilization was new. You have the ability to bear an elfin child. My involvement in sponsoring an elf child is multifold. We can birth a new type of elf that has access to the many levels of Earth life, including the Spirit Guide Realm.

"Healing your inner wounds as well as your physical one will give you a chance to go deep and cleanse yourself from the inside out. I will help."

The orthopedic surgeon prescribed physical therapy, and that helped to ease the constant pain. Angel also sought out acupuncture and various other healing modalities. I made sure to repeat to her that we could heal this injury without resorting to surgery.

"The tendon that has been compromised is deep in the shoulder," I reminded her. "Surgery for this tear would shock the body and take equally as long to heal if not longer. Plus, surgery corrects only the one small problem, in essence, just the tip of the trouble. It will not heal your right side or your karma.

"During this time of healing, it is important for you to keep the body aligned, then use visualizations, proper nourishment, and prayer. Please allow me to help. When you lie and meditate, place that heavily burdened head of yours in my spirit hands. Allow me to draw out the tension and pain. Your body is still twisted with karma. You must slowly untwist as you release the karma. Yes, pain does help burn it away.

"It was a skiing accident that tore your tendon, yet at the time your body was looking for a way to force you to revamp your life. You have the opportunity here to begin again. Close the old chapter and start a new one, especially as regards your physical body and your karma. Nourishment, correct care of yourself, and the energetic pregnancy is the new chapter."

∞

Angel's diary became a journal of pain. On December 8, she wrote, "I thought I might be dead this morning. I wrote a letter 'To be opened in case of my death,' and asked Great Spirit to take me, to take my soul so that I would no longer have to deal with all this pain!"

As her Spirit Guide, I pleaded for assistance from the Master Guides, and received the promise of help. I was able to inform my charge that starting on the winter solstice, we Spirit Guides would place her in an energetic healing box with special instructions each day. "Remember, my dear one," I told her, "you have been given an injury that you can heal. Time, patience, perseverance, dedication, and awareness will lead to a full recovery. You will learn much while you are in the healing box."

Although I could detail the instructions given to Angel during this time of intensive healing, the important fact is that she improved immensely with such focused attention from spirit. At the end of January, she felt well enough to walk by the river once again.

She wrote, "The sunset was beautiful with soft lavender clouds rimmed with phosphorescent pink. Darci said to me, 'That's my love, touching you, caressing you.' I turned south toward the dam and saw great blue streaks in the sky. Darci said they represented the seraphim angels standing in witness to his profession of deep love for me."

When she gave me the chance to elaborate, I told her, "February approaches and so does my desire to have you to myself. We talked about conceiving, and the time is near. Your shoulder injury put you on the track of purification, which is what is needed for such work with the elves. Relax. All is well. Make time for us to be together."

On the last day of January, Angel had a fever, aches, and chills, the final purification before insemination, though I'm not sure she saw it that way. During February, my charge continued to visit the healers who had benefited her the most, receiving acupuncture, Chinese herbal therapy, chiropractic care, as well as healing from the spirit side.

On Valentine's Day, I gave her not one but two gifts. "Twice today when you meditate, begin in the usual way," I suggested. "Then allow me to give you a love bath. Each time will be a little different, so relax and let me bathe you in love. Remember to breathe deeply and see yourself as healed and whole. Smile, dear Angel. Your fortune will change soon."

On February 21, after working with cards from the Daughters of the Moon tarot deck, she expressed both joy and fear in her journal. "Here it is, February, the month Darci suggested for conceiving. The card I drew to represent the past was Kali, the Awakener. Indeed, the injury, even the flu, shook me up, awakening me to the purification process that was occurring. The card for the present was Three of Flames, Loyalty. Three women on the card are holding candles. When two are joined, they become three. The future card was Malama, the big woman with the gourd representing fecundity and abundance. Then I asked for a card for the child, who would, of course, be the outcome. I pulled Bast, play, the joy of the child! All these cards confirm what Darci told me months ago, that I will conceive and bear a spirit child. I'm concerned that I'm not ready. I've said that all my life regarding children. I'm concerned that I don't know enough about this process, for it is so unique and spiritual."

When she listened for my words, I comforted and supported her. "You are unique. You are spiritual. You have been going along, living life, and without being constantly consciously aware of it, you have been preparing. The purification was part. Your removal from an everyday job was part. You are in a space now where such a conception is possible, and I, for one, would like to proceed. This will not be taxing on you, my dear. No, indeed, you shall find much joy and exuberance in this beautiful process. Pray about it. We need only some private time and a sacred space. I am ready if you are. We will be helped and guided all the way."

Aware that time was of the essence, I had to make sure she was willing. Her prayer for years was for guidance on how best she could serve the earth. I decided to emphasize this as the day drew near.

"The elves are jubilant that we have agreed to help them and the dear Earth Mother," I told her as she wrote her morning pages. "Dear one, you are worthy of this effort. You were selected because the high beings know of your dedication, devotion, and intrinsic goodness. They know of our deep connections, for this miracle will take the two of us, though we are using your physical body to house and nurture the energy for this entity to enter the earth plane. Please, love your body. Treat it gently and respectfully for it is the vehicle for an avatar. The elfin being who wishes to come through you, through us, is an evolved entity with a very high vibration. I know you want to know everything about this miracle. We shall go one step at a time. As with human babies, my seed, my energy will be implanted in you, and our united energy shall produce an environment and a form for this entity to use on her Earth walk. We are speaking energetically, of course. This is all energy, but then, the entire universe is energy. Right now, your task is to prepare to receive my contribution by loving yourself and opening to me. Be assured, all this is quite real. I am so pleased you agreed to do this. Drink in the love and joy."

Conception day arrived, February 27, 2001. I instructed Angel to create a clean, quiet environment where we would not be disturbed. After placing fresh white spreads over the futon, she located rose quartz stones all around us. She prayed for protection and guidance, and I encased the two of us in a pyramid of light. As she lay in meditation, I told her, "There will be an initial surge with the impregnation today. I will be giving you a larger amount of my energy than I have ever done before. Part of me will remain in you. You are ready. Relax. I shall guide you. It is a joyful day."

First, I reminded her of other lifetimes when we made love in two physical bodies. This was easy for her to visualize because she had just written about them in my book. I focused on our lifetime in China when our sole purpose was to procreate. In that incarnation, I was Shu and learned to be an effective impregnator because I made sure that every drop ejaculated into Angel, then called Nua.

My sweet charge relaxed as I brought my energy inside of her. Whirling pink and gold light with much sparkling white surrounded us. With deep love, I took extra time filling her with my spirit seed, streaming it into her while she lay in a blissful state.

As the sun set, it resembled a flame in the western sky. Indeed, Angel was pregnant. The flame for the elfin avatar had been lit.

CHAPTER TWENTY-TWO
SPIRIT PREGNANCY

The day after our coupling, Angel was scheduled for an initial visit with a Chinese herbalist, and the timing couldn't have been better. Having spent several lifetimes in China, I was familiar with this culture's medicine and knew it would benefit my charge. Healing with Chinese herbs would move her toward wholeness and good health.

That day as she wrote in her notebook, I reaffirmed her decision to allow me to impregnate her. "Dear one," I told her, "if you could have seen the energy when we joined yesterday! Whirling pink and gold, with much sparkling white surrounded us. You did fine. You allowed me to guide you, and you followed my images and suggestions. Today I am filled to overflowing with joy and so should you be. This is the beginning of a new time, not only for the elves, but also for all who live on or are connected with the earth. Indeed, the Earth Mother rejoices that we do this for her and for her most noble and dedicated servants, the elves. You promised your focus and attention, and we all appreciate this. When you think of our daughter, the avatar, picture your torso glowing from your throat to your thighs, then see your entire body and your aura as bright and radiant. Go with whatever color comes to you. I am close by, loving you, protecting you. The elves and other nature spirits watch over us. The Earth realm is already a better place because of the conception and the promise it brings."

When I had the opportunity a few days later, I reminded my charge that the soul of the avatar, although still on the spirit side, was now close by, connecting to us, monitoring us. The goodness of her essence was helping to protect Angel.

"Mother yourself as you will mother our child," I told her while she wrote. "We three are already linked, even though the avatar's soul has yet to enter your womb. We have time to develop a sacred space for this blessed avatar." I requested that we pray together each day for our daughter.

Both Nyna and Orillo visited that night. We stood around my sleeping charge, spacing ourselves in an equilateral triangle. Reaching our hands toward one another, we joined our energies and created a great sphere of healing light, which shimmered emerald and white in the darkness of Angel's bedroom.

Afterward, concerned about my charge's well-being, I asked Nyna about the pregnancy.

The elfin elder placed her hand on my shoulder, sending comfort and compassion through me. "The struggle of a human birth shows the importance of Earth incarnations. This time, however, Angel will not experience a painful human birth, but will instead experience a spirit birth, an elfin birth. This is not painful for the mother, but instead is energetically transformational. Throughout the pregnancy, we must continually raise Angel's personal vibration so that she can easily handle the intense energy just before and especially during the birth of the avatar. Orillo and I will help."

The prince nodded. "I've moved into the neighborhood and plan to stay. I'm here to help however I can."

I thanked them both, and passed the information on to my charge. Because the pregnancy was in its early stages, I did not see either of them again for a while.

At the vernal equinox, March 20, the world was thawing, the ice and snow melting. While Angel sat writing her morning pages, a chunk of slushy ice slid off the roof.

Wanting her to document more information, I told her, "The elves rejoice at our love and our willingness to help usher in their avatar. She is more than just their queen and leader; she is a being of the transition, one who will make the elfin world more accessible to humans through her presence on Earth. Certain humans who have cultivated their vertical energy flow will easily see her. This will occur once she has grown and been schooled in the ways of elfin royalty. She needs leadership skills as well as spiritual training, and will receive these, some before entering the earth plane and some after being born to us. We will be able to help, a joyous task."

March 28 marked the beginning of Angel's second month of pregnancy. She wrote, "I wish I could tell everyone—or at least my friends—that I'm pregnant with a spirit child, an avatar. Most people would think I've lost my mind in illusion and hallucination, but they don't know what I know."

I replied, "Love, love, love to you as you start your second month. The light within you grows each day. Visualize a spirit fetus, vibrating in your womb with luminosity and high energy. This pregnancy and birth will transform you and me, too. All is well. You are blessed and watched over by many, more than you know. This year will be the most joyous so far in your life! A baby and a book, both brought into the world through our loving collaboration."

The reasons I took every chance to encourage my charge were several. Angel was still in pain, especially at night. Her lower back and hip tightened as she slept, then the resulting ache woke her. Tossing, shifting pillows, she had difficulty getting comfortable so that she could return to sleep. Also, because of the increase in her personal vibration, her stomach was more sensitive to heavy foods. She experienced nausea and other stomach discomfort. Several times her entire digestive system went into distress.

On April 10, after a night full of healing work with Nyna and Orillo, I told her, "Dear one, be of good cheer. Your body is changing rather rapidly and that can be exhausting and disorienting. You will benefit greatly in the long run by experiencing the energy work we do in conjunction with the pregnancy. We will help all we can. I will guide you to comfort, health, and love."

Sometimes I wondered if my words brought much solace when she was suffering. On April 25, she wrote, "My stomach attacked me last night, so I had to climb out of bed to take that thick pink antacid stuff. What a bane! Two weeks of stomach trauma is not good, though I am learning to eat less and eliminate irritants from my diet, once I figure out what they are. Sometimes I eat something and all goes okay, then the next time I eat, my stomach aches horribly. At least I've managed not to vomit everything up in over a week."

Three days later, she took me to task. "Darci, you told me no harm would come to me as a result of this spirit pregnancy. I realize that I'm holding higher and higher vibrations, altering my very being, but shouldn't that make me feel good? Why the awful sour stomach and all the other digestive problems? Do they parallel morning sickness? When will they end?"

"I'm so sorry for your discomfort," I responded. "The stomach problems are temporary and are a tool for positive change. Try eating small amounts. Eat more often, leaving time between for your stomach to rest. Take a moment before putting food into your mouth to bless the food and view it as sacred.

"The pregnancy, of course, has some similarities to a human pregnancy, as you yourself are human. For every moment of discomfort, let there be three of joy! Hold in your heart and mind the fact that, as the mother, you are contributing your body, your solid earthiness, to our daughter's form. No one before now knew that this cross-dimensional mating could be done. Our dear daughter is worth all that we endure."

Worried, I asked for my elfin friends to visit, and Orillo arrived almost immediately. We sat together in the spring grass outside Angel's window, as I explained what Angel was experiencing.

"We are in new territory with this pregnancy," Orillo admitted. "Your charge needs to feel the energy of the child. I will talk to Nyna. We'll see if we can do something to help Angel."

Several nights later, Nyna arrived. She greeted me but did not engage in conversation. Instead, she stood over my sleeping charge, extending her arms, holding her hands, palms down, over Angel's torso. Watching in amazement, I saw ribbons of white and gold light flow from the elder's hands into Angel. When Nyna left, my charge was glowing from head to foot, her womb especially bright.

Concerned that Angel's stomach difficulties were due to a physical cause, I made sure she saw a story on television about testing drinking water. The newsperson said that arsenic in drilled wells is a common problem in Maine. My charge drank a lot of water, and the pregnancy had sensitized her. If the water from her well was not acceptable, she needed to know. After seeing the program, she asked her husband to test their water for arsenic.

On Sunday, May 6, Angel wrote, "Last evening while I was waiting for the squash and onions to bake for supper, I was lying, meditating, when I felt the baby inside me for the first time. Darci then told me that her essence is now there. I thought there would be some great moment when her energy would enter my womb, but it happened quietly."

At the end of May, Angel's pregnant cat, Luna, was near her due date and quite fat. Stretching out on her side along the door to the west porch, the feline enjoyed the cool air seeping in, as Angel made another entry in her journal.

"I'm beginning my fourth month," she wrote. "Do I feel pregnant like my dear kitty? I feel sensitized. I feel my insides energized. I feel loved. This is all so new to me that I am keeping a record of my observations. The thing I notice most definitely is the sensitivity of my stomach. It tightens at the least little thing it doesn't like—or if I eat too fast—or if I don't masticate enough. I don't want to slide back into my old patterns—eating larger portions, eating faster—delighting my taste buds as I screw up my stomach. I'm a different being now; I must conduct myself accordingly."

When she asked for my input, I said, "My love, my wife, you are the jewel in the center of the crown. You shine brightly in your willingness to serve the Earth Mother and her friends. All is well. Breathe deeply. Take your day one step at a time, one project at a time. This way you will not scatter your energy and will accomplish much."

The date was May 31, 2001. The birth of six kittens celebrated the beginning of Angel's second trimester. My charge wrote, "I saw a bear cross route 201 on my way home today. Does the sighting bring extra healing to me? What will happen with my energetic pregnancy? I haven't a clue, except I know I trust the Guides. I trust Darci. I asked him to make sure that this pregnancy would not hurt me on any level. This past year has been one filled with pain. There was the rotator cuff tear, which caused frozen shoulder and severe pain, such that I had to medicate myself heavily. Then there was the stomach pain that left me doubled over for hours. Of course, the chronic pain in my lower back is there every night, kicking in about four hours after I go to bed. According to Darci, I'm burning karma as I move through the pain. Then there are the blasted hot flashes that flare whenever they want to. I request some periods of relief, please. Otherwise, I'm ready to abandon this physical form."

I tried to comfort her. "I hate seeing you in pain, dear Angel. I do all I can. You must help yourself move through it. Let go. Release the pain. It will move. Pain does have a purpose. It burns your karma like old newspapers in a blazing fire. Please know that you are well energetically. You are beautiful. Your aura is strong and vibrant. You are now pregnant with our child. Our dear daughter grows within you. She is acclimating to Earth through your body and through our love. It is a joyous time."

On June 2, the water test results came back. Unacceptable levels of arsenic were present in their drinking water. They immediately ceased drinking it. I hoped that this alone would ease my charge's stomach discomfort.

During June Angel was too busy for her condition. She was gardening, planting all the warm weather crops. She was painting a large fiberglass bear for a festival on the coast. I didn't like her breathing the fumes of the enamel paint, but she had promised to do the art piece, and it was her nature to follow through. She was participating in the Fourth of July play, writing a song for the women playing the sacred cows. Producing her independent radio show with her husband necessitated a weekly deadline. Sitting with the new kittens seemed to relax her.

July 9, after all the visitors from the Fourth of July celebration had gone, Angel had an emotional breakdown. She strode out into the woods to vent and find some peace. First came wild anger, then tears after she reinjured her shoulder on the walk. The elves surrounded her. She could hear them telling her over and over that she was loved, very loved by them.

The next day, she made the following entry in her journal: "I wonder if I will ever know true enlightenment. I feel so burdened, yet I want to feel light—be light. I know I hold a lot of anger. I own that. I'm not sure how to process it. Life has kicked me around, so I have a naturally defensive attitude. I want to learn to automatically let it go, let it flow. Bless me, I want to do better."

My heart overflowed with compassion and love for her. I was so happy that I could communicate this to her.

On Sunday, July 22, Angel accompanied her husband to his family's summer camp on a lake. On the drive she and I had a discussion on naming our child. I told her I was surprised that she had not been more curious about the baby's name. She replied telepathically that she knew the elves would name her. I told her that, as the child's mother, she had some input, too. I also informed her that the entity herself had asked that her name begin with the first letters of the word "emerald" to pay respects to the green world she will represent. Nyna had called the child Emer-Aye, so Angel chose the middle name Leela. My charge began writing a song, a chant, using the name.

Several days later, Angel hiked alone to one of her favorite waterfalls. As the sunlight glistened on the rushing, foaming water, I sent the request in a telepathic whisper to her: "We are a pair that time and death cannot part. With that in mind, be brave, for you know with certainty that I am with you every minute of every day. Whatever you choose to do, I will help you, especially with the birth of our child."

On August 1, my charge made the following entry in her journal. "A few days ago I began my sixth month of this spirit pregnancy. I do feel laden, not physically but energetically. I seem to nod off when I meditate, especially the afternoon meditation. Sometimes I doze after dinner, too. My dreams are very vivid."

When she gave over the page to me, I told her, "Despite your lack of energy, your aura shines with new radiance. Our union has made possible the arrival of a new form of being. She is an elf, it is true, but an elf imbued with new sacred attributes that allow her to materialize in the carbon-based world. This phenomenon is beyond anything I can explain to you. For now, I will just thank you again for trusting the process. Thank you for trusting me. Thank you for allowing the universe to alter your energy field to make the birth of this hybrid entity possible. Once she is here, so many things may change on Earth. The potential for healing the planet increases many times. Let's talk about Emer-Aye Leela every day. I will help you prepare for her arrival as a good birthing partner should. I am a loving and proud father."

Angel led a past-lives workshop on August 4. For seventeen minutes, the participants sat deep in meditation experiencing a guided visualization during which their Spirit Guides showed them glimpses of their past lives. For Angel and me, those seventeen minutes were amazing.

As my charge relaxed into the meditation, she visualized me guiding her through a blindingly bright archway, where we were greeted by a group of Guides and elves standing among bushes bearing hundreds of white roses. I led her to an ornately carved bench and sat beside her. She moved close to me, and I pulled her into my arms so that she was sitting on my lap.

Two elves came forward, almost as if Angel and I were holding court. The first, an elf I had not yet met, appeared muscled and strong. He handed Angel a sheaf of sweetgrass, saying that elves love sweetgrass and she should always have plenty on hand. Next a female elf stepped forward. She looked much like Nyna, but younger. She handed me a clear stone, which radiated a bright white light. We thanked them.

Next we heard the voice of our daughter-to-be. After confirming that she has brought some of her energy into Angel's womb, she explained that she was still preparing for her arrival on Earth. Then she told Angel what I already knew, that she had been born to us long ago when we were people of the Cree Nation. In that lifetime, she was Naquahris, an advocate for peace, sacred ceremony, and honoring the Earth Mother.

The hot weather persisted through the first half of August. I told Angel that the next few months were crucial for both mother and child. I suggested that she relax and rest, just as if she were experiencing a normal physical pregnancy.

"You look well," I said gently. "Your aura sparkles with white, pastel pink, and yellow. This pregnancy agrees with you. As long as you stay rested and keep yourself healthy and well, the added energy in your body and aura will not deplete you. It is only when you become overtired that you feel low."

Reminding her of a passage from *The Dawn Book*, which we wrote together in 1990, I asked for a pre-birth ceremony to welcome the avatar's soul. "Have the welcoming ceremony in September near the full moon. There will still be many flowers and warm enough weather."

Later in August, Angel told her friend and healer, Carol, about the energetic pregnancy. Carol was helping Angel with her health issues and reported that she had noticed the shift in my charge's energy.

"Darci, I could feel the electric sparks as Carol worked on me," Angel confided. "Ever since I just surrendered, gave over to the universe, I've been better. I guess I had to let go, surrender my ego, my petty wishes, and allow the magic to happen. I drew the raven card months ago. It portends magic coming into my life and says not to analyze it or try to understand it. Ever since Emer-Aye spoke to me in class meditation, I have felt more centered and more stable."

I gave her the following response, which she wrote in her notebook. "Dear one, although the connection you make with me, with any of the Guides, is in your mind, I am a real entity. I am your partner through time. The original dance of souls, as Shirley McClain describes, was the dance we did together. Our union through space and time and dimension is very real, though this connection does come through your mind. Of course your heart is involved. Your soul is involved! We are about to become parents! The upcoming birth has many, many Guides excited, to say nothing of the nature spirits and elves. A few humans have a sense of it. All will know eventually."

Toward the end of August, Angel had an appointment with Danielle, her Chinese herbalist. To my surprise, my charge told the practitioner about the "project" she was doing with the guides and the elementals. She added that it might be affecting her energy.

"I don't tell many people," admitted Angel. "I'm aware that I would be called delusional."

"I would never call you that," responded Danielle.

She checked Angel's tongue, then felt the pulses in her forearms. When she felt the pulse in the right arm, her eyebrows lifted and her eyes grew wide. "You have the pulse of a pregnant woman!" she exclaimed. "Yes! You are pregnant!"

"The baby will be named Emer-Aye," said Angel.

Danielle replied the same way Carol had earlier that month. "That's a beautiful name."

On the drive home, Angel talked to me. "Darci, it's as if these women know in their hearts that Emer-Aye's arrival means a new era for the earth is beginning, a new era for the flora and for humans. That's why I'm involved, right? My participation as her mother ensures her connection to the human race. You say she will be able to manifest to humans. That will be a huge step in opening people's eyes to the realms beyond earthly reality."

"The spirit world adores you and protects you from harm," I replied. "Feel your pregnancy. Embrace it. Feel your body's energy increase and expand. Soon you will be able to hold our dear daughter's soul within you. I encourage you to continue to write. One day the world will know our story."

On August 28, the day my charge and wife began her third trimester, Nyna and Orillo visited. While Angel slept, Nyna expressed her concern.

"She is not quite ready, Darci. Emer-Aye's soul must reside in Angel's womb for at least one moon cycle for the effects to be as we wish. Longer if possible."

"How is she not ready?" I asked. "She's feeling much better."

Orillo looked on as the elfin elder continued. "After all you've learned about the soul who comes as our avatar, surely you realize that the energy contained in this being is immense. I fear Angel cannot yet handle it, but the time is drawing near for the avatar to arrive."

"What can I do?" My voice trembled with concern for my dear wife.

"Advise her to rest, indeed to meditate, three times a day. When she does, work on her to increase her capacity to hold high energy. We will visit every night if necessary to work with Angel while she sleeps."

The two of them again joined me in energizing Angel, finishing just before the pain in her lower back woke her. I saw a difference right away.

September brought increased activity to Angel's life. I warned her. "Rest is essential for you now. Days like yesterday when you have no break to rest and meditate are unacceptable in this final trimester. There is hardly enough time as it is for me and the others to work on you and adjust your energy. You must give us every chance. I know I am stating this strongly, but it is important, indeed, critical for a successful birth."

When writing together on September 10, I informed Angel that the pregnancy was progressing well. "Thank you for doing as I asked. The three meditations a day are helping you a great deal. I'd like you to do something special as soon as you are able. Lie down outside on a blanket and allow the elves to visit you. Some will pay their respects, some will bring gifts, some will offer a few words or a gentle touch. I will sit with you." I drew a deep breath and added, "Please, dear Angel, be not downhearted at the world's turmoil."

CHAPTER TWENTY-THREE
CHAOS AND COMPASSION

On September 11, 2001, the world changed, especially for Americans. Terrorists hijacked four U.S. passenger jets in flight and used them as weapons, killing thousands. Angel was actually watching on television when the second jet hit the south tower of the World Trade Center. Chaos ensued. I'd gotten a message from Sottrol alerting me to the probability that something like this was about to happen, but he gave me no details.

As Angel wrote in her journal, I comforted her. "Yes, many souls are passing over together," I said. "Those that are involved are working out karmic imbalances. They are being well cared for by their Spirit Guides and other spirit helpers.

"The tragedies to your south are unsettling, yet strangely they bring the energies on Earth into a better state of balance. As you send love to those passing over and their families, send love also to the Earth, for she is in need of healing, too.

"I know you are concerned with the repercussions of these catastrophes, and all I can say is—greater forces are at work here, greater than any government. The Earth is demanding balance and respect. Let us give that to her and more."

Angel wrote, "Darci, it's hard to believe that the situation on Earth is actually improving, energetically speaking. I'd like to think that you and I are helping enhance positive energy on Earth. Emer-Aye can bring all peoples together with a new view of life on this planet. She is the avatar that the white buffalo portends. She is a link between the seen and the unseen. She will bring great knowledge, great connections, great wisdom, and great love. It is time. Many know it. Not many know about Emer-Aye yet, but many look for an avatar, and she is coming. On this morning of disaster, she brings hope for a better world."

The next day, she penned, "The tragedies happened yesterday—so many people dying, so much drama. It's an extraordinary event, a horrible thing, this deliberate taking of lives and destruction of property. There is a positive side. People forget the petty things and pull together. They pray. They look at their own mortality, which means looking within. Now I see what Darci means. Strange as it may seem, the energy on Earth has been raised significantly by this event due to the worldwide outpouring of compassion."

That afternoon, my charge walked up to the high fields with a blanket and sat under the giant ash tree. A light breeze played with her hair as puffy white clouds floated across a deep blue sky. The peace and beauty were far from the acrid smoke and devastation eight hundred miles to the south.

Once Angel settled and said a prayer, she invited any elves wishing to interact with her to come to her. There was an immediate rush forward of many elfin entities. My charge was overwhelmed and asked me to handle it. I immediately chose four elves who each had something in particular to share with her. The others gathered around to listen.

The first elf was a cherubic entity, rosy and joyful with curly brown hair. Shy when stepping toward Angel, she became enthusiastic once the words flowed. "My name is Teekee, and I'm here to tell you that there is so much joy now that Emer-Aye is finally coming to the earth plane. It is a long-awaited event! Be joyful in your life because you are a part of this. Appreciate all that is around you. Give love to everything you see. Let the joy pour forth. Celebrate! As much as you can, celebrate! Joy and love, that's the atmosphere into which we want Emer-Aye to come. Despite the tragedies in the outer world, despite what happened yesterday, despite the great exodus of souls moving on from the earth plane, despite the fear and the terrible torturous ways that people died, or perhaps because of all this—there is a great outpouring of empathy, compassion, love, and prayers. This clears the way for Emer-Aye's energy. This shift had to happen before our avatar could arrive on Earth."

Angel then asked Teekee, "Are other avators coming to Earth besides Emer-Aye?"

"Yes," replied the little one. "There are other arrivals on Earth, none of them the elfin avatar, though. The others do have a similar purpose, which is to manifest through the veil, and have it happen in a way that humans know." Spreading her little mint green skirt, she curtsied. "I am very pleased to speak with you. I'll be at every party."

When Angel saw the next elfin entity move in front of her, she thought for a moment it was her Spirit Guide Esther because of the veil-like appearance and floating pastel colors, pinks, whites, and light blues. However, Esther is tall and statuesque, and this being was much smaller, though she exhibited a similar vertical striping in her energy field.

Introducing herself as Anarakua, she spoke with confidence. "The elves are real. The nature spirit energy is real. Your work will connect many to it. That's one of the things you are here to do, Angel. It's very important that you spend lots of time outside with the elves during the next few weeks. In this way, we elves can help you prepare and set the stage, make sure everything is ready. Give us as much time as you can. We do have emissaries who are with you in your home. Most of the time we elves like to interact outside because the plant realm is also our realm. It helps that you have many plants in your home. Treat them as elfin friends. One elf can come inside your home for each plant you have."

"That's wonderful to know," exclaimed Angel. "I now have a new outlook on my plants. Thank you!"

Anarakua continued, "You can call me Akki. Know that you are honored among the elves. Your attention, your focus, your abilities, your willingness, your immersion, and your love of nature are all appreciated."

Angel then observed, "There's a lot of amazing spirit activity here. This is a great gathering. It's a little overwhelming for me, so I'm glad you're coming forward one at a time."

Akki nodded and went on. "This is a celebration for the increased energy on the earth. Humans did this themselves in response to yesterday's events. It's important that humans recognize that they have done this. It's important for people to hold and build upon this high level of compassion and cooperation."

"I understand," replied my charge. "But many want revenge."

"Continue to pray," Akki responded. "Continue to visualize a peaceful world. If it takes more disasters to bring the peoples of the world together, then more disasters will occur."

Angel raised her eyebrows in surprise. "So—if we humans choose to make this transition ourselves, then we may spare ourselves some cataclysmic Earth changes down the line?"

"Absolutely true," she said. "The goal is to raise humanity to the next level of being, which is for humans to operate from the heart with love and compassion. It's time to remind your current leaders that this is their role—to act and interact with all world leaders compassionately. Think about this. It is a positive thing that the dastardly acts of yesterday were not perpetrated by a specific country. There was a reason for this. Countries must aid each other in the face of terrorism. That is why the villains are not associated with one country, but with several countries."

Angel and I thanked her.

The next elfin entity came bounding forward. Joyous and jubilant, he jumped into Angel's lap and hugged her. I could tell that Angel felt she knew him somehow. He sensed this, too, and told her, "Oh, we've known each other in so many lifetimes. Family, family, family. Lovers and connections— but we don't need to go back over all that. What's important is that you are now in a human body, and I am in elfin form, though we were in human form together before."

"Your name, sir?" I asked.

"Spaekey."

I nodded. His vertical vibration did have distinctive spikes, and it oscillated much faster than the other two elves who had stepped forward. Angel seemed to be watching the flashing vertical light around this entity.

"Time for jubilation!" said Spaekey. "The rain is coming. The fall brings rains. Winter brings snows. All is well." He did a quick little jig, then went on. "I want to tell you how special Emer-Aye is. First, she has a long royal elfin name. She comes through a line of elfin energy that is extremely high, rare, sacred, beautiful, excellent, and emerald. Thank you for doing this!"

I saw a frown wrinkle Angel's brow and I realized that the energy level was too high for her, and she had experienced a shooting pain in her temple. Asking the group to help her adapt, I put her in a sphere of protective white light.

Spaekey, however, would not slow down. "Emer-Aye is a leader soul," he orated. "She is an alpha soul, a soul that wants to break boundaries because essentially that's what needs to happen here. The boundaries need to be opened between the Earth plane and associated planes."

A breeze rose, and light yellow butterflies appeared around us, some flying in pairs. The faeries were joining us. I smiled. They deserved to be a part of this, though they would welcome their own avatar soon.

"Angel, dear, please take good care of yourself," Spaekey went on, "especially during the time Emer-Aye resides within you. The avatar's vibration is very strong. She will be using your body and your energy to acclimate to Earth and to her purpose here. It's very important that you rest, meditate, and most of all remain joyful! Do deep breathing. This will help with the birth. You have the best teacher for breathing, right, Darci? Listen to your tall handsome Spirit Guide, Angel. He knows what's what."

The energetic elf winked at me, jigged, bowed, and stepped back.

The fourth elf to come forward was an elder, one I had not yet met. I could tell that she had been on Earth for hundreds of years, had seen many changes, experienced much tumult, and had felt the Earth herself transform. She was a white-haired grandmother figure wearing a blue hooded cloak. I saw a streak of deep blue in her white hair and noticed much pink light radiating from her. Walking over to Angel, she hugged my charge and kissed her third eye. The grandmother elf sat down in front of her, gently took her hand, and gazed into her eyes.

"Bless you, my child," she spoke quietly. "You may call me Gran." She smiled. "Angel, dear, please know that you are going to make such a difference for all of the generations to come—generations of elves, of elementals, and of humans. It is an important thing that you do." Releasing Angel's hand, she wore a serious expression. "I know you've heard this from every quarter, but you must take good care of yourself, especially while you are hosting Emer-Aye. The avatar will be gentle and loving with you, my dear. Know that she will bring a tremendous amount of love and joy and an overwhelming amount of energy. We elves along with the Spirit Guides are working with you every day to try to prepare you for this. Breathe easy. You are almost there. Keep at your meditations and rest. All is well. I promise we will not allow any harm to come to you. In fact, a great deal of joy and ecstasy are possible through this process."

She glanced at me, then returned her gaze to Angel. "The elder elves, those of us who have been around on Earth for hundreds of years, we are available for consultation. We have been waiting for this! We've known that the potential and opportunity were there and were hoping that such an event would occur. We've known that the shift in energy on Earth was going to present itself along with an opportunity to improve conditions here on this plane."

"We've heard there are others," I spoke up. "Seven Avatars, in fact."

"Yes," Gran nodded. "Other spirits are bringing in other entities." She looked at Angel.

"We are so pleased that you chose the elves and chose to help the elfin avatar enter."

"Tell us about the others, Gran," Angel requested.

"Seven in all, as you know. These entities began coming to the earth after the start of the new millennium and the official beginning of the Aquarian Age. Now is a good strong time for Emer-Aye to come through. All the avatars have come to cement love and compassion as the reigning emotions here, and to support the shift in human energy and the energy of the planet. All manner of beings understand that this shift must stabilize and stay! What happened yesterday is just the first of a number of tragedies unless humans begin to operate consistently from their hearts, from a place of love and compassion." Her face took on a worried look. "It's important for the leaders to understand this and make decisions accordingly."

"Would the U.S. president understand this?" asked my charge.

Gran shook her head. "Probably not." She patted Angel's hand. "Enough for today. Go home. Meditate with Darci. Relax. Keep in mind that there's a continuous celebration, constant joy bubbling here on the planet as these Seven Avatars come in. All are being assisted by the Creator, Spirit Guides, Master Guides, angels—and you, my dear."

On the walk home, I suggested that Angel write her government representatives and let her voice be heard, because now she possessed the spirit perspective. I knew that if the U.S. retaliated with force, the compassion that the world now held would dissipate.

The new moon occurred on September 17. When Angel went to start her vehicle and make a run to town, the car was dead. I consoled her.

"The elves want you to stay here so they can take care of you," I told her. "You have to realize that you are not the same. Nothing is the same. You have no business running to town in your condition."

"My condition?" she retorted.

"Yes. The world is not the same, and you are not the same. These events are linked, don't you see? There has been a surge of energy around the globe in conjunction with this event. Besides, your time of preparation for Emer-Aye is in full swing. Rest is needed … and joy."

Seeing her brow wrinkle in frustration, I said, "Don't worry about the car. We'll get it going for you. You have to promise to take care of yourself and rest. Budget your time. Driving into town takes time, energy, and resources. Your trips must be carefully planned. Much can be done by phone and even email. Reorganize your life."

She sighed. "Okay, Darci. I will try to be frugal with my time and give you the attention and focus I promised."

A couple of days later, she wrote, "The kittens are romping, oblivious to the world's turmoil. I didn't sleep well at all. It seemed to take a week for the enormity of the terrorist attack to set in. It has affected everybody. Punishing the men responsible through the world court is definitely the direction to take as opposed to striking back militarily, but I doubt our leaders have the patience or foresight to take the high road.

"It's been difficult for me to muster joy. The elves and Guides say that Emer-Aye must be born into an atmosphere of joy and love. I need help with this. I'm so sensitive to the masses, their feelings and concerns, which right now include sorrow, grief, anger, and revenge mixed with prayer and compassion. Darci says that the elves attend me. I humbly ask for their help and the help of my Spirit Guides to heal me so that I may proceed."

"Be not discouraged," I empathized. "Much help is on the way for you and Emer-Aye. The setting is altogether good, just as we wish it to be. There is an opening made wider and brighter by the events of last Tuesday and the global response of prayer and compassion. All is well, though it may not seem so. The flora rejoices at the shift in energy. The Earth sighs with relief at the change. Joy from the Spirit Guide Realm and the angelic realms is pouring through the opening to Earth. It is a glorious time. Consider what I have said, and please be joyful."

On the autumnal equinox, Angel wrote a letter to her representatives in Congress. She titled it "Heartfelt Plea," and asked that the United States break the cycle of revenge by not going to war. She pointed out that such actions would turn many countries against us.

During one of her three meditations, I suggested that she paint a portrait of Emer-Aye. I told her that the elfin avatar is a symbol of joy, and her arrival heralds a new golden age on Earth.

On September 29, Angel hosted a welcome party for Emer-Aye. Her husband and another friend attended. My charge had placed cut flowers in a circle around the three of them, and they sang songs to welcome the baby. For the first time since the disasters, I could tell Angel was happy, almost giddy.

Frost descended on October 1 bringing a crystalline sheen to the landscape. The hills flamed with autumn colors. Angel was still struggling. She wrote, "Anxiety is everywhere. There is still plenty about the terrorists' attacks on television and in the newspapers. I fear that I will not be able to do enough for Emer-Aye. I guess all mothers feel that way. I need to sleep to do well and to keep my energy levels up for our daughter, yet sleep eludes me. I do rest. I did three meditations yesterday, yet I still fell asleep in my chair at 8:30 p.m., then couldn't sleep once I went to bed."

"Dear wife," I comforted, "I see your weariness. Take care to fill your eyes and your head with pleasant relaxing visions and thoughts before retiring. The three daily meditations help immensely. Go slowly today. Take it easy. Love and cherish yourself. You need time with the elves. The temperatures are warming, and this promises to be a beautiful day. Go outside and enjoy the company of the many elves who love you."

Nyna and Orillo visited that evening. The grandmother elf said that it was time to give Angel specific information. She informed me that the elder elves had evaluated Angel's condition, talked with the Master Guides, and ascertained that Emer-Aye needed only a minimum of five days in Angel's womb to acclimate before birth.

"Five days to two weeks," added Orillo. "We originally thought that the avatar would need one entire moon cycle within Angel's body, but we have revised that."

"Good." I was relieved. "Angel might not be able to take a month of the intense energy that comes with this soul. She is struggling as it is."

"We are close, Darci," said the elder with sparkles in her emerald eyes. "The babe will be born before the end of October. Tell Angel that the avatar's soul will enter her womb mid-month, depending on her preparedness. Give your charge extra attention. We will hold her in the light."

With Mother Earth's autumnal splendor outside every window, Angel should have been reveling in the beauty, but she was again upset by global events. On October 7, the United States attacked Afghanistan. My dear charge prayed for those who were bombed and for those who were ordered to do the bombing.

"Keep praying," I told her. "Keep talking and writing. You see the bigger picture. You know what must happen for peace and compassion to prevail on Earth. I will call attention to opportunities you may have to put forth the spirit view. Meanwhile, enjoy your pregnancy and the beautiful countryside around you. Emer-Aye's arrival is all-important now. Rest, play with the elves, pray, and just be with the increased energy. I'm right here beside you at all times."

∞

Misty rain blurred the landscape on October 17 as Angel meditated on her slant board. I could see she was ready. Orillo and Nyna arrived as soon as I had that realization. We knew it was time. They stood with me as we welcomed the avatar's soul to Earth. At first Emer-Aye's essence filled the room with blindingly bright, swirling green, gold, and white light. We watched as she slowly condensed her energy into a small orb of bright light.

Angel wrote about the experience in her journal. "Even though it was a misty, moisty English sort of day, I did outdoor chores, digging carrots and dahlias. This seemed to ground me. A raven called to me as I went inside to do one of my daily meditations. To my surprise, Emer-Aye came to me. Her essence was huge. At first I thought I would be smothered by it. I said, "Please don't overwhelm me!" I felt the vibration soften, and I had the sense that the high vibration of the avatar surrounded me gently, allowing my neck and head to be above it so I could see and breathe. Emer-Aye told me telepathically that she was going to condense further to enter my energy field and my womb. I must admit that I swooned several times during the process. I had to let go and trust that I was being aided and watched over as this powerful soul came to rest inside me. Now that I am up and about, I find the only physical effect so far is slight vertigo."

As the proud father, I smiled. "Angel, you are a natural mother. You will do well with this. Your instincts are compassionate and nurturing. Be joyful. All is well. She is here with us now. These are precious days. The three of us bond as a family more closely with each passing moment. Do not fear the upcoming birth. You will have much help. For now, simply love her. Show our daughter the earth through your loving eyes."

Two days later, Angel's vertigo increased. Her body was still adjusting to carrying our daughter and her intense and powerful energy. She wrote, "Yesterday Danielle told me that the Chinese see dizziness as inner wind. Later in the session, she added that the Chinese see Spirit as wind, so it makes sense that I would experience dizziness once Emer-Aye's spirit entered my womb. In fact, when Danielle checked the pulses in my wrists, she detected two distinct heartbeats! Other than the dizziness, I feel fine, though I need to rest a lot. Even three meditations a day may not be enough. Yesterday in my third meditation, I felt the kundalini energy very strongly. I sensed it rise up into the area of my heart. My body vibrates a great deal these days. In this instance, the white vibrating light reached my stomach, breasts, and heart. I got a glimpse of what true enlightenment might be."

"Words fail me today, Angel," I told her. "You are so beautiful, so radiant, so full of life. Emer-Aye is settling in and adjusting. Thank you for relaxing and allowing her all the time she needs. She will not tax you longer than she needs to. She still requires a bit more time. We are all around you, helping you, so feel free to give over any stresses or worries."

Every day that the weather cooperated, Angel walked in the fields and woods. The elves showed her special power spots where she could sit comfortably. I was always by her side, of course. On October 21, my charge ventured to one of these areas. A curved tree supported her as she sat, the knobs on the trunk massaging her back in just the right places. Beautiful little elfin plants covered the forest floor. As my charge rested, Nyna and three elfin midwives introduced themselves to her. They instructed her in breathing and relaxation techniques and gave her a healing.

"I feel so pregnant!" she wrote in her journal. "I'm moving very slowly and carefully. I feel big. I feel laden. Even though I'm moving slowly, I don't feel sluggish. I'm buzzing! My entire body is electric, but I move slowly because the baby has such a giant energy field that if I make sudden moves, I lose my balance and become dizzy. I am holding the soul, the energy, as any human mother holds the soul and energy of her baby. I am honored to help the elfin avatar in this way."

For my part, I stayed close as breath and supported her with my words. "My dear sweet wife, you do well with this. You glow unbelievably brightly. Know that your connection with the spirit side is as real as the bombing that continues in Afghanistan. The goodness you foster is helping to shift the energies on Earth. Continue to pray, and I will pray with you. Rest, relax, and enjoy the bliss that comes with holding Emer-Aye's spirit with your own. She loves you and appreciates you, as do I. The birth is near."

CHAPTER TWENTY-FOUR
BLESSED BIRTH

Frost covered the landscape at dawn on October 23. Angel named this post-foliage season "the time of russet and gold" in her song "New Harvest Waltz." After her first meditation of the day, she came to me with questions about the elves.

"Darci, I know so little about them. I feel like I'm adopting a baby from a foreign culture. I need to learn more. Can you help me?"

"Ask me anything."

"This is the first full day of the Sun sign Scorpio. I guess I've known for a while that Emer-Aye would be born with the Sun in Scorpio."

"It's a power sign," I reminded her.

"Do elves have birth imprints like humans do? Could I draw up a natal chart for Emer-Aye?"

"Yes and yes."

"Do elves sleep?"

"Most do. The daylight activates the flora, which is their realm. They work with the vegetation during the day and rest when it's dark. The elves are closely connected to the plant world, yet are separate entities unto themselves."

"So how long they sleep depends upon the time of year?"

"Correct. Some elves, like Nyna and Orillo, assist Spirit Guides with various projects, and some of that work occurs during the night."

"Do the elves watch over animals as well as plants?"

"No."

"Do elves eat or drink?" she asked.

"No. The elves are energetic beings, as we Spirit Guides are, and can be nourished only with energy. You can feed us love energy anytime." I smiled, and she saw it. "The elves are souls who have come to the earth plane to learn different lessons from humans, but the two worlds intertwine through the flora."

The evening of October 24, a moderate earthquake shook Maine. It was centered north of Bangor and reverberated throughout the hills. Angel and I saw this as a sign that the arrival of the elfin avatar was imminent.

Thursday, October 25, my charge spent time outside, walking by the headwaters of Michael Stream. A raven called to her. Angel had heard ravens throughout the pregnancy, and since this raptor symbolizes magic, she saw the bird as Emer-Aye's totem.

Nyna, Orillo, and I joined her on the walk. The two elves had come to ask her to do another daily exercise in preparation for the birth.

"We are concerned that Angel will not stay grounded enough," Orillo told me. "The baby's energy is immense. If Angel is not grounded, she may become even dizzier and lose focus. Besides, this will help the avatar."

Nyna explained. "Have your charge dig all ten of her fingers into rich soil, and let the earth energy fill her and flow through to the baby."

I relayed the information, though Angel had caught some of the conversation. Upon returning home, she immediately went to the garden and performed the exercise, using one of the beds that had been cleared and dug. Another raven flew overhead, its deep throaty caw echoing against the trees.

"The raven is thanking you," I told her. While I had her attention, I put forward a request of my own. "After the birth, can we take a few days to be with each other and our beautiful daughter? Even two days. This is precious time. I suggest that we travel to the ocean as we did on our honeymoon, though it doesn't really matter where we are. I request privacy for our tenth wedding anniversary, and we deserve some special sacred time as a family."

Saturday, October 27, the first gunshot of deer hunting season sounded in the woods behind my charge's home. Angel whispered a prayer for the deer. "Great Spirit, please bless and protect these beautiful, gentle four-leggeds in this time of peril. Thank you. Aho."

Danielle had given Angel a formula of Chinese herbs specifically designed to help her with the birth and recovery. Neither Angel nor I knew exactly when Emer-Aye would be born. Angel asked that it not be on Halloween, even though the day is a sacred cross-quarter point in the wiccan calendar.

"Be patient," I advised. "Emer-Aye needs this time to orient herself. Because she has you as a human mother, she will go through a different process from other elves when adapting to Earth. Her first few months after birth must be spent close to you and me and a few caretaker elves. As she becomes accustomed to her unique situation on Earth, she will be able to spend more and more time with the elves. This will most likely occur in the spring. Let us look forward to this winter, an excellent time to nest and care for our daughter. She will need attention and love from us both."

Sunday, October 28, marked eight months to the day since I impregnated Angel. The babe would come any day now since elves need only eight months to gestate. The three elfin midwives, Angel's prenatal tutor Isadora, Nyna, and Orillo camped out in the field outside Angel's window. One of them always seemed to be by Angel's side.

"Because the birth is an unusual one, the elves are especially attentive right now," I informed her. "We do them a great service in ushering in one of their own, one with special powers. Yes, she has earned these throughout many lifetimes, but the fact that we are her parents adds another level to her abilities." I sent her a ray of rose-colored love light, which swirled around her. "Rest and spend time out-of-doors. That's really all you have to do. Remember, all is well. All is as it should be. Be of good cheer. Birthing is joyful."

Angel walked up to the high fields later that day, her face into the wind. "It was as if I were putting my face into the stream of terror, agony, stress, insomnia, and despair that's rampant in this country and in the world," she wrote in her journal. "I think it was positive for me to be in that wind for just a few minutes so that I understand—and Emer-Aye understands—what's going on. Once I sensed the global turbulence and had that realization, I had to take myself out of the stream and find sheltered protection. A raven flew in front of me as I walked home."

That evening, Nyna took me aside as Orillo and two of the midwives tended to a sleeping Angel.

"The birth will be Tuesday, October 30," she told me. "Things will begin unfolding tomorrow, so focus on your charge and stay very close to her."

"Is it a good day for our daughter to be born?" I asked her.

"A very good day." Nyna smiled.

Monday, October 29, a lone raven sat atop the giant maple tree cawing Angel awake. During her morning meditation, I gave my charge the following instructions. "Stay hydrated and lighten up on heavier foods. As usual, do two more meditations and spend time out-of-doors. When outside, stand with your feet apart, your knees slightly bent, and breathe deeply. Also remember to dig your fingers into earth, though it may be chilly. Perform all this and you will be in good shape. Remember—the birth will occur tomorrow."

Angel took a walk at the end of the day, ending in the garden for the exercise she had been given. She wrote, "I took a chance wandering around at the end of the day during hunting season. Anyway, as requested, I just put all ten of my fingers into the garden soil and allowed the energy of the Earth to come up and fill the baby. I sent some energy back to the Earth through the arches in my feet, and I pulled some down through my crown chakra, too. I did this for as long as it felt right. My fingers were getting cold. The sun was setting. I received information from Isadora today on how to eat for the next few days. She suggested soups and teas, staying away from the heavier foods such as eggs and cheese. She also told me that the stance, feet apart, knees flexed, along with deep breathing, are things I ought to practice every hour. Evidently some work with the birth will be done in this position. Basically she said that I will have to hold a pretty high charge of energy, so she wants me to be very hydrated in order to birth this entity."

October 30 dawned cold, bright, and still. The sun streamed into Angel's home as she sat clad in her nightgown writing in her journal, awaiting the birth. I passed along the information that the birth would be tonight when the moon is high in the sky. I told her to focus and prepare.

Here is her journal entry. "Yesterday I began to dilate. Darci had me all to himself for a few precious moments and took exquisite care of me. Last night I could feel movement in my belly. Once I awoke in the night because my womb was vibrating and pulsing. Later I felt a slight cramp in my left side.

"I need to move more plants into the birthing room to make it easier for the attending elves. I want my elfin midwives to be present in full strength. I will also light candles, beautiful for an evening birth. Darci just told me to smudge the house and the birthing room thoroughly with lavender so that the vibration is very high. I feel full. I feel ready. I feel the floor of my pelvis relaxing. I feel as though I am opening. I trust the magic that is Emer-Aye's arrival."

Of course I stayed very close to my charge all day. Each time she meditated, she experienced a major influx of energy. When her husband, Graham, came home, they shared a light dinner. He agreed to program music for the evening's events.

At 7:30 p.m. on my instruction, she entered the shower. I asked her to hang on to the safety bar, breathe deeply, then huff fast forceful exhales until her lungs were nearly empty, then repeat. When this exertion made her dizzy, I said, "Assimilate the energy." She alternated this activity with squatting, forcing her knees outward by placing her arms inside them.

"Relax. Dilate," I whispered. After thirty minutes of these preparations, we moved to the birthing room, the bedroom on the lower floor. After she settled in, we did more breathing. I asked her to visualize a large column of light passing vertically through her. I saw it clearly. I wanted to make sure she did, too.

The midwives gathered around. Isadora and Nyna stood behind them while Orillo and a large group of elves waited outside in the field. The breathing and visualizing continued for nearly an hour. Angel was in a blissful trance. I could see that she was buzzing from head to foot.

Nyna came to my side, a concerned look on her face. "Darci, we cannot let Angel lose consciousness. She has very nearly done so several times. We need her awake and participating in the birth. Keep her present. Talk to her, please!"

Kneeling by her side, I whispered, "Stay with us, dear one. Please don't drift away. Relax but stay focused. See the light passing through you. You're doing well. The babe will be here soon."

Near 9 p.m., one of the midwives exclaimed, "We have the chute! We have the entry chute!"

Encouraging Angel to continue the deep breathing, I surrounded the entire scene with a sphere of protective light, then resumed my kneeling position by her side and clasped her hand. "Allow the baby to come through. Open and let her come through."

I could hear the elves singing tones to draw Emer-Aye into the world. At 9:12 p.m. our daughter slid out feet-first much as she had in the Cree lifetime when her spirit was born a boy. The midwives cut the energetic cord. The glowing baby was small and lively. Her presence filled the room with a radiance so strong it was nearly blinding. I took the babe, this precious jewel, and placed her over my dear Angel's heart. "Our daughter, our star," I whispered in my wife's ear. "She is here."

I needn't have told her. She knew. She smiled, her eyes glassy with tears.

After a while, Nyna asked to hold the child and show her to the waiting elves. Angel had heard the request and agreed. My dear charge was exhausted. I knew that it was now my job to help replenish her chi, her core energy. As I placed my hands on her, we heard a great cheer arise from the gathering of elves outside the bedroom window.

"Come away with me for our anniversary," I whispered. "You did a great job with this birth, but it has diminished your energy. As an anniversary gift, I will replace it. I will give it back to you stronger than before."

On November 1, All Saints Day, Angel checked in to a small motel on York Beach. My charge and I walked along the shore, white sands stretching in both directions as the surf rolled in. I carried the newborn. Of course I made sure that the new mother rested often, and when she did, I used several techniques to replenish her energy.

While Angel rested, she did some sketches of the baby and wrote in her journal. "Darci takes good care of me," she noted. "He insisted on taking this trip even though I'm financially stretched. It's a long drive, though it flew by. I thought I would be too exhausted from birthing Emer-Aye. Turns out, this is just what I need—rejuvenation time, the honors being done by my very competent and loving spirit husband."

When she turned the page over to me, I told her, "Be of good cheer. Your health is good. Your energy is back up and, in fact, exceeds your pre-birth level. I will do my best to see that you hold this enhanced chi. You have earned it.

"By the way, the elves are holding a thirty-hour celebration to honor Emer-Aye and bless her entrance onto this plane. Nyna told me that we will be surprised at how quickly the baby grows, for she is well nurtured on both sides of the veil.

"Each human being has his or her opportunity to thrive. There's always at least one occasion, often several, for people to face what they have to face, to move through, become stronger, and thrive. Everyone gets a shot at doing what he or she is best at. That's why the Master Guides and the elves gifted us the avatar project. It was perfect for us. You especially thrived by helping in this way. The Master Guides did tailor the project a little so it would suit you better. When the scenario was created, those involved knew that there would be a birth with a cooperative human female who would be able to hold a high level of intense energy. The woman would have to be able to birth an evolved entity and have the needed support in her life. You have me, so we turned out to be the perfect pair for this project. Indeed, I feel like your support person more than anything, as many new fathers do.

"What a marvelous thing we did—for the elves, for the earth, for the Spirit Guides and Master Guides. Now that we are in each other's company, Angel, life is never dull!"

She laughed.

During the next several weeks, we meditated together, the babe between us. Sending love energy back and forth, we filled the baby in the process. When Angel and I were ready to meditate, I would request that the elves bring the baby to us. Sometimes that took a few minutes.

Emer-Aye spent time with the elves every day, for she is their future leader, a sacred being come to Earth to bring their work to a new, higher level. Nyna was in charge of the little one when she wasn't with us, and the elfin elder insisted on spending a large amount of time with the infant. The elves are always first when it comes to the baby because she is their avatar, here to make a major difference on the earth plane. Emer-Aye would be living with them on a full-time basis come spring, but for now, the little one needed daily contact with her spirit father and her human mother, too.

The portrait Angel created of Emer-Aye was beautiful. It captured the radiant little bundle of pink and white with her golden hair, elfin ears, and sparkling green eyes, wrapped in an emerald robe. In the picture, my charge drew the newborn wearing a headdress, for Emer-Aye is elfin royalty. The bright purple ribbon tied around her forehead and temples held a sparkling emerald. It was fitting. She is, after all, the Emerald Avatar.

THE END

EPILOGUE

Seven and a half years later, Emer-Aye stood in the orchard with Nyna, Orillo, and me. She had grown into an energetic rosy-cheeked elfin girl, curious about everything. On this late May day, she was receiving a lesson on how to heal trees, in this case, a floundering young pear.

Angel wasn't aware that, when she was shopping for another tree for her orchard, I had led her to the struggling pear. Nyna had asked me to see that my charge chose a tree on which Emer-Aye could practice, so I made sure Angel bought a sapling that had been mistreated in transit.

I watched while Orillo and Nyna instructed my daughter in how to bring healing energy from the core of the planet up into the roots of the sad little tree. The girl appeared dressed in a simple green frock that came to her knees. She glowed with a golden light, and emerald and white sparkles swirled around her when she moved.

Once the young avatar had golden green energy flowing up through the roots, trunk, and branches of the tree, her instructors then explained how to pull white and gold light from above, from the Creator, and channel it through the dry barren limbs, down the small trunk, into the roots, and the earth. Though the lesson took a while, by its completion Emer-Aye was able to facilitate the vertical energy flowing in both directions.

Nyna placed a gentle hand on the girl's shoulder. "This is your new project, Emer-Aye. Please practice on this tree every day until it flowers. Without your help, this poor tree will die, so please do your best."

Orillo stood with me as the girl went through the exercise again. "All elves learn how to heal the flora," the prince informed me. "There is an entire level of souls who have incarnated onto the earth plane as elementals.

Humans don't realize that this work by these spirits is why the flora on Earth has remained, by in large, very resilient. They work constantly to keep the flora healthy and thriving."

My heart expanded with love when my radiant daughter turned toward me and smiled. She had confidently mastered this lesson.

Midsummer brought Angel to Gardens of Atlantis, a healing center in the countryside outside of Portland. She was teaching another class on connecting with Spirit Guides. Part of Emer-Aye's instruction as the elfin avatar was to attend and participate in Angel's classes.

"One of your daughter's major objectives in coming to Earth as our avatar is to communicate through the veil between worlds," Orillo told me. "Since you and her mother do this on a regular basis, Emer-Aye needs to converse with you both on a regular basis. It helps when the communication takes place in a structured setting."

I nodded. "Nyna said she will be visible to humans."

"In the future," he replied, "once the telepathic centers of their minds are fully activated. Some, like Angel, can see her now."

In the comfortable Victorian home, Angel sat with seven participants. Many Spirit Guides were in attendance as well. The seven Life Guides of those people who chose to take the class were present, plus many Guides who wished to observe. Communications through the veil are a focus for both Spirit Guides and Master Guides because the time is near when telepathy will become a normal part of human life.

In my studies with the Master Guides, I had learned that telepathy works on many levels, and that humans may activate this gift in slightly different ways. For some, telepathic communication is an audio experience, while others find it more sensory, and still others are visually stimulated. Although clairaudience and clairvoyance are the most common manifestations of telepathy, smell, touch, and even taste can be activated.

Angel began by speaking with the attendees, acquainting herself with any experiences or expectations that they had brought into her class. Then she spoke for a while about Spirit Guides. After a ten-minute break, the group reassembled for a guided meditation. The goal was to give each person a chance to connect with his or her Life Guide. Learning and practicing the balanced breath came first, then Angel led them through several grounding and clearing visualizations. Finally, the group relaxed while she detailed their walk through an archway covered with fragrant roses. The gate opened into a beautiful garden filled with radiant flora. Each person could then wander off to find a special corner of the garden in which to experience the spirit meeting.

Although Angel had to keep an eye on the clock to make sure the meditation did not run on too long, she had the opportunity to meet with me and Emer-Aye. Our daughter chose a quiet alcove filled with fragrant white roses, her favorite flower. Once I had led Angel to the marble bench and we had seated ourselves, Emer-Aye raced around the corner and ran into her arms. She hugged her mother first, then me.

"Papa, Mama, I love you so much!" Glowing with a luminescent golden aura, she crawled up into my lap. "Thanks so much for being my parents."

We responded in kind. Emer-Aye appeared clad in a white ankle-length dress with delicate lace overlay. Her golden curls were tied back with a bright green ribbon.

"You're wearing your finery today," I observed.

"I knew I would be seeing you and Mama," she grinned.

"You look lovely," Angel complimented. "Why have you come to my class?"

"Part of what I need to learn right now is to become very good at telepathic communications, especially with humans," she explained, as Angel grasped her small hand. "With Spirit Guides, too, Papa, so this is a perfect setting for me to practice." She stared at Angel with eyes so wise that I could see the many lifetimes she had lived. "Mama, you pick up on visual cues first, so I've learned to send you a strong, vibrant image of myself. Then once I have your attention, I can go ahead and speak, and you hear me easily." She turned in my lap and looked at me. "Papa, you're always easy."

I laughed. So did Angel.

"You know, Mama, you could tell your students that humanity has to prepare for an upgrade."

"An upgrade?" queried Angel.

"You know what I mean," she giggled in response. "Using more of their brains, using their psychic abilities."

"When this occurs," I interjected, "Telepathy will be a major player. It's appropriate that you teach how to activate the telepathic center of the human mind. It's important information."

"That's why I teach it," Angel responded with a smile.

"What have you been learning lately?" I asked the seven-year-old.

"Nyna has been teaching me how to focus, to contain my energy and direct it."

"Direct it how?" asked Angel.

"Mostly to manifest communication. That's my specialty, after all." She sat forward slightly, directing her next words to Angel. "Papa already knows this, but I want you to understand, too. Humans are born with blinders on. They don't remember where their souls have walked before. However, I remember all the previous lifetimes on Earth that have led me to this place."

"Go on," prompted Angel.

"Long ago, I was a girl named Jasmina, born into a matriarchal society. There I learned to honor the Earth Mother and found I could draw courage from her. As Rahid, a boy in India, I developed a rapport with elephants and could communicate telepathically with them. In South America as Leijasa, I learned how to converse with the flora, especially great old trees. Then as the Cree Indian man, Naquahris, I learned to heal with plants and stories. I was a peacemaker who traveled far and wide. Finally, in Tibet as Jing Lei, I studied in the sacred temple with a lama, learned to work through the veil with Spirit Guides, and was able to astral project."

"That's quite a list," responded Angel. "Do you have more to learn?"

"Yes, Mama. I have to adapt to working on this level in elfin form, for this is my first and only time as an elemental. I must tune to the vibration of the flora in particular and allow it to strengthen me. I haven't yet grown into it, really made it my own. Nyna says I'll be fourteen or fifteen years old, as you count time on Earth, before I'm ready to step forward and lead."

"Tell her about the languages," I prompted.

"Oh, right. Since I'm to become a global communicator on behalf of the elves, I am learning many languages. Papa, do you remember how, when I was Naquahris, I could adapt to whatever language was being spoken?"

"I do. There were so many different languages and dialects used from tribe to tribe back in that time. I read that Naquahris would say a prayer and immediately begin to understand the language spoken around him. This talent brought safe passage in his travels."

"It's a psychic gift," Emer-Aye clarified. "After hearing only a few sentences of a language and saying a prayer, I can understand what is being said. One of my names when I was Naquahris was 'The Great Communicator.' I carry that name with me today, though I am still growing into it."

"That's amazing," commented Angel. "Certainly beyond my understanding."

"Nyna insists that I still study the major languages that humanity uses now, so I can be well versed, but I do have that psychic talent, too." She snuggled against my chest. "Time to bring the meditation to a close."

"You are doing well, my daughter," I told her. "You are a powerful, talented entity. I'm glad to see that you are receiving the schooling you need."

Her countenance became serious. "Please remember that the Earth Mother herself called to my soul, asking me to return and become a leader in the new time. The transition on Earth may not be easy, but with us all working together through the veil, we will help."

"May the outcome be positive," Angel whispered.

I simply added, "Aho."

ABOUT THE AUTHOR

Annie Stillwater Gray is a writer, a mystic, an astrologer, a public speaker, a teacher, an audio and visual artist, a healer, a singer-songwriter, and a media veteran. She has been on the air every year since 1974 and currently has her own syndicated radio program, The General Store Variety Show, now in its 18th year. Also she has helped start a community radio station near her home. Annie has studied Integrated Energy Therapy, Reiki, and Bach Flower Remedies. She has been helping people consciously connect with their Spirit Guides since 1989. Annie received a BFA from Boston University in graphic arts and writing. She creates songs and designs all the CD covers and publicity for her bands. At the date this book is released, her band is the western quintet Merry-Go-Roundup.

Books by Annie Stillwater Gray

Education of a Guardian Angel
Published by: Ozark Mountain Publishing

The Dawn Book
Published by: Ozark Mountain Publishing

Work of a Guardian Angel
Published by: Ozark Mountain Publishing

For more information about any of the above titles, soon to be released titles,
or other items in our catalog, write, phone or visit our website:
Ozark Mountain Publishing, LLC
PO Box 754, Huntsville, AR 72740
479-738-2348/800-935-0045
www.ozarkmt.com

Other Books By Ozark Mountain Publishing, Inc.

Guy Needler
Avoiding Karma
Beyond the Source – Book 1, Book 2
The Anne Dialogues
The History of God
The Origin Speaks
James Nussbaumer
The Master of Everything
Mastering Your own Spiritual Freedom
Sherry O'Brian
Peaks and Valleys
Riet Okken
The Liberating Power of Emotions
John Panella
The Gnostic Papers
Victor Parachin
Sit a Bit
Nikki Pattillo
A Spiritual Evolution
Children of the Stars
Rev. Grant H. Pealer
A Funny Thing Happened on the
  Way to Heaven
Worlds Beyond Death
Karen Peebles
The Other Side of Suicide
Victoria Pendragon
Born Healers
Feng Shui from the Inside, Out
Sleep Magic
Michael Perlin
Fantastic Adventures in Metaphysics
Walter Pullen
Evolution of the Spirit
Christine Ramos, RN
A Journey Into Being
Debra Rayburn
Let's Get Natural With Herbs
Charmian Redwood
A New Earth Rising
Coming Home to Lemuria
David Rivinus
Always Dreaming

Briceida Ryan
The Ultimate Dictionary of Dream
  Language
M. Don Schorn
Elder Gods of Antiquity
Legacy of the Elder Gods
Gardens of the Elder Gods
Reincarnation...Stepping Stones of Life
Garnet Schulhauser
Dance of Heavenly Bliss
Dancing Forever with Spirit
Dancing on a Stamp
Annie Stillwater Gray
Education of a Guardian Angel
The Dawn Book
Work of a Guardian Angel
Blair Styra
Don't Change the Channel
Natalie Sudman
Application of Impossible Things
L.R. Sumpter
We Are the Creators
Dee Wallace/Jarrad Hewett
The Big E
Dee Wallace
Conscious Creation
James Wawro
Ask Your Inner Voice
Janie Wells
Embracing the Human Journey
Payment for Passage
Dennis Wheatley/ Maria Wheatley
The Essential Dowsing Guide
Jacquelyn Wiersma
The Zodiac Recipe
Sherry Wilde
The Forgotten Promise
Stuart Wilson & Joanna Prentis
Atlantis and the New Consciousness
Beyond Limitations
The Essenes -Children of the Light
The Magdalene Version
Power of the Magdalene
Robert Winterhalter
The Healing Christ

For more information about any of the above titles, soon to be released titles,
or other items in our catalog, write, phone or visit our website:
PO Box 754, Huntsville, AR 72740
479-738-2348/800-935-0045
www.ozarkmt.com